WETLAND MITIGATION

MITIGATION BANKING AND OTHER STRATEGIES FOR DEVELOPMENT AND COMPLIANCE

Mark S. Dennison
with contributions from
James A. Schmid

Government Institutes
Rockville, Maryland

Government Institutes, Inc., 4 Research Place, Suite 200,
Rockville, Maryland 20850

Copyright © 1997 by Government Institutes. All rights reserved.

01   00   99   5   4   3

No part of this work may be reproduced or transmitted in any form or by any means, electronic or mechanical, including photocopying, recording, or any information storage and retrieval system, without permission in writing from the publisher. All requests for permission to reproduce material from this work should be directed to Government Institutes, Inc., 4 Research Place, Suite 200, Rockville, Maryland 20850.

The reader should not rely on this publication to address specific questions that apply to a particular set of facts. The author and publisher make no representation of warranty, express or implied, as to the completeness, correctness or utility of the information in this publication. In addition, the author and publisher assume no liability of any kind whatsoever resulting from the use of or reliance upon the contents of this book.

Library of Congress Cataloging-in-Publication Data

Dennison, Mark S.
    Wetland mitigation of development impacts / Mark S. Dennison with contributions from James A. Schmid.
       p.   cm.
    Includes index.
    ISBN 0-86587-534-0
    1. Wetlands--Government policy--United States. 2. Wetland mitigation banking--United States. I. Schmid, James A., 1945-   . II. Title.
QH87.3.D44   1996
333.91'85'0973--dc20   96-30343
                                                                       CIP

Printed in the United States of America

For Tracey, the sunshine on my shoulders

Table of Contents

Preface xiii
About the Authors xv
Acknowledgments xvii

Chapter 1. Wetland Functions and Values 1

Introduction   1
Wetland Functions   2
Wetland Values   6
Wetland Losses   7
Consequences of Lost and Degraded Wetlands   8
Clinton Administration's Wetlands Plan   9

Chapter 2. Wetland Identification 13

Wetlands Defined   13
Federal Manual for Delineating Wetlands   16
National Academy of Sciences Wetland Study   18
Wetland Characteristics   19
      Wetland Hydrology   19
      Hydric Soils   20
      Wetland Vegetation   21
Field Testing and Data Collection   22
      Hydrology Indicators   22
      Hydric Soil Indicators   24
      Wetland Vegetation Indicators   25
      Wetland Mapping Criteria   26

Chapter 3. Wetlands Regulation 33

Introduction 33
Clean Water Act Section 404 Program 33
Wetlands Enforcement 35
  Administrative Enforcement 36
  Civil Enforcement 37
  Criminal Enforcement 38
Wetland Regulation under the Swampbuster Program 39
  Wetland Conversion under the Swampbuster Program 40
  Effectiveness of Swampbuster Sanctions 40
  Commenced Conversion Exemption 41
  USDA's Swampbuster Regulations 41
  Federal Agriculture Improvement and
      Reform Act of 1996 42
Related Federal Environmental Laws 43
  National Environmental Policy Act 45
  River and Harbors Act of 1899 46
  Coastal Zone Management Act 46
  Water Resources Development Act 49
  National Flood Insurance Program 52
  Endangered Species Act 54
Special Approaches to Wetlands Management 56
  Advance Identification of Wetlands 56
  Special Area Management Plans 57
  Wetlands and Watersheds 58
State Wetland Regulatory Programs 59
  State Wetland Protection Laws 60
  State Wetlands Grant Program 60
  State Wetland Conservation Plans 61
  State Assumption of the Section 404 Program 62
  Clean Water Act Section 401 Certification 63
  State Water Quality Standards for Wetlands 64

Chapter 4. Wetland Permitting 73

Introduction   73
Section 404 Permit Applications   73
   Application Form   75
   Exemptions   77
Permit Application Process   77
   Army Corps Action on Permit Applications   78
   Public Notice   78
   Public Comment   80
   Public Hearing   81
   Permit Decision   81
General and Nationwide Permits   82
Remedies for Permit Denials   84

Chapter 5. Wetland Mitigation Compliance 89

Introduction   89
Wetland Mitigation Policy   89
State Law Mitigation Requirements   91
Corps/EPA 404(b)(1) Mitigation Guidelines   92
EPA/Corps Mitigation MOA   93
Sequencing Requirement   94
   Avoidance   94
   Minimization   95
   Compensatory Mitigation   95
   Exceptions to the Sequencing Requirement   97
Practicable Alternatives Test   97
   EPA/Corps 1993 Memorandum to the Field   98
   EPA/Corps 1995 Memorandum Regarding
       Small Landowners   101
   Illustrative Cases   102
Achieving Mitigation Compliance   107

Chapter 6. Wetland Mitigation Options 113

Introduction   113
Mitigation Categories   113
Kinds of Wetlands Losses Requiring Mitigation   114
Functional Value Analysis   114
Specific Types of Mitigation   118
Alternatives for Compensatory Mitigation   118
Ensuring Mitigation Project Success   120
Wetland Restoration and Creation Checklist   121

Chapter 7. Wetland Mitigation Banking 129

Introduction   129
Concept of Mitigation Banking   129
How Mitigation Banking Works   131
    Functional Value Assessment   132
    Timing of Credit Withdrawals   133
Types of Mitigation Banks   134
    Single-User Banks   134
    Private Banks   134
    Publicly Owned Banks   135
Advantages of Mitigation Banking   135
    Tenneco-LaTerre Wetland Mitigation Bank   138
Disadvantages of Mitigation Banking   139

Chapter 8. Wetland Mitigation Banking Guidance 143

Introduction   143
Purpose and Scope of Guidance   143
Policy Considerations   144

Planning Considerations   145
   Prospectus   145
   Goal Setting   145
   Site Selection   146
   Technical Feasibility   146
   Role of Preservation   147
   Inclusion of Upland Areas   148
   Mitigation Banking and Watershed Planning   148
Establishment of Mitigation Banks   149
   Mitigation Banking Instruments   149
   Agency Roles and Coordination   150
   Role of the Bank Sponsor   151
   Dispute Resolution Procedure   151
Criteria for Use of a Mitigation Bank   152
   Project Applicability   152
   Relationship to Mitigation Requirements   153
   Geographic Limits of Applicability   153
   Use of a Mitigation Bank vs. On-Site Mitigation   154
   In-Kind vs. Out-of-Kind Mitigation Determinations   155
   Crediting/Debiting/Accounting Procedures   155
   Timing of Credit Withdrawal   156
   Party Responsible for Bank Success   157
Long-Term Management, Monitoring, and Remediation   157
   Bank Operational Life   157
   Long-Term Management and Protection   158
   Monitoring Requirements   158
   Remedial Action   159
   Financial Assurances   159

Chapter 9. Wetland Mitigation Case Studies . . . 161
   by James A. Schmid, Ph.D.

Introduction   161

Case Study 1: Creation of Freshwater Wetland   162
   Project Site   162
   Functional Value of Impacted Wetland   163
   Mitigation as a Condition of Permit Approval   164
   Selection of Mitigation Site   164
   Submission of Mitigation Plan   165
   Mitigation Project Design   165
   Implementation of Mitigation Plan   166
   Post-Construction Monitoring   168
   Success of the Mitigation Project   169
Case Study 2: Creation of Tidal Wetland   170
   Background and Setting   170
   Design/Implementation of Mitigation Plan   171
   Human Disturbance of Mitigation Site   172
Case Study 3: Payment of Fee In-Lieu of Mitigation   172
   Calculation of Fee Payment   174
   Cost Estimate #1   174
   Cost Estimate #2   176
   Cost Estimate #3   177
   Pennsylvania Mitigation Guidelines Concerning
      Cash Contributions   177
Case Study 4: Wetland Mitigation Bank   178
   Background   179
   Location and Description of Bank Site   179
   Bank Establishment   181
Achieving Successful Wetland Mitigation   182
   Past Efforts at Mitigation   184
   Mitigation is Attainable   186

Appendix A **187**
   U.S. EPA Wetland Offices

Appendix B **191**
    Army Corps of Engineers Offices

Appendix C **205**
    State Wetland Offices

Appendix D **215**
    Clinton Administration's Wetlands Plan

Appendix E **243**
    Funding and Technical Assistance for Wetland Acquisition and Restoration

Appendix F **259**
    EPA/Army Corps Memorandum of Agreement Concerning the Determination of Mitigation under the Clean Water Act Section 404(b)(1) Guidelines

Appendix G **267**
    Department of Agriculture, Environmental Protection Agency, Department of the Interior, and Department of the Army Memorandum of Agreement Concerning the Delineation of Wetlands for Purposes of Section 404 of the Clean Water Act and Subtitle B of the Food Security Act

Appendix H **281**
    EPA/Army Corps Memorandum to the Field: Appropriate Level of Analysis Required for Evaluating Compliance with the Section 404(b)(1) Guidelines Alternatives Requirements

Appendix I **289**
    EPA/Army Corps Memorandum to the Field:
        Establishment and Use of Wetland Mitigation
        Banks in the Clean Water Act Section 404
        Regulatory Program

Appendix J **295**
    EPA/Army Corps Memorandum for the Field:
        Individual Permit Flexibility for Small
        Landowners

Index **301**

Preface

One of the most important regulatory requirements for development projects undertaken in wetland areas is some form of "mitigation" to restore or replace lost wetland functions and values. Under the Clean Water Act Section 404 program, mitigation means sequentially avoiding project impacts, minimizing project impacts, and compensating for remaining unavoidable project impacts on wetland ecosystems.

Without a doubt, mitigation is the most onerous prerequisite to wetland permit approval. Developers have incurred considerable expense and repeated delays in negotiating mitigation agreements with the Army Corps in order to carry out land use development activities in wetland areas.

Wetland Mitigation: Mitigation Banking and Other Strategies for Development and Compliance is written as a guide to understanding, evaluating, and implementing various mitigation measures needed to avoid, minimize, or compensate for land use development impacts to wetlands. In practical, easy-to-understand fashion, the book will explain the regulatory framework, permit process, and mitigation prerequisites to obtaining permit approvals to carry out land use development activities in wetland areas. The book contains helpful tables and checklists summarizing key points, numerous "real life" mitigation case studies, and several useful appendices.

The timeliness of the book is apparent. There has been considerable struggle and litigation between private landowners and government regulators over the mitigation requirements for undertaking wetland development activities. Controversy still exists over the wetland identification procedures used to delineate wetland boundaries in the United States. Reforms are, however, on their way. Completion of a study of wetland characterization by the National Research Council in 1995 may aid in formulation of a standardized methodology for wetland delineation. Many components of the Clinton Administration's "40-point" plan for introducing consistency and flexibility into the wetland regulatory regime have now been implemented, including issuance of various Army Corps and EPA guidance memoranda on wetland mitigation, wetland mitigation banking guidance, a new nationwide permit for single-family housing, and guidance on individual permit flexibility for small landowners.

Mark S. Dennison
Westwood, New Jersey

About the Authors

Mark S. Dennison is an attorney and author of numerous books and articles dealing with environmental law and regulatory compliance issues. His books include *Environmental Reporting, Recordkeeping, and Inspections: Compliance Guide for Business and Industry* (1995); *Environmental Due Diligence for Lenders: Practical Guide to Implementing an Environmental Risk Program*, with R. Kenneth Keim and Philip Lee (1995); *Storm Water Discharges: Regulatory Compliance and Best Management Practices* (1995); *OSHA and EPA Process Safety Management Requirements: A Practical Guide for Compliance* (1994); *Hazardous Waste Regulation Handbook: A Practical Guide to RCRA and Superfund* (1994); *Understanding Solid and Hazardous Waste Identification and Classification* (1993); *Wetlands and Coastal Zone Regulation and Compliance*, with Steven Silverberg (1993); *Wetlands: Guide to Science, Law, and Technology*, with James Berry (1993).

Mr. Dennison is also Editor-in-Chief of the monthly newsletter, *Environmental Strategies for Real Estate* and is a regular columnist for the American Planning Association's bi-monthly newsletter, *Environment & Development*. He is in private practice in Westwood, New Jersey, where he specializes in environmental, land use, real estate, and zoning law. He is admitted to practice in New Jersey and New York. Mr. Dennison holds a B.A., *magna cum laude*, from the State University of New York (Oswego), an M.A. from Syracuse University, and a J.D. from New York Law School.

James A. Schmid, Ph.D. is president of Schmid & Company, Inc., an environmental consulting company located in Media, Pennsylvania. The company performs a wide range of services, including environmental assessments, impact statements, permit coordination, and wetlands delineation, restoration, and creation. Dr. Schmid has more than twenty-five years experience as a biologist and has written extensively in the area of wetland ecology, including a field guide to New Jersey wetland plants, *Checklist and Synonymy of New Jersey Higher Plants With Special Reference to Their Rarity and Wetland Indicator Status* (Media, PA: Schmid & Co., 1994). A 1994 U.S. Fish and Wildlife Service audit (1985-1992) found that all of Dr. Schmid's mitigation projects were fully successful in achieving their goals, and that they represented 21 percent of the fully successful wetland mitigations identified by the USFWS in the state during its field survey.

Acknowledgments

I wish to express my appreciation to everyone who played a role in publication of this book. I thank the editorial and production staff at Government Institutes, especially my editor, Alex Padro, for his endless enthusiasm, enduring patience and keen editorial eye.

I must give special thanks to Jim Schmid who provided the useful case studies contained in Chapter 9, as well as for his helpful comments on the rest of the manuscript.

I also wish to thank the many helpful individuals working at different federal and state regulatory offices who answered my questions and provided copies of various forms and government documents.

Additional thanks goes out to family and friends who provided moral support and inspiration, especially Erin Carrather, Jonathan and Jessie Ann Huff, Bobbie Waits, Keith Dennison, and Nikolai Andreivich Budinsky.

Finally, my greatest appreciation is reserved for my dear Tracey, whose sustaining love and support gives a positive direction to my life.

WETLAND MITIGATION

MITIGATION BANKING
AND OTHER STRATEGIES
FOR
DEVELOPMENT AND
COMPLIANCE

Chapter 1

Wetland Functions and Values

INTRODUCTION

Today, regulation of wetlands is one of the most controversial areas of environmental protection law and policy. Private property owners, government regulators, and wetland scientists are engaged in ongoing and vigorous debate concerning which wetlands should be regulated, how they should be regulated, and to what degree they should be regulated. Much of the controversy is driven by the conflicting economic interests of private property rights proponents and land developers who want to use wetlands, and the environmental protectionist goals of various public interest groups who want to preserve them.

The whole body of wetland laws has developed around the scientific study of wetland ecosystems. The scientific delineation of wetlands preceded wetland regulations and formed the basis for the legal criteria defining wetlands. Scientific study of wetland areas spawned the legal protection of wetlands as the data indicated that wetlands provided vital and productive ecosystems for the nation's natural environment. Filling, dredging, and human destruction of wetland ecosystems were decried by wetland scientists, who eventually convinced legislators, and the public, that these habitats needed to be conserved before they disappeared.

Wetland studies were the driving force behind enactment of federal and state environmental laws and regulations aimed specifically at protection of the nation's wetlands. As the public became more environmentally conscious and mindful of the vital role wetland ecosystems played for the environment, the federal government saw it crucial to declare a policy of "no net loss" of wetlands. The future of wetlands is, however, somewhat in question in light of the present effort to redefine the criteria for designating a wetland. Turmoil exists between environmental protectionists and those who hope to develop currently protected wetland areas. Without a doubt, scientific wetland studies continue to play a key role in legal delineation criteria for defining and mapping wetland areas.[1]

Although the law may be in a state of flux, wetland science has developed established principles that identify and explain the wetland ecosystem. Those involved in wetland disputes must understand these principles to know what wetlands are all about.

WETLAND FUNCTIONS

Wetlands are among the most biologically productive natural ecosystems in the world. They can be compared to tropical rain forests and coral reefs in the diversity of species that they support. The valuable functions performed by wetlands include, among other things:[2]

1. *Conveyance and storage of floodwaters.* Wetlands can store large amounts of stormwater, reduce flood levels, and may also form natural floodways that convey floodwaters.
2. *Prevention of erosion and saltwater intrusion.* Coastal wetlands and inland wetlands adjoining large bodies of water reduce the erosional impact of tides and waves.
3. *Sediment control.* Wetlands reduce the velocity of water and thereby reduce soil erosion.
4. *Wildlife habitat formation.* The enormous wetland biomass serves as an excellent habitat for fish and wildlife, including many rare and endangered species.
5. *Recreation.* Wetlands provide recreation in the form of fishing, hunting and wildlife observation.
6. *Water supply and quality maintenance.* Wetlands recharge underground aquifers, serve as a source of surface water supply, and improve water quality by removing excess nutrients and many chemical pollutants.

7. *Food production.* Wetlands produce large quantities of both plant and animal food.
8. *Timber production.*
9. *Archeological value.*
10. *Educational and research value.*
11. *Open space and aesthetic value.*

Wetlands are vital to the survival of various animals and plants, including threatened and endangered species like the wood stork, Florida panther, and whooping crane. The U.S. Fish and Wildlife Service estimates that up to 43 percent of the threatened and endangered species rely directly or indirectly on wetlands for their survival. For other species, such as the wood duck, muskrat, and swamp rose, wetlands are primary habitats. For others, wetlands provide important seasonal habitats where food, water, and cover are plentiful.

Because wetlands are so productive, and because they greatly influence the flow and quality of water, they are of great public value. Wetlands furnish a wealth of natural products, including fish, timber, and wild rice. In the Southeast, 96 percent of the commercial catch, and over 50 percent of the recreational harvest, are fish and shellfish that depend on the estuary-coastal-wetlands system.

Wetlands often function like natural tubs or sponges, storing water (flood-water, or surface water that collects in isolated depressions) and slowly releasing it. Trees and other wetland vegetation help slow floodwaters. This combined action, storage, and slowing, can lower flood heights and reduce water's erosive potential. Thus, wetlands:

- Reduce the likelihood of flood damage to crops in agricultural areas.
- Help control increases in rate and volume of runoff in urban areas.
- Buffer shorelines against erosion.

Wetlands improve water quality, including that of drinking water, by intercepting surface water runoff and removing or retaining nutrients, processing organic wastes, filtering out pollutants, and reducing sediment before it reaches open water. They also control erosion by trapping soil washed from nearby uplands.

Wetlands are important spawning and nursery areas and provide plant food for commercial and recreational fish and shellfish industries. Between 60 percent and 90 percent of U.S. commercial fisheries use coastal wetlands as spawning grounds and nurseries.[3] In 1991, the dockside value of fish landed in the United States was $3.3 billion, which served as the basis of a $26.8 billion fishery processing and sales industry, which in turn employs hundreds of thousands of people. An estimated 71 percent of this value is derived from species that depend directly or indirectly on coastal wetlands during their life cycles. For example, Louisiana's marshes alone produce an annual commercial fish and shellfish harvest of 1.2 billion pounds, worth $244 million in 1991.

More than half of all U.S. adults (98 million people) hunt, fish, birdwatch, or photograph wildlife. These activities, which rely on healthy wetlands, added an estimated $59.5 million to the national economy in 1991. Individual states likewise gain economic benefits from recreational opportunities in wetlands that attract visitors from other states.[4]

Wetlands help stop pollutants from entering receiving waters. For example, the wetlands of the Congaree Bottomland Hardwood Swamp in South Carolina remove sediment and toxic substances and remove or filter excess nutrients. The least cost substitute for these wetlands benefits would be a water treatment plant costing at least $5 million to construct, and additional money would be needed to operate and maintain the plant.

The Minnesota Department of Natural Resources has computed a cost of $300 to replace, on average, each acre-foot of flood water storage. In other words, if development eliminates a one-acre wetland, that naturally holds 12 inches of water during a storm, the replacement cost would be $300. Thus, the cost to replace the water storage of the 5,000 acres of wetlands lost annually in Minnesota would be approximately $1.5 million.

Table 1-1 presents a few examples of potential man-made substitutes for wetland services lost due to wetland destruction.

Table 1-1. Substitutes for Wetland Services

Flood Control	Dams, floodways, dikes, levees, floodwalls, diversions, zoning, relocation of property, land acquisition, flood proofing, detention depressions, reservoirs, land treatment measures.
Shoreline Anchoring	Riprap, bulkheads, jetties, stream restoration, regulation of boat traffic, zoning of erosion-hazard areas, relocation of property, tax policies, land acquisition, flood proofing, flood forecasting, detention depressions, reservoirs, land treatment measures.
Sediment/Toxic Retention	Sedimentation depressions, land treatment measures, dilutional flushing, buffer strip policies, zoning, tax policies, water treatment facilities, dredged removal of contaminants.
Nutrient Retention	Same as Sediment/Toxic Retention, plus chemical treatment, aeration/circulation.
Fishery Habitat, Aquatic Diversity	Creation of replacement habitat, diversion of fishing efforts to unaffected species or non-fishing industries or recreational activities, improvement of habitat (e.g., stream restoration, placement of artificial shelters), stocking, predator management, modification of harvest restrictions, regulation of other limiting factors (e.g., pollutants).
Wildlife Habitat, General Diversity	Similar to Fishery Habitat above.
Ground Water Recharge	Artificial recharge pits, reservoir construction, induced recharge, sediment flushing to increase recharge.

Table 1-1 (Continued)

Active Recreation	Diversion of activities to alternate sites, construction of new sites (e.g., reservoirs, swimming pools), diversion to less water-dependent activities.

Source: The National Fish and Wildlife Foundation, *Fish and Wildlife Service Five-Year Needs Assessment* (December 1, 1988) (revised).

WETLAND VALUES

For many years, there has been considerable interest in revising the Clean Water Act Section 404 program to base permit decisions on the relative values of wetlands as determined in advance by the type or condition of the wetland. In response, several approaches have been proposed to classify or categorize wetlands based on their relative value, with commensurate levels of regulatory protection assigned to each category.

Categorization proponents believe that wetland regulation would be improved by focusing agency resources on protection of the most valuable wetlands. Categorization proponents also believe that this approach could provide greater consistency and predictability in the permit review process and reduce the regulatory burden for activities in lower value wetlands.

On the other hand, concern exists that such a hierarchical approach to wetland protection may result in "writing off" low value wetlands and increase the potential for wetland "takings" claims for high value wetlands. Related concerns include the complexity of evaluating wetland functions and values and the inadequacy of existing methods to do so. In addition, some feel that categorization would only lead to increased reliance on mitigation. Further, state experience indicates that categorization programs require substantial time and financial resources to implement.

Wetland values are currently assessed on a case-by-case basis during the Section 404 permit review process. The level of review is commensurate with the severity of the environmental impact, requiring consideration of both the relative value of the wetland and the impacts of the proposed activity.

In the mid-1980s, efforts to categorize wetlands on a national basis were abandoned because of scientific uncertainties. Some states, including New Jersey, New York, Maine, Pennsylvania, and Vermont, have applied categorization within their wetland protection programs. Alternatively, some states are establishing wetland categories as they incorporate wetlands into their water quality standards programs.

It has been found that categorization works best in the context of local or regional watershed planning initiatives where the relative value of wetlands can be more accurately assessed in the context of particular watershed needs.

WETLAND LOSSES

Over half (53 percent) of the wetlands in the lower 48 states were lost between the late 1700s and the mid-1980s.[5] About 100 million acres of wetlands remain today in the lower 48 states, representing less than 5 percent of the land mass in the continental United States.[6] Twenty-two states have lost at least 50 percent of their original wetlands. Seven of those states, California, Illinois, Indiana, Iowa, Missouri, Kentucky, and Ohio, have lost more than 80 percent of their original wetlands.[7] From the mid-1970s to the mid-1980s, wetlands were lost at an annual rate of 290,000 acres per year.[8]

As of 1985, the year that the Swampbuster provisions of the Food Security Act were enacted to slow the conversion of wetlands to agricultural use, 75 million acres of the nation's cropland had been developed by draining wetlands. From the mid-1970s to the mid-1980s, wetland conversions to agricultural land uses accounted for 54 percent of the wetland losses in the United States.[9] Since the mid-1980s, and passage of the Swampbuster provisions, indications are that wetland losses are slowing on agricultural lands. From 1987 to 1990, programs to restore wetlands under the Food Security Act added about 90,000 acres to the nation's wetlands inventory.

Consequences of Lost and Degraded Wetlands

Losing or degrading wetlands can lead to serious consequences, such as increased flooding, extinction of plant and wildlife species, decline in water quality, and loss of natural beauty. These consequences can be avoided by maintaining valuable wetlands and restoring degraded wetlands wherever possible.

If wetlands are lost or degraded, their ability to control flooding is lost or diminished. For example, the U.S. Army Corps of Engineers determined in a study of the Charles River Basin area in Massachusetts that the loss of 8,422 acres of wetlands near Boston would have resulted in annual flood damage exceeding $17 million. For this reason, the Army Corps elected to preserve the wetlands instead of constructing extensive flood control facilities.[10]

Because many species depend on wetlands, activities that harm wetlands also harm these species. For example, the well-being of waterfowl populations is tied directly to the status and abundance of wetland habitats. Populations of mallard and northern pintail ducks in North America have declined since 1955. The loss and degradation of wetlands is one of the major causes of the decline. In 1994, duck populations increased by 24 percent over the 1993 estimate and were the highest since 1980. Scientists believe that improved wetland conditions and increased cover on Conservation Reserve Program lands may be major factors for the increase.[11]

Degraded wetlands may not provide sufficient habitat to support species commonly found there. Wetlands in the Kesterton National Wildlife Refuge were continuously flooded with irrigation return flow that had high concentrations of selenium. As a result, large-mouth and striped bass and catfish disappeared from the refuge in 1982. In the spring of 1983, eggs from water birds at the site hatched less frequently and had more deformities in the embryos.[12]

Overlogging of mature U.S. bottomland hardwood forests is believed to have caused the extinction of North America's largest woodpecker, the Ivory-Billed Woodpecker.[13]

Destroying or degrading wetlands results in lower water quality. For example, forested wetlands reduce nutrient loading into water bodies, such as the Chesapeake Bay. Forested riparian (streamside) wetlands in predominantly agricultural watersheds have been shown to remove approximately 80 percent of the phosphorus and 90 percent of the nitrogen from the water. If wetlands do not perform this function, however, results will include an increase in undesirable weed growth and algal blooms. When algal blooms decompose, large amounts of oxygen are used up, depriving fish and other aquatic organisms. Algal blooms are a major cause of fish kills.

CLINTON ADMINISTRATION'S WETLANDS PLAN

On August 24, 1993, President Clinton's White House Office of Environmental Policy announced a comprehensive wetlands protection plan.[14] The "40-point" plan contains various proposals for administrative and congressional action aimed at reforming federal wetlands protection programs.[15] The primary goal of the plan is to improve federal wetlands policy by:

- Increasing cooperation with private landowners to protect and restore wetlands;
- Increasing public participation and state and local government involvement in wetlands protection;
- Streamlining wetlands permitting programs; and
- Basing wetland protection on good science and sound judgment.

A number of actions have already been undertaken to achieve these goals, including:

- Clarification, through regulation, that "prior converted" croplands are not to be regulated as wetlands under either the Food Security Act's "Swampbuster" program or the Clean Water Act's Section 404 program.
- Issuance of policies that have increased flexibility in wetland permitting and reduced burdens on permit applicants.[16]
- Responsibility to be given to USDA for identifying all wetlands on agricultural lands for both the Swampbuster and Section 404 programs.[17]

- New guidance on use of mitigation banks.[18]
- Greater flexibility in permitting requirements for Alaska due to unique circumstances in that state.[19]
- Development of administrative mechanisms to minimize the regulatory burden on landowners and farmers for small projects on their land.[20]
- Approval of state assumption of the Section 404 program for most inland wetlands by New Jersey.[21]
- Requested increased funding for the Wetlands Reserve Program to assist farmers who wish to restore wetlands.
- Increased funding to state and local governments for administration of wetlands programs.

In addition, a number of other initiatives are under consideration, including:

- Allowing administrative appeals of permit denials and wetland jurisdictional determinations as an alternative to expensive and time-consuming litigation.
- Establishing a wetland delineator certification program to increase the government's reliance on wetlands delineations performed by private experts, thereby providing greater flexibility and certainty to applicants.[22]
- Improvement of assessment techniques to allow for better consideration of wetland functions and values in permit decisions.
- Development of guidance to facilitate use of programmatic general permits, thus giving state/local governments more flexibility in wetlands protection and reducing unnecessary duplication.
- Expansion of the Wetlands Reserve Program into all 50 states and allowing more types of land into the program.

ENDNOTES

1. *See* Chapter 2 for a discussion of the 1995 study released by National Academy of Sciences.

2. *See Protecting America's Wetlands: An Action Agenda,* Final Report of the National Wetlands Policy Forum (1988).

3. *See The Impact of Federal Programs on Wetlands, Vol.II,* U.S. Dept. of Interior, Report to Congress (Mar. 1994), p. 31.

4. U.S. Congress, Office of Technology Assessment, *Preparing for an Uncertain Climate: Vol. II*, OTA-O-568, U.S. Gov't Printing Office, Washington, D.C., 1993.

5. Dahl, *Wetland Losses in the United States 1780s to 1980s,* U.S. Fish and Wildlife Service, Washington, D.C., 1990.

6. Dahl and Johnson, *Status and Trends of Wetlands in the Conterminous United States*, U.S. Fish and Wildlife Service, 1989.

7. Mitsch and Gosselink, *Wetlands, Second Edition*, Van Nostrand Reinhold, New York, N.Y., 1993.

8. Dahl and Johnson, *Status and Trends of Wetlands in the Conterminous United States, Mid-1970s to Mid-1980s*, U.S. Fish and Wildlife Service, 1990.

9. In the period of the mid-1950s to the mid-1970s, agricultural conversions represented 87 percent of all wetland losses. *See The Impact of Federal Programs on Wetlands, Vol.II,* U.S. Dept. of Interior, Report to Congress (Mar. 1994), p. 2.

10. Army Corps of Engineers, *Water Resources Development Plan, Charles River Watershed, Massachusetts*, Army Corps, New England Division, Waltham, MA, 1976.

11. U.S. Fish and Wildlife Service, *Waterfowl Population Status 1994*, Office of Migratory Bird Management, U.S. Gov't Printing Office, Washington, D.C., 1994.

12. Harris, *Death in the Marsh* (Island Press, Washington, D.C., 1991).

13. Gosselink, et al., eds., *Ecological Processes and Cumulative Impacts* (Lewis Publishers, Chelsea, MI, 1990).

14. White House Office of Environmental Policy, *Protecting America's Wetlands: A Fair, Flexible and Effective Approach*, (Aug. 24, 1993).

15. A copy of this wetlands policy statement is reproduced as Appendix D.

16. *See* EPA/Army Corps, *Memorandum for the Field: Individual Permit Flexibility for Small Landowners* (March 6, 1995).

17. *See Memorandum of Agreement Among the Department of Agriculture, the Environmental Protection Agency, the Department of the Interior, and the Department of the Army Concerning the Delineation of Wetlands for Purposes of Section 404 of the Clean Water Act and Subtitle B of the Food Security Act* (January 6, 1994).

18. *See* "Federal Guidance for the Establishment, Use and Operation of Mitigation Banks," 60 Fed. Reg. 58605 (Nov. 28, 1995). *See also* EPA/Army Corps, *Memorandum to the Field: Establishment and Use of Wetland Mitigation Banks in the Clean Water Act Section 404 Regulatory Program* (Aug. 23, 1993).

19. *Alaska Wetlands Initiative (Final)*, May, 13, 1994. Copies may be ordered by calling the EPA Wetlands Information hotline at (800) 832-7828.

20. *See also* "Issuance of Nationwide Permit for Single-Family Housing," 60 Fed. Reg. 38650 (July 27, 1995).

21. *See* 59 Fed. Reg. 9933 (Mar. 2, 1994).

22. *See* "Wetland Delineator Certification Program; Proposed Rule," 60 Fed. Reg. (Mar. 14, 1995).

Chapter 2

Wetland Identification

WETLANDS DEFINED

Wetlands are generally found in topographical landscape depressions where water collects, and between dry land and water along the edges of streams, rivers, lakes, and coastlines. Wetlands of various types exist throughout the United States.[1] Examples are bogs, bottomland hardwoods, fens, mangrove swamps, marshes, and emergent wetlands. Bogs typically have a thick layer of floating root masses or peat on the surface and are highly acidic. Bogs have no regular inlet or outlet of water and are dependent upon precipitation. Bottomland hardwoods are deciduous forested wetlands found along rivers and streams. Fens have a defined outlet and are supported by mineral-rich groundwater that has seeped to the surface. Mangrove swamps are coastal saltwater shrub or forested wetlands that may be flooded with water all year around or only during high tides. Marshes are emergent wetlands with a regular inlet and outlet of salt or freshwater and are found in coastal and inland areas. Emergent wetlands are characterized by free-standing, nonwoody plants and can be either freshwater or saltwater.

Perhaps because of the variety of wetland types, a consequent variety of wetland definitions have emerged. A 1988 report by the National Wetlands Policy Forum estimated that over fifty definitions existed among the various federal agencies.[2] Of these fifty definitions, only two have primary importance. The U.S. EPA, the Army Corps of Engineers, and the National Resource Conservation Service, the primary agencies in charge of overseeing the federal regulation of wetlands, use the following general definition for wetlands:

Wetlands are "[t]hose areas that are inundated or saturated by surface or groundwater at a frequency and duration sufficient to support, and that under normal circumstances do support, a prevalence of vegetation typically adapted for life in saturated soil conditions. Wetlands generally include swamps, marshes, bogs, and similar areas."[3]

The U.S. Fish and Wildlife Service's Wetland Classification System provides the other principal wetlands definition.[4] The Fish and Wildlife Service defines wetlands as "lands transitional between terrestrial and aquatic systems where the water table is usually at or near the surface or the land is covered by shallow water. For purposes of this classification wetlands must have one or more of the following three attributes:

1. At least periodically, the land supports predominately hydrophytes.
2. The substrate is predominately undrained hydric soil.
3. The substrate is nonsoil and is saturated with water or covered by shallow water at some time during the growing season of each year."[5]

The Fish and Wildlife Service definition is more expansive because it includes non-vegetated wetlands such as mud-flats, sandflats, rocky shores, shallow open waters, and sand bars.[6] This definition has been used primarily by the Fish and Wildlife Service to prepare a national wetland inventory and map system.[7] This definition has indirectly impacted the Section 404 permit program because the Fish and Wildlife Service has an advisory role in the permit process and may comment on whether particular wetlands serve as valuable wildlife habitats.[8]

In common language, wetlands are areas where the frequent and prolonged presence of water at or near the soil surface drives the natural system, including the kinds of soils that form, the plants that grow, and the fish and wildlife that habitat the area. Swamps, marshes, and bogs are well-recognized types of wetlands which are generally easier to identify than drier and more variable wetlands, such as vernal pools, playa lakes, and prairie potholes.

However, determining whether a particular area is a wetland is much more difficult than this general characterization might lead one to believe. The old adage that "it looks and sounds like a duck so it must be a duck" is hardly applicable in the case of wetlands. In fact, there is considerable conflict of opinion between the scientific, regulatory, and regulated community over the means for determining which areas should be classified as wetlands.[9]

It is generally accepted that wetlands can be identified by the hydrology, soil conditions, and plant growth in an area. When the upper part of the soil is saturated with water at growing season temperatures, soil organisms consume the oxygen in the soil and cause conditions unsuitable for most plants (*i.e.*, anaerobic soil conditions). Such chemial conditions also cause the development of recognizable soil characteristics (such as color and texture) of so-called "hydric" soils. The plants that can grow in such conditions, such as marsh grass, are called "hydrophytes." Together, hydric soils and hydrophytes provide evidence that an area is a wetland.

The presence of water—by ponding, flooding, or soil saturation—is not always a good indicator of wetlands. Except for wetlands that are flooded by ocean tides, the amount of water present in wetlands varies as a result of rainfall patterns, snow melt, dry seasons, and droughts. Some of the best known wetlands, such as the Florida Everglades and the Mississippi bottomland hardwood swamps, are often dry. In contrast, many upland areas are very wet during and shortly after wet weather. Such natural fluctuations must be considered when identifying wetlands based on hydrologic indicators.

It may be rather obvious in some cases that a given area contains wetlands, such as an area saturated with water and dominated by wetland plant species for long periods during the year; however, in many cases wetland boundary identification at the margins is problematic and subject to differing opinions. This is further confounded by inconsistent application of rules for evidence and lack of scientifically based thresholds for wetland delineation. Even in situations where a wetland clearly exists, it is generally difficult to place an exact boundary line at the margins where wetlands end and uplands begin. Regulators are on a seemingly never-ending quest to formulate reliable wetland maps and regulated parties continually call the wetland boundaries into question.

Obviously, wetlands must be identified to be regulated and/or protected; however, wetland delineation—despite ongoing scientific refinements—is yet to be an exact science. Even if a complete and precise scientific methodology existed for wetland identification, true application of any methodology would surely be hampered by human factors, including resources and time available for determination, the relative expertise of the delineator, and the influence of competing political interests (*i.e.*, environmental protectionists, government regulators, private property owners).

FEDERAL MANUAL FOR DELINEATING WETLANDS

On January 10, 1989, the U.S. Environmental Protection Agency, the Army Corps of Engineers, the Soil Conservation Service (now called the Natural Resources Conservation Service) of the U.S. Department of Agriculture, and the Fish and Wildlife Service of the U.S. Department of Interior introduced a *Federal Manual for Identifying and Delineating Wetlands.* The manual was devised to provide technical criteria, field indicators, and other types of information necessary to make consistent wetland determinations among the various federal agencies in charge of regulating wetlands. Each agency had its own legal definition of what a wetland was, so the federal manual was devised to coordinate interagency regulation of wetlands.

During the following two years, the 1989 Manual was used by the agencies for wetland delineation, chiefly for identifying and delineating wetlands subject to federal regulations under the Clean Water Act. Use of the manual coupled with policy changes (*e.g.*, farmed wetlands) led to a significant increase in federal jurisdiction over wetlands in many areas of the country. Unfortunately, during this time, misconceptions concerning use of the 1989 Manual (*e.g.*, classifying any area mapped with hydric soil as wetland without considering other criteria), also led to exaggerated claims of expanded federal regulation. This atmosphere of misinformation and public concern over regulation created an obvious need to review the 1989 Manual and revise it as necessary.

Critics of the manual contended that many of the approximately 7,000 plant species used as wetland indicators also occur with some frequency in non-wetland areas. The manual was also opposed because it created thirteen special conditions under which land may be deemed wetland by satisfying only one or two of the three required technical criteria for identifying wetland.[10] Critics further contended that the manual was replete with technical flaws, including the failure to recognize significant regional differences in vegetation and soil across the country.[11]

In the wake of controversy, the four agencies recognized that additional clarification and/or changes might be required, and had planned to review the situation after the first year of implementation. Thus, in May 1990, the agencies initiated an evaluation of the 1989 Manual, concluding that while the manual represented a substantial improvement over pre-existing approaches, several key issues needed to be re-examined and clarified. Some of the key technical issues needing re-examination were:

1. The wetland hydrology criterion.
2. The use of hydric soil for delineating the wetland boundary.
3. The assumption that facultative vegetation indicated wetland hydrology.
4. The open-ended nature of the determination process, which created opportunities for misuse.

In response to the expansive nature of the manual and subsequent political repercussions, the Army Corps initiated efforts to limit the manual's scope. Specifically, on September 26, 1990, the Corps issued a regulatory guidance memorandum providing that farmers are no longer required to obtain Section 404 permits to change previously converted wetlands from agricultural to other uses.[12] The Corps reasoned that the converted croplands would not support a "prevalence of hydrophytic vegetation" and therefore should not be classified as wetlands.[13]

In August 1991, the EPA issued proposed revisions to address the inadequacies of the 1989 Manual.[14] Further controversy has surrounded the proposed revisions. EPA received a virtually unprecedented 80,000+ public comments, reflecting conflicting public and private interests on the proposed revisions.[15] While a new delineation manual is being developed, Congress has forbidden use of the 1989 Manual.[16] For the time being, the EPA and the Army Corps have agreed to use the previous 1987 Corps Manual[17] to delineate wetlands.[18]

NATIONAL ACADEMY OF SCIENCES WETLAND STUDY

In 1992, in response to the controversy over the federal manual for delineating wetlands, Congress commissioned the National Academy of Sciences (NAS) to conduct a study of scientific approaches to wetlands characterization. The study was carried out by a committee overseen jointly by the Water Science and Technology Board (WSTB) and the Board on Environmental Studies and Toxicology (BEST), with input from other relevant units of the National Research Council. The results of the study were released in May 1995. The study reviewed and evaluated the consequences of alternative wetland delineation approaches based on an understanding of how wetlands function. The wetland characterization committee, comprised of representatives from science, academia, business, and conservationist groups, concluded that a single regulatory definition, single delineation manual, and consolidation of regulatory authority within a single federal agency would substantially improve the regulation of wetlands.

In its report, entitled *Wetlands: Characteristics and Boundaries*, the wetland characterization committee focuses on the science of identifying and delineating wetlands. It establishes a reference definition of wetlands, providing a standard by which regulatory definitions and actions can be assessed. It also calls for increased recognition of regional differences, better training of wetland delineators, and further research into the characteristics and functions of wetlands.

The report states that three factors must be considered when wetlands are identified: water, soil, and plants. Of these, water has special status because the soils and plants characteristic of wetlands cannot develop without the proper hydrologic conditions. But assessing the hydrology of an area is often difficult, in part because the water conditions needed to produce a wetland may occur for very short periods. In such cases, those responsible for delineating wetlands often use the soil and vegetation as the most feasible and reliable evidence for the presence of wetlands. But these factors are not infallible. For example, if water conditions have been altered, the presence of soil or plants characteristic of a wetland does not necessarily indicate that a wetland still exists. The new reference definition established by the committee takes these considerations into account by emphasizing the primacy of water conditions while also citing soil and vegetation conditions as important indicators.[19]

WETLAND CHARACTERISTICS

Although the wetland picture is frequently blurred, there are still some widely accepted criteria that can be used to help put a wetland into focus. Scientific analysis of hydrology, soils, and vegetation form the basis for classifying a particular tract of land as a wetland. In fact, these three basic elements comprise the criteria for the legal delineation of all wetlands. Generally speaking, a wetland will have water-saturated soil that is alternately inundated and drained with a low diffusion of oxygen. Plants may have honeycombed stems with big air spaces to aid the plant in diffusing oxygen down to the roots. Gray and black silts and clays of very fine texture are commonly present.

Parties who are challenging wetland regulation need to understand these basic components, whether contesting the government's wetland classification and/or permit denial or whether seeking to protect an area as a wetland.

Wetland Hydrology

The crucial factor leading to creation of all wetlands is a permanent or periodic inundation, or soil saturation for a significant period[20] during the growing season in most years. The frequency and duration of inundation or soil saturation is one indicator that separates wetland from nonwetland areas. Wetland hydrology is, however, usually the most difficult indicator to verify in the field because of annual, seasonal, and daily fluctuations in the amount of water present.[21]

Wetlands of all types, tidal and nontidal, are formed along rivers, lakes, and estuaries where flooding is likely to occur, or may be found in isolated depressions surrounded by upland where surface water collects. When water is present in the soil from inundation for 15 or more consecutive days or saturation from surface water or from groundwater to the surface occurs for 21 or more consecutive days during the growing season in most years, anaerobic conditions typically affect the types of plants that can grow and the types of soils that develop.[22]

Hydric Soils

Wetland hydrology results in formation of hydric soils. Hydric soils are defined as soils that are saturated, flooded, or ponded long enough during the growing season to develop anaerobic conditions in the upper part.[23] Wetness during the growing season will cause anaerobic soil conditions that normally lead to a chemical reduction of some soil components, mainly iron oxides and manganese oxides. The reduction of these oxides is reflected in the soil color and other physical characteristics that are indicative of hydric soils. Soil saturation and inundation also impedes aerobic decomposition of the organic materials, such as leaves, stems, and roots, and encourages their accumulation over time as peat or muck.

Hydric soils are separated into two major types on the basis of material composition: organic soil and mineral soil.[24] In general, soils with at least 16 inches of organic material in the upper part of the soil profile and soils with organic material resting on bedrock are considered organic soils (histosols). Soils largely composed of sand, silt, and/or clay are mineral soils.

Hydric organic soils are subdivided into three groups based on the presence of identifiable plant material:

1. *Muck* (saprists) in which two-thirds or more of the material is decomposed and less than one-third of the plant fibers are identifiable;
2. *Peat* (fibrists) in which less than one-third of the material is decomposed and more than two-thirds of the plant fibers are still identifiable; and
3. *Mucky peat* or *peaty muck* (hemists) in which the ratio of decomposed to identifiable plant matter is more nearly even.[25]

Hydric organic soils can be easily identified as black-colored muck to dark brown-colored peat.[26] These soils form where the land is very poorly drained. Distinguishing mucks from peats based on the relative degree of decomposition is fairly simple. In mucks, almost all of the plant remains have been decomposed beyond recognition. When rubbed, mucks feel greasy and leave hands dirty. In contrast, the plant remains in peats show little decomposition and the original constituent plants can be recognized fairly easily. When the organic matter is rubbed between the fingers, most plants fibers will remain identifiable, leaving hands relatively clean. Between the extremes of mucks and peats, organic soils with partially decomposed plant fibers can be recognized. In peaty mucks up to two-thirds of the plant fibers can be destroyed by rubbing the materials between the fingers, while in mucky peats up to two-thirds of the plant remains are still recognizable after rubbing.

When less organic material accumulates in soil, the soil may be a hydric mineral soil. Although some mineral soils may have thick organic surface layers due to heavy seasonal rainfall or a high water table, these soils are still composed largely of mineral matter.[27] A thick dark surface layer, grayish subsurface and subsoil colors, the presence of orange or reddish brown (iron) and/or dark reddish brown or black (manganese) mottles near the surface, and the wet condition of the soil may help identify the hydric character of many mineral soils.[28] When drained, however, these characteristics persist for very long periods.

Wetland Vegetation

Wetlands are generally dominated by numerous species of plants.[29] Vegetation is a primary indicator for wetland habitats.[30] The growth of these plants is influenced by the frequency of inundation and the drainage of the soil, the amount of salinity, soil sediment type, and oxygen levels in the soil.[31] All plants growing in wetlands have adapted in one way or another to life in permanently or periodically inundated or saturated soils. Some plants have developed structural or morphological adaptations to inundation or saturation, while others have broad ecological tolerances. On the other hand, many important "upland" species cannot survive in wetlands. Because the growth of each plant species is influenced by these factors, presence of particular species in different areas is suggestive of the type of soil and hydrology present in that location. Wetland vegetation is therefore heavily relied upon as an indicator for wetlands.

FIELD TESTING AND DATA COLLECTION

The scientist uses field testing methods to arrive at a conclusion as to whether a particular tract of land constitutes a wetland. In performing the field testing, the scientist will collect data on hydrology, soils, and vegetation of the area to make the wetland assessment. Each of these components must be investigated before an accurate identification of wetland areas can be made. If an area is a wetland, boundaries will be drawn and the wetland may then be shown as such on federal, state, or county maps.

Hydrology Indicators

In identifying a wetland, the duration and frequency of inundation by flooding in some locations may be established by evaluating long-term stream or tide gauge data[32] or by examining aerial photos covering at least a 5-year period.[33] Historical recorded hydrologic data may provide both short- and long-term information on the frequency and duration of flooding, but little or no information on soil saturation periods. Historical recorded data include stream gauge data, lake gauge data, tide gauge data, flood predictions, and historical flood records. Use of these data is commonly limited to areas adjacent to streams and other similar areas.

Recorded data may be available from the following sources:

- Army Corps of Engineer district offices (data for major waterbodies and for site-specific areas from planning and design documents).
- U.S. Geological Survey (stream and tidal gauge data).
- National Oceanic and Atmospheric Administration (tidal gauge data).
- State, county, and local agencies (flood data).
- Natural Resource Conservation Service state offices (small watershed projects and water table study data).
- Private developers or landowners (site-specific hydrologic data, which may include water table or groundwater well data).

Surface saturation may be determined by making observations in an unlined borehole and discovering whether the soil is saturated to the surface for 21 or more consecutive days during the growing season in a majority of years. If surface soil saturation is observed for 21 or more consecutive days during the growing season, or the area is inundated for 15 or more consecutive days, wetland hydrology probably exists. An accurate interpretation of these field observations must always take into account recent and long-term rainfall conditions that occurred before and during the time the hydrologic data was gathered. Both the season of the year and the preceding weather conditions must be considered, because excess water may not be present during parts of the growing season in some wetlands due to high evaporation and plant transpiration rates that lower the water table.[34] Alternatively, nonwetlands may exceed the hydrology threshold in abnormally wet years.

Many times surface soil saturation will be apparent from a ground surface that is clearly soggy or mucky. At other times, it may be necessary to dig a hole and observe the level at which water stands in the hole once sufficient time has passed to allow any water to drain into the hole from the surrounding soil. By observing the walls of the hole, it may also become possible to determine the upper level at which water is flowing into the hole. Still, in some heavy clay soils, water may take a long time to accumulate in the hole even when the soil is saturated. Therefore, whenever attempting to observe the level of free water in a bore hole, it is crucial that adequate time be allowed for water in the hole to reach equilibrium with the water table.

Another simple test for soil saturation at the surface is the "squeeze test" or "shake test" method. By taking a surface soil sample and squeezing or shaking the sample, soil saturation may be determined if water can be extracted. Other signs that may reflect the geophysical extent of wetland hydrology include water marks, drift lines, water-borne deposits, surface-scoured areas, wetland drainage patterns, and certain plant morphological adaptations,[35] although none of these indicators address the duration of wetness.

Aerial photographs may also provide direct evidence of inundation or soil saturation at the surface in an area. Inundation (flooding or ponding) is best observed during the early spring in temperate and boreal regions when snow and ice are gone and leaves of deciduous trees and shrubs are not yet fully developed. This allows detection of wet soil conditions that would be obscured by the tree or shrub canopy at full leaf-out. For marshes, this season of photography may be desirable, except in regions characterized by distinct dry and rainy seasons, such as southern Florida and California. Wetland hydrology would be best observed during the wet season in these latter areas. It is most desirable to examine several consecutive years of early spring or wet season aerial photographs to document evidence of wetland inundation or soil saturation. In this way, the effects of abnormally dry or wet springs, for example, may be minimized. In interpreting aerial photographs, it is important to know the antecedent weather conditions. This will help eliminate potential misinterpretations caused by abnormally wet or dry periods. Contact the U.S. Weather Service for historical weather records or the U.S. Geological Survey for hydrologic records. Aerial photographs for agricultural regions of the country are often available at county offices of the Agricultural Stabilization and Conservation Service.

Hydric Soil Indicators

A detailed examination of soil conditions provides a good indication of whether hydric soils are present. However, examination of soil indicators is complex because over 2,000 soil types occur in wetlands.[36] Soil colors are strongly influenced by the frequency and duration of soil saturation. A gray layer with dark dominant colors[37] and brighter colored mottles[38] near the surface are common indicators of hydric soils in the United States.

In hydric soils, the distinctive colors result from a process known as gleization.[39] Prolonged saturation of mineral soil converts iron from its oxidized (ferric) form to its reduced (ferrous) state. These reduced compounds may be completely removed from the soil, resulting in gleying. Gleyed layers are predominantly gray in color and occasionally greenish or bluish gray, as shown on the gley page of Munsell color charts. Mineral soils that are always saturated may develop uniform gleyed colors. Soils gleyed shallower than ten inches from the surface are evidence of formation under wetland hydrology and anaerobic soil conditions. These soils may show evidence of oxidizing conditions only along root channels.[40]

Mineral soils that are alternately saturated and oxidized (aerated) during the year are usually mottled in the part of the soil that is seasonally wet. The abundance, size, and color of the mottles usually reflect the hydrology—the duration of the saturation period—and indicate whether or not the soil is saturated for long periods. Mineral soils that are predominantly grayish with common or many, distinct or prominent brown or yellow mottles are usually saturated for long periods during the growing season and are hydric soils. Soils that are predominantly brown or yellow with gray mottles are saturated for shorter periods and may be hydric depending on the depth to the gray mottles and the color of the overlying layer. Mineral soils that are never saturated are usually bright-colored and are not mottled—they are nonhydric soils.[41] Soils that developed gray and mottled colors under saturation will retain those colors indefinitely after the water has been removed. Hence, care must be taken when inferring current wetness from soil colors alone. Evidence of hydrology is essential where field conditions suggest a likelihood of hydrologic change.

Wetland Vegetation Indicators

Field identification of the species composition present in a possible wetland will aid in proper wetland delineation. Plant identification requires that the scientist use field guides or more technical taxonomic manuals to properly identify the genus and species of each kind of plant found in a potential wetland area.[42] More than 7,000 plant types in the United States may occur in wetlands.[43] Indicators of wetland plants include among other things "trees having shallow root systems, swollen trunks ..., or roots found growing from the plant stem or trunk above the soil surface."[44]

Because not all wetland plant species grow only in wetlands, plants alone cannot be the sole criterion for identifying and delineating wetlands.[45] The majority of plant species growing in wetlands also grow in nonwetland areas in varying abundance. Many plants that require saturated soils to compete successfully in the wild (obligate hydrophytes) do not require those saturated conditions throughout the year. Further, many more kinds of plants not only have roots capable of growing in the oxygen-poor conditions of saturated soils but also can compete successfully in well-drained uplands (facultative hydrophytes). For example, in New Jersey, there are about 3,000 species of higher plants that grow in the wild. Of these, 20 percent are obligate hydrophytes, 46 percent are facultative hydrophytes, and 34 percent are obligate upland plants considered to be intolerant of wetland conditions.[46] This variability in habitat occurrence makes identification of wetlands from a purely botanical standpoint very difficult in many cases. For this reason, it is crucial that the scientist also evaluate soils and hydrology when identifying wetlands.[47]

Wetland Mapping Criteria

In response to scientific study of wetland ecosystems, governments at the state and local level have designated particular areas as wetlands. Long before specific laws and regulations were enacted to protect these areas, geographic and topographic maps were drawn that showed where some wetlands were found. The various environmental protection agencies rely heavily on these maps when permits for development and dredge or fill activities are sought. Activities taking place in areas designated as wetlands on these maps may be closely scrutinized for compliance with environmental protection laws. Any attorney or wetland consultant advising a client who wishes to carry out an activity on a specific property with wetland characteristics must understand how to read these maps and be on guard for normal technical errors to properly advise the client regarding the legality of carrying out activities on the property. Published maps are no substitute for onsite delineation of wetlands.

Once an area has been delineated as a wetland based on the field study and findings of hydrology, hydric soils, and wetland vegetation, the area is typically denoted as such on site plans for construction projects. The U.S. Fish and Wildlife Service maintains U.S. Geological Survey maps overprinted with wetlands identification, known as National Wetlands Inventory Maps.[48] Each state is broken down into quadrangles and a map is available for each quadrangle. The National Wetlands Inventory (NWI) has produced over 32,000 1:24,000-scale and 1:63,360-scale wetland maps covering 74 percent of the lower 48 states and 24 percent of Alaska. More than 1,450,000 copies of these maps have been distributed by NWI.[49] They are useful documents but are not regulatory maps.

Mapping priorities are based principally on the needs of the FWS and other federal and state agencies. High priority is given to the coastal zone (which includes the coastline of the Great Lakes), prairie wetlands, playa lakes, floodplains of major rivers and other areas that support the goals of the North American Waterfowl Plan. The NWI produces wetland maps at a rate of five percent per year in the lower 48 states and two percent annually in Alaska. The NWI will have to increase the rate of map production in Alaska to approximately 12 percent of the state annually to comply with the new mandate of the Wild Exotic Bird Conservation Act Amendments to the Emergency Wetlands Resources Act. By law, the NWI is required to complete the mapping of the remainder of the contiguous United States by September 30, 1998 and by September 30, 2000 for Alaska and non-contiguous portions of the United States.

The NWI is also constructing a digitized, geographically referenced wetland database. All map data are stored in a common, ground-based, geographic reference system. These digital data are being used for such applications as resource management planning, impact assessment, wetland trend analysis and information retrieval. As of 1994, more than 6,000 NWI maps, representing 11.5 percent of the continental United States, have been digitized.[50] Statewide databases have been built for New Jersey, Delaware, Maryland, Illinois, Indiana, and Washington and are in progress in Minnesota, Virginia, South Carolina, South Dakota, and Florida. NWI digital databases are also available for portions of 33 other states. Copies of database files can be purchased at cost from the NWI offices in St. Petersburg, Florida.[51]

The states also maintain their own wetlands maps with wetlands delineated in accordance with state criteria. Some state maps are regulatory while some are not. A property owner or developer should consult both the state and federal maps to determine whether wetlands are located on the property, and if so, how the state and federal laws and regulations restrict activities in wetland areas.[52]

ENDNOTES

1. "Proposed Revisions to the Federal Manual for Delineating Wetlands," 56 Fed. Reg. 40446 (Aug. 14, 1991).

2. *See Protecting America's Wetlands: An Action Agenda,* Final Report of the National Wetlands Policy Forum (1988), at 36.

3. 33 C.F.R. §§ 328.3; 230.3.

4. U.S. Fish and Wildlife Service, *Classification of Wetlands and Deepwater Habitats of the United States*, U.S. Dept. of the Interior, FWS/OBS-79/31 (1979), at p. 3.

5. *Id.* at p. 3 (footnotes omitted).

6. *Id.* at p. 8.

7. *Id.* at p. 3.

8. 33 U.S.C. § 1344(m).

9. *See* Schmid, "Wetlands in the Urban Landscape of the United States," in *The Ecological City: Preserving and Restoring Urban Biodiversity* (Platt, Rowntree, and Muick, eds.) Univ. of Massachusetts Press, Amherst, MA, 1994, pp. 106-133.

10. *See* "Impacted Community Seeks to Scale Back Overly 'Broad' Federal Wetland Guide," 11(35) *Inside EPA* 12 (Aug. 31, 1990).

11. *Id.*

12. *See* "Millions Of Acres Of Converted Wetlands No Longer Subject To Federal Water Act Permits," 21 *Env't. Rep. (BNA)* 1121 (Oct. 5, 1990).

13. *Id.*

14. 56 Fed. Reg. 40446 (Aug. 14, 1991).

15. A January 1992 report by the Environmental Defense Fund and the World Wildlife Fund indicated that the proposed changes to the manual would strip

federal protection from approximately one-half the remaining wetlands in the United States. *How Wet Is a Wetland? The Impacts of the Proposed Revisions to the Federal Delineation Manual,* Report by Environmental Defense Fund and World Wildlife Fund (Jan. 16, 1992), reproduced in *Daily Env't Rep. (BNA)* at E-1 (Jan. 17, 1992).

16. Pub. L. No. 102-377, 106 Stat. 1315, 1324 (1992).

17. U.S. Army Corps of Engineers, *Corps of Engineers Wetlands Delineation Manual,* ADA 176-734, Technical Report Y-87-1 (Jan. 1987).

18. 58 Fed.Reg. 4995 (Jan. 19, 1993) (agreement to use 1987 Corps manual). The Department of the Interior, although not formally agreeing to use the 1987 manual, has agreed to defer to the delineation decisions of the EPA and Army Corps for purposes of Section 404.

19. Copies of the committee's report are available for $37.95 by calling the National Academy Press at (800) 624-6242.

20. The Federal Delineation Manual requires inundation for 15 or more consecutive days or saturation from surface water or from groundwater to the surface for 21 or more consecutive days. *Federal Manual for Delineating Wetlands* (1989).

21. Numerous factors influence the wetness of an area, including the amount of precipitation, the topography of the area, soil permeability, and plant cover. *Federal Manual for Delineating Wetlands* (1989).

22. Anaerobiosis does not necessarily occur in all wetlands and those where it may not occur include vegetated sand bars, seepage areas, springs, and the upper edges of salt marshes. *Federal Manual for Delineating Wetlands* (1989).

23. 56 Fed. Reg. 40456 (Aug. 14, 1991).

24. For technical definitions, *see Soil Taxonomy,* U.S.D.A. Soil Survey Staff, 1975.

25. *See Id.*

26. 56 Fed. Reg. 40457 (Aug. 14, 1991).

27. *Id.*

28. *Id.*

29. For example, salt hay, black grass, saltworts, sea lavender, tall cordgrass, hightide bush, cattail, groundsel, marsh mallow and intertidal low marsh cordgrass are common tidal wetland plant species. N.Y. Envtl. Conserv. Laws § 25-0103(1)(b) (McKinney).

30. 56 Fed. Reg. 40460 (Aug. 14, 1991).

31. Day, Hall, Kemp, and Yanez-Arancibia, *Estuarine Ecology*, John Wiley & Sons, Inc., New York, N.Y, 1989, p. 211.

32. 56 Fed. Reg. 40453 (Aug. 14, 1991).

33. *Id.*

34. *Id.*

35. *Id.*

36. *See* Army Corps of Engineers, *Recognizing Wetlands* (1987), at 4.

37. These are the low chroma colors, such as black, various shades of gray, and the darker shades of brown and red, as shown on the gley page of the Munsell color charts.

38. Mottles are spots or blotches of different colors or shades of colors interspersed with the dominant (matrix) color. 56 Fed. Reg. 40453, 40457-40458 (Aug. 14, 1991).

39. 56 Fed. Reg. 40453, 40457-40458 (Aug. 14, 1991).

40. *Id.*

41. *Id.*

42. For example, the U.S. Fish and Wildlife Service publishes such guides. *See* Reed, *National List of Plant Species that Occur in Wetlands*, U.S. Fish and Wildlife Service, 1988, 188 pp.; Tiner, *Field Guide to Nontidal Wetlands Identification,* U.S. Fish and Wildlife Service, 1988, 283 pp.

43. Reed, *National List of Plant Species that Occur in Wetlands*, U.S. Fish and Wildlife Service, Wetland Ecology Group, Biological Report 88(24), 1988, 188 pp.

44. *See* Army Corps of Engineers, *Recognizing Wetlands* (1987), at 4.

45. Of the nearly 7,000 vascular plant species which have been found growing in U.S. wetlands, only about 27 percent are "obligate wetland" species that nearly always occur in wetlands under natural conditions. Reed, *National List of Plant Species that Occur in Wetlands*, U.S. Fish and Wildlife Service, Wetland Ecology Group, Biological Report 88(24), 1988, 188 pp.

46. *See* Schmid, *Checklist and Synonymy of New Jersey Higher Plants With Special Reference to Their Rarity and Wetland Indicator Status*, Media, PA: Schmid & Co., 1994.

47. The proposed revisions to the Federal Manual would require that all three criteria be met before an area could be classified as a wetland. Proposed Revisions to the Federal Manual for Delineating Wetlands, U.S. EPA, August 14, 1991.

48. For example, the state of New Jersey is broken into 179 quadrangles. To determine where wetlands are located in specific area in the state, one would purchase the quadrangle map for the particular location. The maps are produced on a scale of 1 to 24,000 with one inch equaling 2,000 feet.

49. Information on the availability of NWI maps may be obtained by calling 1-800-USA-MAPS. In area code (703), the phone number is (703) 648-6045.

50. All maps will be in digital format by September 30, 2004.

51. To order NWI digital wetland data, call 1-800-USA-MAPS. In area code (703), the phone number is (703) 648-6045.

52. *See* Chapter 3 for an overview of wetlands regulation.

Chapter 3

Wetlands Regulation

INTRODUCTION

A variety of federal, state, and local laws and regulations affect development activities in wetland areas. The types, sizes, and locations of wetlands governed by these regulations vary. As a result, applicants for wetland permits must conduct a case-by-case review of the applicable laws and contact relevant federal, state, and local authorities prior to project development. For large-scale projects, the developer may elect to hire an environmental consultant and/or attorney to coordinate the permitting process.

The primary federal laws that regulate wetland development activities are Sections 404 and 401 of the Clean Water Act, and Section 10 of the Rivers and Harbors Act. Other federal laws may also apply, including the National Environmental Policy Act (NEPA), the Coastal Zone Management Act (CZMA), and the Swampbuster provisions of the Food Security Act of 1985, as amended in 1990 and 1996. Various state laws may also regulate wetland development, including state freshwater and tidal wetland laws, state environmental quality review acts, and state coastal zone management regulations. Finally, some localities may also have municipal ordinances governing activities in wetland areas. This chapter provides a comprehensive overview of this regulatory framework.

CLEAN WATER ACT SECTION 404 PROGRAM

The principal federal law regulating activities in wetland areas is the Federal Water Pollution Control Act, commonly referred to as the Clean

Water Act (CWA).[1] Section 404 of the CWA provides the primary federal authority for protecting the nation's wetlands.[2] The U.S. Army Corps of Engineers (Army Corps) is charged with primary oversight responsibility for the Section 404 program with guidance from the U.S. Environmental Protection Agency (EPA).

The Army Corps was first given authority to regulate construction activities involving dredging, filling, or obstructing "navigable waters" under the Rivers and Harbors Act of 1899,[3] however, this authority did not expressly include wetlands.[4] The Rivers and Harbors Act had very limited impact on the protection of wetlands because such areas are usually outside the mean high water mark. For this reason, the Army Corps operated its permit program for almost seventy years while paying little attention to the protection of wetlands. This approach changed, however, when passage of the National Environmental Policy Act of 1969 (NEPA)[5] empowered the Army Corps to consider environmental factors in its permitting process. Under NEPA, all federal agencies are required to consider the possible environmental impact of their proposed actions and projects.[6]

In 1972, three years following the passage of NEPA, Congress amended the Federal Water Pollution Control Act (commonly known as the Clean Water Act), which created the Clean Water Act Section 404 program. On its face, the express language of CWA Section 404 is limited to requiring permits for the "discharge of dredged or fill material" into "navigable waters."[7] Army Corps regulations define dredged material as "material that is excavated or dredged from waters of the United States."[8] Fill material is defined as "any material used for the primary purpose of replacing an aquatic area with dry land or of changing the bottom elevation of a waterbody."[9]

The "navigable waters" language of Section 404 has been interpreted broadly to mean all "waters of the United States,"[10] which may include wetlands. The Army Corps defines "waters of the United States" to mean "[a]ll waters which are currently used, or were used in the past, or may be susceptible to use in interstate or foreign commerce, including all waters which are subject to the ebb and flow of the tide...."[11] This definition also includes "[a]ll other waters such as intrastate lakes, rivers, streams (including intermittent streams), mudflats, sandflats, wetlands, sloughs, prairie potholes, wet meadows, playa lakes, or natural ponds, the use, degradation, or destruction of which could affect interstate or foreign commerce...."[12] The Army Corps' regulations also encompass wetlands "adjacent" to waters associated with interstate commerce, and have been interpreted to include jurisdiction over certain "isolated wetlands."[13] Several courts have upheld various aspects of the Army Corps' expansive interpretation of its wetland jurisdiction.[14]

Under the Section 404 program, the Army Corps and EPA share jurisdictional authority over the dredging and filling of waters of the United States, including wetlands. Although the Clean Water Act is essentially silent on which agency has authority to make jurisdictional determinations under the Section 404 Program, EPA and Army Corps have formulated agreements detailing their respective jurisdictional responsibilities.[15]

Once there has been a determination of jurisdiction over a wetland, the next inquiry involves determining whether the activity requires a permit. Until recently, EPA, the Army Corps, and courts have held that Section 404 regulates only physical discharges of dredged or fill material into navigable waters.[16] On its face, this language indicates that many activities that destroy wetlands are not regulated under the Clean Water Act.[17] This narrow "discharge rule" has, however, been eroded by regulatory guidance and judicial decisions.[18]

For example, in a 1990 Regulatory Guidance Letter (RGL)[19] the Army Corps expressly indicated that all landclearing activities using mechanized equipment are subject to Section 404 permit requirements. Further, in another RGL,[20] the Army Corps addressed the applicability of Section 404 to projects constructed with pilings. In that RGL, the Army Corps stated its intention to regulate projects placed on pilings when the placement of such pilings "is used in a manner essentially equivalent to a discharge of fill material in physical effect or functional use and effect."

WETLANDS ENFORCEMENT

In addition to jointly implementing the Clean Water Act's Section 404 program, the U.S. Environmental Protection Agency (EPA) and the U.S. Army Corps of Engineers (Army Corps) share Section 404 enforcement authority. Violations fall into two general categories: (1) the failure to comply with the terms or conditions of a Section 404 permit; or (2) the discharge of dredged or fill material into waters of the United States without a permit. Depending on the nature of the Section 404 violation, the EPA and Army Corps have three types of enforcement alternatives to choose from: (1) administrative compliance orders; (2) civil enforcement proceedings; and (3) criminal enforcement actions. Each of these three types of enforcement actions are discussed here.

Administrative Enforcement

Under Sections 309(a)(3) and 404(s) of the Clean Water Act, the EPA and Army Corps may issue administrative compliance orders.[21] In administrative enforcement under Section 309(a)(3) of the Clean Water Act, the EPA can issue an administrative compliance order requiring a violator to stop any ongoing illegal discharge activity and, where appropriate, to remove the illegal discharge or otherwise restore the site. The Army Corps, pursuant to Section 404(s) may issue "cease and desist" orders to require a violator to comply with the terms and conditions set forth in a Section 404 permit.

Under Section 309(g), the EPA and the Army Corps are empowered to assess administrative civil penalties of up to, but not exceeding, $125,000 per action.[22] Penalties may be assessed for two classes of violations: Class I—lesser violations; and Class II—serious violations.[23] Class I violations carry a penalty of up to $10,000 per violation, with a maximum penalty of $25,000. Class II violations carry a penalty of up to $10,000 per day of violation, with a maximum penalty of $125,000.

The EPA will seek penalties for unpermitted discharges of dredge or fill materials into navigable waters. In assessing the penalty amount, the EPA has developed guidance for calculation of administrative penalties based on six factors:[24]

1. The nature, circumstances, extent, and gravity of the violation;
2. The economic benefit to the violator;
3. The violator's ability to pay;
4. Prior violations of the Clean Water Act;
5. The violator's degree of culpability; and
6. Other factors that justice may require.

The Army Corps has authority to issue administrative penalties for violations of any condition or limitation in a Section 404 permit, although they differ in amount and procedure from the EPA's penalty structure. The Army Corps may assess penalties of up to $10,000 for each permit violation, with a maximum penalty of $25,000.[25] Army Corps penalty proceedings are initiated by the District Engineer who is preparing and processing a proposed order, specifying the amount of the penalty and stating the nature of the violation.[26]

The failure of a violator to pay the administrative penalties assessed by the EPA or Army Corps after all administrative appeals have failed, allows the EPA or Army Corps to request that the Attorney General bring a civil action for recovery of the amount assessed.[27]

Civil Enforcement

Sections 309(b) and (d) and 404(s) of the Clean Water Act give the EPA and the Army Corps authority to initiate civil judicial actions, seeking restoration and other types of injunctive relief, as well as civil penalties.

In 1989, the EPA and Army Corps entered into a Memorandum of Agreement (MOA) on enforcement to ensure efficient and effective implementation of their joint authority.[28] Under the MOA, the Army Corps, is the lead agency concerning violations of permits issued by the Army Corp. For unpermitted discharges, the EPA and the Army Corps jointly determine the appropriate lead agency based on criteria outlined in the MOA. As a practical matter, the Army Corps is usually the lead enforcement agency for wetland permit violations and unpermitted discharges because the agency has more field resources; however, the EPA may take the lead in cases of repeat or particularly egregious violations.

EPA and the Army Corps consider a wide variety of factors when deciding whether to initiate an enforcement action. These factors include the amount of fill, the size of the water body (acres of wetlands filled and the environmental significance), the discharger's previous experience with Section 404 requirements, and the discharger's compliance history. In most instances, the EPA and the Army Corps seek to resolve Section 404 violations through voluntary compliance or administrative enforcement.

Criminal Enforcement

Under Section 309(c), the agencies also have authority to bring criminal judicial enforcement actions for knowing or negligent violations of Section 404.[29] The criminal penalty for negligent violations is a fine of not less than $2,500, nor more than $25,000 per day of violation, or by imprisonment for not more than one year, or both.[30] If the defendant already has one or more previous convictions, the maximum amount of the fine and the jail term are both doubled. Knowing violations are punishable by a fine of not less than $5,000, nor more than $50,000 per day of violation, or by imprisonment for not more than three years, or both.[31] False statements on permit applications and tampering with monitoring devices may draw a fine of not more than $10,000, or imprisonment for not more than two years, or both.[32]

For example, in one case, a jury convicted John Pozsgai on 40 counts of knowingly filling wetlands in Bucks County, Pennsylvania without a Section 404 permit. Mr. Pozsgai was sentenced to three years imprisonment, ordered to restore the site upon his release, and assessed a fine.[33] Even prior to purchasing the 14-acre tract in 1987, Mr. Pozsgai was told by private consultants that the site contained wetlands subject to permitting requirements of Section 404. He purchased the property at a reduced price due to the presence of wetlands, and then proceeded to ignore no fewer than ten warnings from the U.S. EPA and Army Corps' field staff to stop filling the wetlands without first applying for a Section 404 permit. He also defied a temporary restraining order issued by a federal court judge.

In another case, William Ellen was found guilty by a Maryland jury of knowingly filling 86 acres of wetlands without a Section 404 permit. He was sentenced to six months in jail and one year supervised release. The U.S. Supreme Court denied review of the conviction and sentence.[34]

Mr. Ellen, a consultant, was hired to assist a landowner in locating a suitable site for a private hunting club and wildlife preserve on Maryland's Eastern Shore. With Mr. Ellen's assistance, the landowner selected a 3,000-acre site in Dorchester County that bordered on the Chesapeake Bay tributaries and consisted largely of forested wetlands and tidal marshes. As project manager, Mr. Ellen was responsible for acquiring environmental permits and complying with all applicable environmental laws and regulations. His own consulting engineer repeatedly told him that a Section 404 permit was required. Nevertheless, he supervised extensive excavation and construction work, destroying wetlands at the site, without first obtaining a Section 404 permit. Despite repeated warnings to Mr. Ellen from the Army Corps, this unpermitted activity did not stop until the Army Corps contacted the subcontractors directly.

WETLAND REGULATION UNDER THE SWAMPBUSTER PROGRAM

As part of the Food Security Act of 1985 (FSA),[35] as amended by the Food, Agriculture, Conservation, and Trade Act of 1990 (FACTA) and the Federal Agriculture Improvement and Reform Act of 1996 (FAIRA), Congress enacted conservation provisions designed to eliminate the historic detrimental effect of agricultural programs on wetlands and highly erodible lands, including the so-called "sodbuster" and "Swampbuster" programs.[36] These programs were designed to encourage participants in United States Department of Agriculture (USDA) programs to adopt land management measures by linking eligibility for USDA program benefits to farming practices on highly erodible land and converted wetlands.

In particular, the highly erodible land provisions of the "sodbuster" program provide that after December 23, 1985, a program participant is ineligible for certain USDA program benefits for the production of an agricultural commodity on a field in which highly erodible land is predominant.[37] Additionally, the wetland conservation provisions of the "Swampbuster" program provide that after December 23, 1985, a program participant is ineligible for certain USDA program benefits for the production of an agricultural commodity on a converted wetland, or after November 28, 1990, for the conversion of a wetland that makes the production of an agriculture commodity possible.[38] In addition to price and income supports, violators are ineligible for insured or guaranteed loans, disaster relief, crop insurance, conservation and environmental easement payments, and participation in small watershed protection and flood prevention projects. This section focuses on the wetland conservation requirements of the Swampbuster program.

Wetland Conversion under the Swampbuster Program

The Swampbuster program reduced the incentives to convert wetlands to croplands by denying eligibility for almost all farm program benefits on all acres operated by a grower who either converts a wetland or plants on a converted wetland. A converted wetland is defined as a wetland that has been drained, dredged, filled, leveled, or otherwise manipulated for the purpose or to have the effect of making the production of an agricultural commodity possible if such production would not have been possible but for the action and, before such action, the land was a wetland and was neither erodible land nor highly erodible cropland.[39] The ineligibility for benefits triggered by wetland conversion applies not only to the converted wetland but on all lands in which the operator has at least a 20 percent interest during the crop year.

A violator can regain eligibility for future farm program benefits by restoring the converted wetland to its original condition. In addition, Swampbuster violators who convert wetlands inadvertently may receive only a partial penalty, provided they agree to restore the wetlands within one year. However, a violator may invoke this inadvertent conversion/ partial penalty provision only once every ten years.

Effectiveness of Swampbuster Sanctions

Because the commodity programs constitute the major source of benefits for most farmers, Swampbuster will have its greatest impact where commodity program participation is high. Its effect will be limited where growers of program crops tend not to participate in commodity programs or where non-program crops predominate (*e.g.*, dairy price support programs). It is also possible that in the near future the attractiveness of participating in the commodity programs will diminish because statutory benefit levels are scheduled to decline and continuing budget deficits generate interest in restricting the subsidies. Although the effectiveness of Swampbuster will be diminished if commodity program benefits are reduced, there are other program benefits which are denied to Swampbuster violators, including price and income support payments, farm storage facility loans, grain storage payments, FmHA loans, crop insurance, disaster payments, and loans used to convert wetlands. Thus,

Swampbuster would continue to deter wetland conversion, though at a reduced rate.

According to one study, of an estimated 78.4 million acres of nonfederal wetlands left, only about 17 million acres (22%) have some probability of being converted to cropland. Swampbuster may halt conversion on about 6 million acres but is likely to be ineffective on another 6.3 million acres.[40]

Commenced Conversion Exemption

The Swampbuster provisions provide that wetland conversion commenced prior to December 23, 1985, does not render a person ineligible for benefits.[41] Under 7 C.F.R. § 12.5(b)(3)(i)-(ii), conversion is deemed commenced if there have been physical efforts to convert the wetland, or if substantial funds have been committed to the conversion. "A person must show that the commenced activity has been actively pursued or the conversion will not be exempt under this section."[42] In addition, "[o]nly those wetlands for which the construction has begun or to which the [committed funds] relate may qualify for a determination of commencement."[43] All wetland conversion activities allowed under the commenced conversion exemption had to be completed on or before January 1, 1995.[44] Thus, this exemption to the Swampbuster provisions of the Food Security Act is no longer available.

USDA's Swampbuster Regulations

The USDA's implementing regulations for the Swampbuster program are found at 7 C.F.R. Part 12. The regulations provide the terms of program ineligibility, describe the exemptions from ineligibility, outline the responsibilities of the different USDA agencies involved in implementing the provisions, and generally establish the framework for administration of the provisions. The implementing regulations mirror the structure of the FSA, as amended, by listing the activities that will cause a person to lose program benefits, the program benefits that are at risk, and the conditions under which these activities can occur without losing program eligibility.

Subpart A of the regulations describes the terms of ineligibility, USDA programs encompassed by its terms, the list of exemptions from ineligibility, the agency responsibilities, and the appeal provisions for persons adversely affected by an agency determination. Subpart C describes the technical aspects of the wetland conservation provisions, including the criteria for determining a wetland, the criteria for determining a converted wetland, and the uses of wetlands and converted wetlands that can be made without losing program eligibility.

Federal Agriculture Improvement and Reform Act of 1996

Meeting the objectives of the Swampbuster program has been difficult for some producers. The Federal Agriculture Improvement and Reform Act of 1996 (FAIRA), enacted April 4, 1996, made several modifications to the wetland conservation provisions of the Swampbuster program designed to increase USDA's ability to help individual program participants address their unique resources concerns in a more flexible manner. FAIRA made the following changes to the implementation of the wetland conservation requirements:

- Adds new programs to the list of USDA program benefits covered.
- Deletes some programs from the list of USDA program benefits covered.
- Permits a person to cease using farmed wetlands, or farmed-wetland pastures, as identified by National Resource Conservation Service (NRCS), for cropping or forage production, and allows the lands to return to wetland conditions, and subsequently bring these lands back into agricultural production after any length of time without loss of eligibility for USDA program benefits, given certain conditions.
- Allows flexibility in determining the programs for which a person who violates wetland conservation provisions will become ineligible.
- Ensures that persons the right to request and appeal a certified wetland determination.

- Provides that a certified wetland delineation will remain in effect until the person requests a new determination and certification.
- Ensures that wetlands that were certified as prior-converted cropland will continue to be considered prior-converted cropland even if wetland characteristics return as a result of lack of maintenance of the land or other circumstances beyond the person's control provided the prior-converted cropland continues to be used for agricultural purposes.
- Requires USDA to identify on a regional basis which categories of activities constitute a minimal effect on wetland functions and values.
- Provides persons who convert a wetland greater flexibility to mitigate the loss of wetland functions and values through restoration, enhancement, or creation of wetlands.
- Allows the Farm Service Agency (FSA) to waive a person's ineligibility for benefits if FSA believes the person acted in good faith and without intent to violate the wetland provisions.
- Provides for a pilot program for wetland mitigation banking.
- Repeals the requirements for consultation with the Fish and Wildlife Service (FWS).
- Provides that benefits of affiliates of a business enterprise who violate wetland conservation requirements will be reduced in proportion to the interest held by the affiliate in the business enterprise.
- Defines "agricultural lands" for the purpose of implementing a January 6, 1994, interagency memorandum of agreement on Federal wetland delineations on agricultural lands.

On September 6, 1996, the USDA issued an interim final rule amending the wetland conservation provisions of the Swampbuster program.[45] The interim final rule incorporates specific changes required by the Federal Agriculture Improvement and Reform Act of 1996 and makes other changes to improve the administration of these provisions.

RELATED FEDERAL ENVIRONMENTAL LAWS

An applicant seeking Army Corps approval for a Section 404 permit must keep in mind that final issuance of a permit requires compliance with other state and federal laws. The most important state approvals include water quality certification under Section 401 of the Clean Water Act[46] and a determination of consistency with state Coastal Zone Management Programs. Crucial federal law approvals include compliance with the National Environmental Policy Act and Endangered Species Act. The following list outlines many other important federal environmental laws that may impose additional permitting and regulatory compliance requirements on activities undertaken in wetland areas:

- Clean Air Act, 42 U.S.C. § 7401 *et seq.*
- Clean Water Act, 33 U.S.C. § 1251 *et seq.*
- Coastal Barriers Resources Act, 16 U.S.C. § 3501 *et seq.*
- Coastal Zone Management Act, 16 U.S.C. § 1451 *et seq.*
- Endangered Species Act, 16 U.S.C. § 1531 *et seq.*
- Fish and Wildlife Coordination Act, 16 U.S.C. § 661 *et seq.*
- Magnuson Fishery Conservation and Management Act, 16 U.S.C. § 1801 *et seq.*
- Marine Mammal Protection Act, 16 U.S.C. § 1361 *et seq.*
- Marine Sanctuaries Act, 16 U.S.C. § 1431 et seq.
- National Environmental Policy Act, 42 U.S.C. § 4321 *et seq.*[47]
- National Flood Insurance Act, 42 U.S.C. § 4001-4128.
- National Historic Preservation Act, 16 U.S.C. § 470 *et seq.*
- Preservation of Historical and Archaeological Data Act, 16 U.S.C. § 469 *et seq.*
- Rivers and Harbors Act, 33 U.S.C. § 401 *et seq.*
- Water Resources Development Act.

Obviously, discussion of each of these federal environmental laws is beyond the scope of this volume. A brief discussion of some of these laws is provided merely to alert the reader to the extensive federal system of environmental laws that may affect wetland development activities. Of course, the type and magnitude of the particular activity will determine which federal laws will impose additional regulatory requirements. Again, it is important to stress that further regulatory requirements may come from the state and local levels.

National Environmental Policy Act (NEPA)

Various federal and state laws and regulations are specifically designed to control the adverse environmental impact of development projects. Federal and state environmental quality review acts demand special scrutiny of the environmental consequences of a given project. These laws provide a detailed screening process for evaluating and mitigating environmental impacts before development permits may be issued. Thus, the first step toward achieving regulatory compliance and securing necessary project approvals is successful management of the environmental quality review process according to the National Environmental Policy Act (NEPA), for federal permits, and the applicable state environmental quality review act (referred to as "little NEPAs"), for state permits.

In 1969, Congress enacted the National Environmental Policy Act (NEPA)[48] to address a growing concern over the environment and the need for environmental protection. NEPA requires that all federal agencies participate in achieving environmental protection goals. The statute sets forth procedures for federal agencies to incorporate environmental considerations in their decision making processes.[49]

The most important procedural requirements are contained in NEPA's action-forcing provisions, which are designed to ensure consideration of environmental factors and public participation in major federal agency decision making. To satisfy NEPA's procedural requirements, agencies must prepare environmental assessments (EAs) for proposed activities, unless the action falls within a categorical exclusion.[50] Based on determinations made in the EA, the agency is then required to decide whether a full environmental impact statement (EIS) is needed or whether it may issue a finding of no significant impact (FONSI).[51] The federal agency may also choose to bypass the EA step and prepare an EIS for the proposed activity if it is one for which agency regulations usually require an EIS.[52]

NEPA requires that an EIS be prepared and included "in every recommendation or report on proposals for legislation and other major federal actions significantly affecting the quality of the human environment ...."[53] Once an agency determines that an action requires the preparation of an EIS, it must initiate the "scoping" process, during which the agency notifies and invites all concerned agencies and individuals to participate in the decision making process.[54] The agency identifies the issues to be analyzed and determines the scope and depth of the environmental analysis. Then the agency prepares the EIS, which concisely describes how NEPA's policies will be achieved and analyzes a range of alternatives to the proposed action. The environmental analysis in the EIS must take a "hard look" at the environmental consequences of the proposed action.[55]

Most states have enacted their own "little NEPA" environmental quality review acts modeled after the federal statute.[56] Like the federal act, the basic purpose of these state laws is to incorporate consideration of environmental impacts into decisions on permit applications and other discretionary actions taken by state agencies.

River and Harbors Act of 1899 (RHA)

Under Section 10 of the Rivers and Harbors Act of 1899 (RHA), a developer or landowner may need to apply for an Obstruction and Alteration Permit from the Army Corps of Engineers.[57] Section 10 of the RHA prohibits the "creation of any obstruction not affirmatively authorized by Congress, to the navigable capacity of any of the waters of the United States...." Generally, the RHA requires that a landowner secure a Section 10 permit from the Corps before building any wharf, pier, or other structure in any water of the United States outside established harbor lines.[58] Section 9 of the RHA also requires application to the Corps for a permit to construct a bridge, causeway, dam, or dike in navigable waters.[59]

Coastal Zone Management Act (CZMA)

In 1972, Congress enacted the Coastal Zone Management Act (CZMA)[60] aimed specifically at management of coastal environmental problems. With passage of the CZMA, the federal government set up a complex coastal zone management scheme, implemented primarily at the state and local government levels, which places stringent controls on activities that adversely impact the coastal environment. Further, 1990 amendments to the Coastal Zone Management Act added new nonpoint source pollution control requirements.

Under the CZMA, coastal states may apply for grants to develop coastal management plans (CMPs). Before a state CMP can be approved by the federal government, the state must assure that certain mandatory elements are contained in the state management program. CZMA Section 306(d) outlines the federally required content of individual state CMPs.[61]

As long as the substantive requirements of the CZMA are met, each of the coastal states has a choice of how best to implement its CMP. Some states use a policy format, which outlines specific goals to be achieved by the CMP in accordance with the federal Act. This approach utilizes existing state laws and regulations to implement the policies outlined in the CMP (*e.g.*, New York, Massachusetts, New Jersey, and Florida). This method is popular because it does not require the adoption of a new statutory scheme solely for coastal zone management. Other states have codified a specific statute as its coastal zone management program (*e.g.*, Connecticut, North Carolina, and South Carolina).

Under the CZMA, each state determines the boundaries of its coastal zone. Varying geography of each state has resulted in different ways of mapping the state coastal zone. Some states employ setback boundaries from the mean high water mark. Others use the boundaries of counties located on the coast. In Florida, the entire state is considered the coastal zone for purposes of the state's coastal management plan. A landowner or developer wishing to carry out a land use activity needs to know where the coastal zone boundary of his state is located in order to determine whether the activity is subject to consistency review.

Once a state has a federally approved CMP, it possesses a powerful tool for regulating activities affecting its coastal zone. Section 307 of the CZMA provides that all federal activities and projects affecting the state's coastal zone, as well as activities carried out by private parties that require a federal permit or license, be consistent with the state's approved CMP. Applicants for a federal permit must demonstrate to the state coastal zone authority that the proposed activity complies with the policies of the state's CMP. If the state authority finds that the proposed activity is inconsistent with the CMP, the federal agency may not issue the necessary permits unless the Secretary of Commerce overrides the state's objection on appeal or by his own initiative.

Applicants for a federal permit or license should first consult with the designated state agency to obtain the views and assistance of that agency regarding the means for ensuring that the proposed activity will be conducted in a manner consistent with the state's management program. This is the most common sense method of assuring that the project will not later be contested for failure to comply with the state CMP. Consultation with the state agency gives the developer the best information concerning what the state would expect him to do to mitigate adverse coastal impacts.

The developer should also consult the coastal management program document to determine its policies and goals. Included in the CMP is a list of federal license and permit activities which the state deems likely to affect the coastal zone and which the state will expect to review for consistency with its program. This list is mandatory as part of the approved program and must describe the types of federal licenses and permits involved.

After the federal permit applicant determines that his activity will be consistent with the state CMP, he provides a certification to that effect in the federal permit application (*e.g.*, Section 404 wetland permit). The applicant must simultaneously submit a copy of the certification to the designated state agency. The consistency certification must contain the following language: "The proposed activity complies with (name of state) approved coastal management program and will be conducted in a manner consistent with such program."[62]

State agency review of an applicant's consistency certification commences as soon as the state agency receives a copy of the certification and supporting information. The state is required to notify the applicant and the relevant federal agency "at the earliest practicable time" whether it concurs with or objects to the consistency certification. If the state has not determined whether the proposed activity is consistent with the CMP within three months, it must advise the applicant and federal agency of the status of the matter and the basis for any further delay. If no decision has been rendered by the state after six months, consistency is conclusively presumed. Should the state object to the consistency certification, it must notify the applicant, federal agency, and the Assistant Administrator. The state's objection must describe how the proposed activity will be inconsistent with the CMP and provide possible means for the applicant to carry out the activity in a way that would be consistent with the CMP if any such alternative measures exist.

Water Resources Development Act

The Water Resources Development Act of 1986 (WRDA-86) established new cost-sharing requirements for the planning, construction, and operation and maintenance of projects for navigation, flood control, and other purposes, and also established national and local users fees, ensuring that non-federal interests play an important role in planning, financing, and maintaining water projects.

The non-federal share of navigation projects increased dramatically with WRDA-86. During construction of navigation channels, local interests must pay at least 10 percent for projects with depths of less than 20 feet (often projects on inland waterways), 25 percent for projects between 20 and 45 feet deep, and 50 percent for projects over 45 feet deep. These percentages are payable in cash, not in kind. In each case, non-federal sponsors are required to provide any necessary lands, easements, rights-of-way, relocations, and dredged material disposal areas necessary for the project. Credit is allowed for the value of these contributions against the additional 10 percent cash requirement. The federal government remains responsible for all costs of operation and maintenance of navigation projects maintained to a depth of 45 feet. Non-federal interests are responsible for one-half the incremental cost required to maintain depths over 45 feet. WRDA-86 also authorized funding of specific modifications to the inland waterway system with one-half of the costs from the Inland Waterways Trust Fund. WRDA-86, as modified by the Water Resources Development Act of 1990 (WRDA-90), now provides for the recovery of 100 percent of the eligible operations and maintenance costs assigned to commercial navigation of all harbors and inland harbors within the United States.

For all flood control projects—reservoirs, levees, floodwalls, and channels—local interests must contribute at least 25 percent of the project's construction costs and 100 percent of the maintenance costs. The federal government will no longer pay all land, construction, and maintenance costs for major reservoirs or all construction costs for local protection projects, such as levees, floodwalls, and channel improvements. In-kind contributions by non-federal sponsors, such as lands, easements, rights-of-ways, and relocation costs, count as credit against the 25 percent cost share. While the legislation did provide for reduction in the otherwise standard cost-sharing requirements for situations where a non-federal sponsor lacked the ability to pay, there have been few instances where the non-federal share was reduced. Projects lacking a positive benefit-cost ratio may still proceed, but non-federal sponsors must pay all costs in excess of benefits. For shoreline protection, the Act requires 35 percent local cost sharing as opposed to the 30-50 percent local cost sharing required prior to passage of the Act.

The cost-sharing provisions of the Act apply to all projects or separable elements of projects whose construction starts after April 30, 1986, except for harbor projects where the applicability date is November 17, 1986. Local interests must also pay a portion of the design studies on the same basis as construction. Moreover, the Act limited the Army Corps' annual obligation for civil works projects to $1.4 billion in 1987 and $1.8 billion in 1991, and placed controls on cost-overruns.

WRDA-86 also continued the de-emphasis on construction of federal water projects. Although work had continued on previously authorized projects, Congress had not authorized any new starts for Army Corps water resource projects in the 10-year period 1976-1986. With the WRDA-86, Congress went further than this and deauthorized $11.3 billion worth of Army Corps projects. Although the Act called for the study or construction of 270 new projects, it subjects them to the new cost-sharing rules and to more rigorous mitigation requirements.

New project authorizations and modifications in WRDA-90 did not alter the general mitigation and cost-sharing reforms of WRDA-86. However, WRDA-90 contains new provisions that should have an overall positive effect on protection and restoration of wetlands.

WRDA-90 established environmental protection as a primary mission of the Army Corps in planning, constructing, operating, and maintaining water resource projects. Further, the Act established an interim goal of "no overall net loss of the Nation's remaining wetlands base, as defined by acreage and function, and a long-term goal to increase the quality and quantity of the Nation's wetlands, as defined by acreage and function." In order to implement the no-net-loss goal, the Army Corps is directed to use all appropriate authorities to restore and create wetlands, and is directed to develop a wetlands action plan, in consultation with the EPA, FWS, and other appropriate federal agencies. In addition, WRDA-90 authorizes a wetland restoration demonstration program to determine the feasibility of wetland restoration, enhancement, and creation as a means of contributing to the goal of no-net-loss of wetlands.

The changes mandated and authorities provided for by WRDA-86 and WRDA-90 concerning cost sharing, mitigation, and the environmental mission of the Army Corps should help to protect and restore wetlands and constrain the demand for new projects. It should be noted, however, that the new revisions apply only to projects constructed by the Army Corps, not those built by other federal agencies.

The WRDA-86 contains a number of provisions that specifically address wetland protection. Most significant are its mitigation requirements. Prior to passage of WRDA-86, mitigation policy for wetlands losses resulting from water projects had not been well-articulated by Congress, and mitigation occurred irregularly. Now, when proposing a project to Congress, the Army Corps must develop mitigation plans for every new project or explain why the project will have negligible effects on fish and wildlife. Mitigation costs for new projects are among those to be shared by non-federal sponsors, and mitigation will have to proceed prior to or concurrent with construction, not afterward. This should slow the loss of wetlands resulting from new Army Corps projects, especially losses of bottomland hardwoods which are to be mitigated in-kind to the maximum extent possible. To repair past damages to wetlands, the Act established a new continuing authority funded at $30 million annually for mitigation. The amount on a single project may not exceed $7.5 million or 10 percent of the project cost. Despite proposals from the State of Florida, no budget request has yet been made to draw on the $30 million authority and no funds have been appropriated by Congress.

Although the WRDA-86 established the importance of mitigation as a concept, it applies only to Army Corps projects. Further, it lacks specificity regarding what types of mitigation are acceptable and preferable. This lack of specificity is important because there has been a long-standing disagreement between development-oriented and resource-oriented agencies regarding the Council of Environmental Quality (CEQ)'s definition of mitigation.[63] The disagreement centers on whether the mitigation actions listed by the CEQ are listed in order of preference.

Some agencies, primarily resource agencies, have favored considering mitigation options sequentially, while others have argued for the greatest flexibility in setting mitigation requirements. This issue of sequencing was partially resolved in February 1990 when the Army Corps and the EPA signed a Memorandum of Agreement (MOA) in mitigation. The MOA established policies and procedures to be used by the two agencies in implementing mitigation sequencing under the Section 404 program. The issue remains controversial, however, and has attracted congressional debate.

National Flood Insurance Program

Administered by the Federal Emergency Management Agency (FEMA),[64] the federal government has instituted its National Flood Insurance Program (NFIP) in 1968 to provide subsidized insurance and flood hazard mitigation strategies to flood-prone communities.[65] Federal regulations define floodplains as land areas that are prone to flooding, a temporary condition of partial or complete inundation of normally dry land from the overflow of inland or tidal waters, or the unusual and rapid accumulation or runoff of surface waters from any source.[66] States contain areas which have been designated as floodplains by the Federal Emergency Management Agency (FEMA).

The NFIP is a voluntary federal program which provides subsidized flood insurance to property owners in communities which join the program by enforcing adequate floodplain development regulations. Floodplain management measures or plans are generally implemented on the local level through coordination with federal, state and local officials. Municipalities prepare floodplain management programs, which must meet certain minimum requirements of the National Flood Insurance Program regulations.[67] If a community fails to develop its own local program, the state may impose its own regulatory scheme on the community to ensure that the community's residents are eligible for federal flood insurance.

The federal floodplain program is a combination of insurance and hazard mitigation measures. Though participation in the program is voluntary, the purchase of flood insurance is mandatory as a condition to receiving federal or federally related financial assistance for acquisition or construction of buildings in federally designated "Special Flood Hazard Areas."[68] In order to be eligible to purchase flood insurance through the NFIP, the community in which property is located must have an approved floodplain management program. Flood-prone communities are identified by FEMA, which works with state and local governments to publish a Flood Hazard Boundary Map (FHBM).[69] Once a FHBM is issued for a community, it is eligible to participate in the "emergency phase" of the NFIP.[70] To participate in this emergency phase, the community must enforce floodplain regulations that are not as extensive as those required under the later regular phase.[71]

During the emergency phase of the program, FEMA may perform a flood risk study as a basis for issuing a Flood Insurance Rate Map (FIRM) for the community.[72] Engineering computations from the study are used to determine the 100-year floodplain boundaries. Areas inside these boundaries are designated as the Special Flood Hazard Areas (SFHAs), which are further subdivided into insurance risk rate zones based on their level of flood hazard risk. If property falls inside one of these SFHAs, the developer or landowner must obtain necessary permits and comply with the local floodplain management ordinance.

Federal, state, and local governments coordinate efforts to identify and map Special Flood Hazard Areas (SFHAs), which are susceptible to periodic flooding. These areas are subdivided into insurance rate risk zones, which are used to determine the premiums for federal flood insurance.[73] Eligibility for flood insurance is dependent on a communities development of a local floodplain management program, which meets certain standards set forth in the FEMA regulations.[74] Although participation in the NFIP is voluntary, most states mandate that local governments develop floodplain management programs to ensure that residents are eligible for federal flood insurance.[75]

Local floodplain ordinances contain requirements relating to development and substantial improvements of existing structures found in SFHAs, including minimum elevation, floodproofing, and permitting requirements.[76] In order to obtain a permit, the landowner or developer must meet the standards in the ordinance, which are designed to minimize flood damage. The state may have model local laws to guide flood-prone communities in implementing their floodplain management programs, however, local governments may choose to institute more stringent regulations than the state's model program. Thus, it is important for the developer or landowner to find out the specific requirements of the community.

Endangered Species Act

The ultimate goal of the Endangered Species Act (ESA)[77] is "to provide a means whereby the ecosystems upon which endangered species and threatened species depend may be conserved, [and] to provide a program for the conservation of such endangered species and threatened species ..."[78] Congress enacted the ESA in 1973 in response to its finding that "various species of fish, wildlife, and plants in the United States have been rendered extinct as a consequence of economic growth and development untempered by adequate concern and conservation."[79] The ESA reflects congressional recognition of the benefits of species preservation and diversity.

The ESA directs the Secretary of the Interior to list those wildlife species that are "endangered" or "threatened" because of habitat modification or destruction, over-utilization of the species, disease or predation, inadequate regulation, or other natural or man-made factors. Once a species is listed, it is unlawful (among other things) to "take" it—which under the Act means "to harass, harm, pursue, hunt, shoot, wound, kill, trap, capture, or collect, or to attempt to engage in any such conduct."[80]

Sections 7 and 9 of the ESA are the two primary provisions for implementing endangered species preservation. Section 7 protects against federal agency actions, either undertaken by the federal government or subject to federal approvals, which jeopardize the continued existence of endangered or threatened species or that destroy or adversely affect critical habitats. With the large number of projects involving federal permits, approvals, funding, or participation, the potential impact of Section 7 is quite extensive.

Section 9 of the ESA applies to a much larger groups of people, entities, and projects than those covered by Section 7 restrictions on federal actions. Section 9 prohibits all "takings" of endangered species by any "person" under the jurisdiction of the United States. This broad authorization is meant to include private individuals and entities, as well as federal, state, and local governments and officials. Section 9 prohibits persons from "taking," within the United States and its territory or on the high seas, any species of wildlife or fish that is on the endangered species list.

Section 10(a) authorizes the granting of incidental taking permits, which allow for some harm to individual members of a species if certain stringent mitigation measures are met.[81] To apply for relief under this provision, landowners and developers must comply with the following conditions:

1. The taking be incidental to otherwise lawful conduct.
2. The applicant prepare and submit a conservation plan.
3. The plan demonstrate (a) that the applicant will minimize and mitigate the impacts of the taking to the maximum extent practicable, (b) that adequate funding will be available to implement the plan, and (c) that the taking will not appreciably reduce the likelihood of the survival and recovery of the species in the wild.

The Secretary may also specify any other measures deemed "necessary or appropriate". This sweeping mandate has resulted in far reaching, onerous prohibitions by the federal government on the use and development of private and public lands.

Regulations promulgated by the U.S. Fish and Wildlife Service (FWS), the primary agency that administers the ESA, define "harm" as "an act which actually kills or injures wildlife. Such act may include significant habitat modification or degradation where it actually kills or injures wildlife by significantly impairing essential behavioral patterns, including breeding, feeding, or sheltering."[82] According to the agency's interpretation of this definition, "take" includes not only *direct* conduct which causes *immediate* harm, but also *indirect* effects which *may* cause *speculative future* harm. In numerous situations, including court proceedings, the FWS has asserted that this regulation protects species habitat and restricts habitat modification, even where no direct physical impact to a particular animal can be shown. In 1995, the U.S. Supreme Court, in *Babbitt v. Sweet Home Chapter of Communities for a Great Oregon*[83] concluded that the FWS reasonably construed congressional intent behind the ESA when the agency issued regulations defining "harm" to include habitat modification.

SPECIAL APPROACHES TO WETLANDS MANAGEMENT

In addition to the comprehensive wetland regulatory programs in existence at the federal, state, and local levels, specialized approaches have been developed that combine wetland management with land use planning. This section evaluates several planning approaches to wetland management.

Advance Identification (ADID) of Wetlands

One of the newest and most promising mechanisms available for governmental protection of wetlands is the "Advance Identification of Wetlands" (ADID) process which is authorized by the EPA's Section 404(b)(1) regulations. Under the regulations, EPA and the Army Corps, on their own initiative or at the request of any other party (and after consultation with any affected state), "may identify sites which will be considered as: (1) possible future disposal sites, including existing disposal sites and non-sensitive areas; or (2) areas generally unsuitable for disposal site specification ...."[84]

The designation of an area as acceptable for Section 404 dredge and fill disposal activities does not, however, constitute a Section 404 permit, nor does identification of an area as not available necessary preclude a Section 404 permit in the future.[85] On the other hand, it operates as a form of notice to property owners as well as local, state, and federal agencies of the likely acceptability of an individual or general Section 404 permit in an affected area, and may facilitate permit approval. As such, the ADID is a valuable and powerful planning tool that is increasing in popularity across the nation.[86]

The ADID process involves collecting and distributing information on the values and functions of wetland areas. The EPA conducts the process in cooperation with the Army Corps and in consultation with states. Local communities can use this information to help them better understand the values and functions of wetlands in their areas. It also serves as a preliminary indication of factors likely to be considered during review of a Section 404 permit application.

The ADID process is intended to add predictability to the wetlands permitting process as well as better account for the impacts from multiple projects within a geographic area.

As of February 1993, 38 ADID projects had been completed and 33 more were ongoing. The projects ranged in size from less than 100 acres to more than 4,000 square miles and are located throughout the United States. ADID projects can be resource-intensive activities, although some have been completed in as little as six months.

Regional EPA experience indicates that the smaller or more local the ADID project boundaries, the more complete and effective the analysis and results will be. ADID projects have been initiated by local entities to facilitate planning efforts. For example, in the Wetlands Special Area Study in West Eugene, Oregon, local efforts led to issuance of a Section 404 permit. Because the ADID was incorporated into the city's general comprehensive plan, and because Oregon's land use policies have the effect of local land use law, the ADID effort streamlined the regulatory process.

These local efforts have been proven to be one of the more successful ways of generating support for wetlands protection. Local cooperation and support are vital to the success of ADID projects.

The number of ADID projects has increased over time, and the EPA expects more states, localities, and private organizations to become involved in providing funds and otherwise supporting ADID or other comprehensive planning efforts. Because ADID efforts are usually based on watershed planning, they are extremely compatible with geographic and ecosystem initiatives such as the EPA's Watershed Protection Approach.

Special Area Management Plans

The Special Area Management Plan (SAMP) process is a comprehensive plan providing for natural resource protection and reasonable economic growth, which contains detailed statement of policies and criteria to guide land and water uses in specific geographic areas. The Coastal Zone Management Act[87] defines "special area master plan" as: "a comprehensive plan providing for natural resource protection and reasonable coastal-dependent economic growth containing a detailed and comprehensive statement of policies; standards and criteria to guide public and private land uses of lands and waters; and mechanisms for timely implementation in specific geographic areas within the coastal zone."[88]

A SAMP provides predictability to developmental interests by establishing an area-wide basis for regulatory actions founded on cumulative effects of changes in the environment. The Corps Regulatory Guidance Letter No. 86-10 discusses the development of SAMPs. The SAMP requires extensive study and planning by federal, state, and local environmental and land use planning authorities. The nature of the geographic area targeted for SAMP development will determine the degree of involvement of various government and private interests in the process.

Because development of a SAMP would most likely be considered a major federal action under the National Environmental Policy Act, a SAMP would usually be developed in conjunction with an Environmental Impact Statement (EIS). The function of the EIS for the SAMP is to develop management plan alternatives, assess potential environmental, social, and economic consequences of each alternative, and identify the preferred alternative. A benefit of the EIS process is that it provides a forum for the informed identification and evaluation of management plan alternatives, while allowing opportunity for interested individuals and groups to participate in the development of the SAMP.

A SAMP can be especially useful as a wetlands mitigation plan for an area. The Army Corps/EPA joint MOA on mitigation determinations provides that mitigation consistent with an EPA—and Army Corps—approved comprehensive plan, such as a SAMP, would satisfy the avoidance, minimization, and compensatory mitigation requirements.[89]

Wetlands and Watersheds

Wetlands are important elements of a watershed because they serve as the link between land and water resources. Wetland protection programs are often more effective when coordinated with other surface and groundwater protection programs and with other resource management programs, such as flood control, water supply, recreation, control of stormwater, and nonpoint source water pollution.

A watershed, also called a drainage basin, is the area in which all water, sediments, and dissolved materials flow or drain from the land into a common river, lake, ocean, or other body of water.

The quality of the nation's wetlands and other water resources is directly linked to the quality of the environment surrounding these waters. However, resource protection programs have historically focused on single goals or a small set of goals. These programs have succeeded in identifying and controlling, to some extent, the larger point sources of water pollution.

A watershed-based approach to water and wetlands protection considers the whole system, including other resource management programs that address land, air, and water, to successfully manage problems for a given aquatic resource. The watershed approach thus includes not only the water resource, but also the surrounding land from which the water drains. This area can be as large as the Mississippi River drainage basin or as small as a back yard.

EPA's Office of Water is actively pursuing a Watershed Protection Approach within EPA and other agencies. EPA's Wetlands Division incorporates a watershed approach in much of its work with other agencies, states, and organizations. Current activities include the following:

- Developing guidance linking wetlands protection programs to watershed planning efforts.
- Funding state watershed projects through State Wetland Protection Grants.
- Integrating a watershed approach into federal floodplain management activities.
- Supporting a series of national and regional meetings on wetlands and regional watershed planning.

STATE WETLAND REGULATORY PROGRAMS

Landowners and developers who wish to carry out activities in wetland areas must find their way through a maze of federal, state, and local laws and regulations before finally securing the necessary approvals for a specific activity or project. Federal wetland approvals cannot be obtained if necessary state wetland approvals have been denied.[90] A certification of water quality may be necessary under federal and state law. For some projects, an environmental impact assessment may be required pursuant to a state's environmental quality review act. Local zoning regulations, including wetland ordinances, may impose additional requirements. The landowner or developer may need to certify that coastal wetland activities will be carried out in a manner consistent with a state's coastal management program.

State Wetland Protection Laws

The landowner or developer should consult state wetland maps to determine if the project is in an area subject to state wetland regulation. Since state regulatory schemes for wetlands vary, it is necessary to determine the appropriate procedures and consult the state's wetland regulations when applying for a state wetland permit. The degree of regulation may be minimal in some states, while quite stringent in others.

Some states have separate regulations for tidal and freshwater wetlands. The regulations themselves may be difficult to locate. Some states may have enacted a specific law to govern wetlands, while others have tagged wetlands regulation onto an already existing environmental law. Finally, a number of states have delegated authority to local governments to regulate wetlands. In these states, an enabling law is usually passed that contains certain standards that must be maintained when municipalities enact local wetland ordinances.[91] Thus, a landowner or developer may need to comply with three layers of regulation from federal, state, and local authorities.

State Wetlands Grant Program

Since 1990, a federal grant program has supported state efforts to protect wetlands by providing funds to enhance existing programs or develop new ones. The State Wetlands Protection Grant Program was initiated in FY90 with a $1 million appropriation. In FY95, Congress appropriated $15 million to support the grant program. State interest in the grant program continues to increase.

- States usually request more than double the amount of grant funds available each year.
- Each state has received at least one grant to develop or enhance wetland protection programs.
- In FY94, 101 grants were awarded from the 166 applications received.

Grant funds can only be used to enhance existing or develop new wetland protection programs. Grants cannot be used for operational support of state wetland protection programs. Lack of funds for operational support will likely continue to be a serious impediment to state involvement in wetland protection.

State Wetland Conservation Plans

A tool that states are using to protect wetlands is the State Wetland Conservation Plan (SWCP). A SWCP is a strategy for states to achieve no-net-loss and other wetland management goals by integrating both regulatory and non-regulatory approaches to protecting wetlands.[92]

A large number of land- and water-based activities impact wetlands. These activities are not addressed by any single federal, state, or local agency program. While many public and private programs and activities protect wetlands, these programs are often limited in scope and not well-coordinated. These programs also do not address all of the problems affecting wetlands.

States are well-positioned between federal and local government to take the lead in integrating and expanding wetland protection and management programs. They are experienced in managing federally mandated environmental programs under the Clean Water Act and the Coastal Zone Management Act. They are uniquely equipped to help resolve local and regional conflicts and identify the local economic and geographic factors that may influence wetland protection.

The SWCP for Texas focuses on non-regulatory and voluntary approaches to wetland protection designed to complement the state's wetland regulatory program. The plan encourages development of economic incentives for private landowners to protect wetlands and educational outreach for state and local officials.

The SWCP for Tennessee focuses on a strategy to collect wetland information for outreach and education to private owners of wetlands as well as regional and local decision makers. Current implementation efforts include identification of critical functions of major wetland types, priority sites for acquisition and/or restoration, as well as maintenance and restoration of natural floodplain hydrology through digitization and use of remote sensing.

The SWCP for Maine focuses on ways to establish better coordination between state and federal regulatory programs, as well as new non-regulatory mechanisms to foster voluntary stewardship. In addition, the state expects to use an ecosystem framework to guide the prioritization of wetlands for comprehensive protection, and review and improve compensatory mitigation policies.

State Assumption of the Section 404 Program

Section 404(g) of the Clean Water Act authorizes individual states to assume the responsibilities for administering the Section 404 dredge and fill permit program by applying to EPA for approval of its program.[93] Once its program has been approved, a state, rather than the Army Corps, may issue Section 404 permits directly. To date, the only states that have assumed responsibility for the Section 404 program are Michigan and New Jersey. Florida has also been considering state assumption of the Section 404 program.[94]

Limited federal oversight authority is retained even after the state's assumption of the Section 404 program. The EPA retains authority to veto a permit, or to withdraw its approval of the state's Section 404 authority, if statutory and regulatory requirements are not followed.[95] Pursuant to its retained oversight authority, a state is required to present to the EPA copies of all permit applications which are submitted to the state for approval. In addition, the state must notify the EPA of any action that it takes with respect to such applications.[96] The EPA Administrator must, within 10 days, provide copies of the application to the Army Corps, the Department of the Interior (DOI), and the Fish and Wildlife Service

(FWS). The state must be notified within thirty days if the Administrator intends to comment on the state's handling of the application. The administrator's comments must be submitted within ninety days.

Once a state is notified that the EPA intends to comment, it may not issue the permit until after it has received the comment, or until ninety days have passed. If the EPA objects to the application, the state "shall not issue such proposed permit" even after the ninety days have elapsed.[97] The aggrieved state may request a hearing to air its complaints. However, if the state does not request a hearing, or if it fails to modify its plan so as to conform to the EPA's objections, authority to issue the permit is transferred to the Army Corps.[98]

Clean Water Act Section 401 Certification

States are required by Section 401 of the Clean Water Act to provide a water quality certification before a federal license or permit can be issued for any activity that may result in a discharge into intrastate navigable waters, including wetlands. The certification must "set forth any effluent limitations and other limitations ... necessary to assure that any applicant" will comply with various provisions of the Act and "any other appropriate" state law requirement.[99] Under EPA regulations, the standards must also include an antidegradation policy to ensure that "[e]xisting instream water uses and the level of water quality necessary to protect [those] uses [are] maintained and protected."[100]

The major federal licenses and permits subject to Section 401 are Section 402 and Section 404 permits, Federal Energy Regulatory Commission (FERC) hydropower licenses, and Rivers and Harbors Act Section 9 and 10 permits. In most cases, Section 401 certification review is conducted at the same time as the federal agency review. Many states have established joint permit processing to ensure this occurs.

States primarily make their decisions to deny, certify, or condition permits or licenses by ensuring that the activity will comply with state water quality standards. In addition, states look at whether the activity will violate effluent limitations, new source performance standards, toxic pollutants, and other state water resource regulation requirements.

Section 401 certification allows states to address associated chemical, physical, and biological impacts, such as low dissolved oxygen levels, turbidity, inundation of habitat, stream volumes and fluctuations, filling of habitat, impacts on fish migration, and loss of aquatic species as a result of habitat alteration.

In 1988, the National Wetlands Policy Forum recommended that states "make more aggressive use of their certification authorities under Section 401 of the CWA to protect their wetlands from chemical and other types of alterations." In response, in 1989, the EPA issued guidelines to states on applying Section 401 certification to protect wetlands.[101] Twenty states have been awarded State Wetlands Protection Grants to support use of Section 401 certification to protect wetlands.

Some states rely on Section 401 certification as their primary mechanism to protect wetlands in the state. In addition, most states denied or conditioned Section 401 certification for some Section 404 nationwide permits to reduce problematic wetland losses. In particular, many states denied certification of Nationwide Permit 26 because they felt that individual review of projects in isolated or headwater wetlands is critical to achieving CWA goals in their states.

State Water Quality Standards for Wetlands

In 1990, the EPA issued guidance to states on development of specific water quality standards for wetlands.[102] Wetland water quality standards are important because they are the primary tool used in water quality certification decisions.

The EPA asked states to develop or improve their wetland water quality standards by the end of September 1993. Water quality standards have three primary components: (1) designated uses, (2) criteria to protect those uses, and (3) an anti-degradation policy. At a minimum, these uses must meet the CWA goals to protect and propagate fish, shellfish, and wildlife, and for recreation in and on the water. States may also designate uses associated with unique functions and values of wetlands, such as floodwater storage and groundwater recharge.

States also adopt criteria to protect those uses. Criteria can be general narrative statements, such as "maintain natural hydrologic conditions, including hydroperiod, hydrodynamics, and natural water temperature variations necessary to support vegetation which would be present naturally." Criteria may also include specific numeric values, such as a dissolved oxygen concentration of 5.0 mg/l.

State anti-degradation policies include provisions for full protection of existing uses (functions), maintenance of water quality of high-quality waters, and a prohibition against lowering water quality in outstanding resource waters. In addition, a state's anti-degradation policy addresses fill activities in wetlands by ensuring no significant degradation occurs as a result of fill activity.

Narrative criteria in conjunction with anti-degradation policies can provide the basis for addressing hydrologic and physical impacts to wetlands (not discerned through numeric criteria) caused by nonpoint source pollution, storm water discharges,[103] groundwater pumping, filling, and other sources of wetland degradation. When combined with a strong implementation policy, wetland water quality standards can provide the basis for such tools as quality management practices,[104] monitoring programs, and mitigation plans, as well as serve as the primary basis for Section 401 certification decisions.

ENDNOTES

1. 33 U.S.C. § 1251 *et seq.*

2. 33 U.S.C. § 1344.

3. 33 U.S.C. § 401 *et seq.*

4. The original purpose of Rivers and Harbors Act regulation of dredge-and-fill activities was to protect and promote navigation. 33 U.S.C. § 403.

5. 42 U.S.C. § 4321 *et seq.*

6. 42 U.S.C. § 4332.

7. 33 U.S.C. § 1344.

8. 33 C.F.R. § 323.2(c).

9. 33 C.F.R. § 323.2(e). The draining of wetlands, which is a major source of wetland losses, is not expressly regulated or prohibited by Section 404.

10. 33 U.S.C. § 1362(7). *See Natural Resources Defense Council, Inc. v. Callaway*, 392 F. Supp. 685 (D.D.C. 1975).

11. 33 C.F.R. § 328.3(a)(1). The regulations call for a case-by-case determination concerning whether a given wetland has the required effect on interstate commerce. *See also* 40 C.F.R. § 230.3(s) (EPA regulations).

12. 33 C.F.R. § 328.3(a)(3).

13. 33 C.F.R. § 328.3(a)(5),(7).

14. *See United States v. Riverside Bayview Homes, Inc.*, 474 U.S. 121 (1985) (discussion of meaning of "waters of the United States").

15. EPA/Department of Defense, *Memorandum of Understanding on Geographical Jurisdiction of the Section 404 Program (MOU)*, 45 Fed. Reg. 45018 (July 2, 1980); Department of the Army/EPA, *Memorandum of Agreement Concerning the Geographic Jurisdiction of the Section 404 Program and the Application of the Exemptions under Section 404(f) of the Clean Water Act (MOA)* (January 19, 1989).

16. *See United States v. Lambert*, 589 F. Supp. 366 (M.D. Fla. 1984).

17. This is consistent with the plain language of Section 404, which regulates only "discharges" of pollutants. 33 U.S.C. § 1311(a).

18. *See Avoyelles Sportsmen's League, Inc. v. Marsh*, 715 F.2d 897 (5th Cir. 1983) (certain land-clearing activities, which resulted in redeposits of material taken from the wetland, constituted a discharge of a pollutant and, therefore, required a dredge-and-fill permit).

19. Regulatory Guidance Letter No. 90-5 (July 18, 1990).

20. Regulatory Guidance Letter No. 90-8 (Dec. 14, 1990).

21. 33 U.S.C. § 1319(a)(3); 33 U.S.C. § 1344(s).

22. 33 U.S.C. § 1319(g).

23. 33 U.S.C. § 1319(g)(2).

24. *Clean Water Act Section 404 Civil Administrative Penalty Actions: Guidance on Calculating Settlement Amounts* (December 14, 1990).

25. 33 C.F.R. § 326.6(a)(1).

26. 33 C.F.R. § 326.6(b)(1).

27. 33 U.S.C. § 1319(g)(9).

28. *Memorandum of Agreement Between the Department of the Army and the Environmental Protection Agency Concerning Federal Enforcement for the Section 404 Program of the Clean Water Act* (Jan. 19, 1989).

29. 33 U.S.C. § 1319(c).

30. 33 U.S.C. § 1319(c)(1).

31. 33 U.S.C. § 1319(c)(2).

32. 33 U.S.C. § 1319(c)(4).

33. *U.S. v. Pozsgai*, No. 88-00450 (E.D. Pa. Dec. 30, 1989), aff'd, 897 F.2d 524 (3d Cir.), *cert. denied*, 498 U.S. 812 (1990).

34. *U.S. v. Ellen*, 961 F.2d 462 (4th Cir. 1992), cert. denied, 121 L.Ed.2d 155 (1992).

35. 16 U.S.C. §§ 3801-3845.

36. 16 U.S.C. §§ 3811-3823.

37. 16 U.S.C. § 3811.

38. 16 U.S.C. §§ 3821-22.

39. 16 U.S.C. § 3801(a)(4)(A).

40. *See* Heimlich, "The Swampbuster Provision: Implementation and Impact," Proceedings of the National Symposium on Protection of Wetlands from

Agricultural Impacts, U.S. Fish and Wildlife Service, Dept. of the Interior, Washington, D.C. (1988), pp. 87-94.

41. 16 U.S.C. § 3822(b)(1)(A).

42. 7 C.F.R. § 12.5(b)(5)(ii).

43. 7 C.F.R. § 12.5(b)(5)(iv). See, for example, *Von Eye v. United States*, 1996 WL 447739 (8th Cir., Aug. 9, 1996).

44. 7 C.F.R. § 12.5(b)(5)(iii).

45. 61 Fed.Reg. 47019 (Sept. 6, 1996). The interim final rule may also be accessed, and comments submitted, via Internet. Users can access the NRCS Federal Register homepage and submit comments at http:/astro.itc.nrcs.usda.gov:6500.

46. 33 U.S.C. § 1341.

47. The Council on Environmental Quality's implementing regulations are found at 40 C.F.R. parts 1500-1508.

48. 42 U.S.C. §§ 4321-4370c.

49. 42 U.S.C. § 4332(2)(C); 40 C.F.R. § 1502.3.

50. 40 C.F.R. § 1501.4(a)(2).

51. 40 C.F.R. § 1501.4(c), (e). *See Committee to Preserve Boomer Lake Park v. Department of Transportation*, 4 F.3d 1543 (10th Cir. 1993).

52. 40 C.F.R. § 1501.4(a)(1).

53. 42 U.S.C. § 4332(C). *See also* 40 C.F.R. §§ 1502.3, 1508.18.

54. 40 C.F.R. § 1501.7(a)(1).

55. *See Landmark West! v. U.S. Postal Service*, 1993 WL 541366 (S.D.N.Y. Dec. 29, 1993); *Friends of the Payette v. Horseshoe Bend Hydroelectric Co.*, 988 F.2d 989 (9th Cir. 1993).

56. *See,* for example, N.Y. Envt'l Conserv. Law §§ 8-0101-8-0117 (McKinney).

57. 33 U.S.C. § 403.

58. *See State of New York v. DeLyser*, 759 F.Supp. 982 (W.D.N.Y. 1991).

59. 33 U.S.C. § 401.

60. 16 U.S.C. § 1451 *et seq. See also* P.L. 101-508, 104 Stat. 1388 (1990) (1990 Reauthorization); P.L. 104-150, 110 Stat. 1380 (1996) (1996 Reauthorization).

61. 16 U.S.C. § 1455(d).

62. 15 C.F.R. § 930.57(b).

63. The CEQ's mitigation guidelines call for avoiding the wetland if the proposed project is not water dependent or if alternatives exist. If the project is water dependent and no alternatives exist, minimize the impact by modifying the project. If modification is not possible, rectify the impact by restoring the environment. *See* 40 C.F.R. § 1508.20.

64. FEMA replaced HUD as the responsible agency in 1978.

65. National Flood Insurance Act of 1968, 42 U.S.C. §§ 4001-4128.

66. 44 C.F.R. § 59.1.

67. 44 C.F.R. § 59.22.

68. Flood Disaster Protection Act of 1973, tit. I § 102(a); 42 U.S.C. § 4012a.

69. 44 C.F.R. § 64.3(a)(2).

70. 44 C.F.R. § 64.5(a).

71. 44 C.F.R. Part 59 (detailing the general provisions of the NFIP, including the emergency and regular program phases, as well as the actions a community must take to become and stay eligible under the program).

72. 44 C.F.R. § 64.3(a)(1).

73. 44 C.F.R. § 64.3(1)(a).

74. 44 C.F.R. § 59.22; The minimum requirements for local floodplain programs are found at 44 C.F.R. Part 60.

75. *See, e.g.,* N.Y. Envt'l Conserv. Law §§ 36-0101 to 36-0115 (McKinney).

76. *See* 44 C.F.R. § 60.3.

77. 16 U.S.C. § 1531-1544.

78. 16 U.S.C. § 1531(b).

79. 16 U.S.C. § 1531(a)(1).

80. 16 U.S.C. § 1532(19).

81. 16 U.S.C. § 1539(a).

82. 50 C.F.R. § 17.3.

83. *Babbitt v. Sweet Home Chapter of Communities for a Great Oregon, 115 S.Ct. 2407 (U.S. 1995).*

84. 40 C.F.R. § 230.80(a).

85. 40 C.F.R. § 230.80(b).

86. *See Summary of ADID Projects Under Section 230.80 of the 404(b)(1) Guidelines,* U.S. EPA Office of Wetlands, Oceans, and Watersheds, Wetlands Division (June 10, 1991).

87. 16 U.S.C. § 1451 *et seq.*

88. 16 U.S.C. § 1453(17).

89. "Section 404(b)(1) Guidelines Mitigation MOA," 55 Fed.Reg. 9210 (Feb. 7, 1990).

90. 33 C.F.R. § 320.4(j).

91. *For example, see* Va. Code Ann. § 28.2-1302, which provides for adoption of local wetland zoning ordinances. In Connecticut, each local government is required

to establish an "Inland Wetlands Agency" or else authorize an existing board or commission to carry out the state's wetlands regulations. Conn. Gen. Stat. § 22a-42(a). Other state laws governing local oversight of wetland regulation include: Fla. Stat. Ann. § 403.916; Mass. Gen. L. ch. 131, § 40; N.Y. Envt'l Conserv. Law §§ 24-0501, 25-0507.

92. *See* EPA, "Why Develop a State Wetlands Conservation Plan?" (Feb. 1993) (available from the EPA Wetlands Information Hotline by calling 800-832-7828).

93. 33 U.S.C. § 1344(g)-(i).

94. *See* Dix and Denson, "Florida's Assumption of Federal Dredge-and-Fill Jurisdiction: Clearing the Permitting Stream Bed or Muddying Administrative Waters?" 67 *Fla.B.J.* 56-59 (1993).

95. 33 U.S.C. § 1344(i)-(j).

96. 33 U.S.C. § 1344(j).

97. *Id.*

98. *See Friends of Crystal River v. U.S. E.P.A.*, 1994 WL 511221 (6th Cir. Sept. 21, 1994), *aff'g,* 794 F. Supp. 674 (W.D. Mich. 1992).

99. 33 U.S.C. § 1341(d).

100. In *PUD No. 1 of Jefferson County v. Washington Dept. of Ecology*, 114 S.Ct. 1900 (U.S. 1994), the U.S. Supreme Court upheld a minimum stream flow requirement as a permissible condition of a Section 401 certification.

101. EPA, *Wetlands and 401 Certification: Opportunities for States and Eligible Indian Tribes* (April 1989).

102. EPA, *Water Quality Standards for Wetlands: National Guidance*, EPA/S-90-011 (July 1990).

103. *See* EPA, *Natural Wetlands and Urban Stormwater: Potential Impacts and Management*, EPA 843-R-001 (Feb. 1993).

104. *See* Dennison, *Storm Water Discharges: Regulatory Compliance and Best Management Practices* (CRC Press/Lewis Publishers 1995).

Chapter 4

Wetland Permitting

INTRODUCTION

In many instances, wetland regulation has been, and will continue to be, a major regulatory hurdle for developers to overcome. By understanding and complying with regulatory requirements and permit procedures, and effectively communicating early with regulatory authorities, developers can often meet wetland restrictions while still maintaining a successful project.

Whether a particular area is regulated as a "jurisdictional" wetland is not always apparent The prudent developer always inquires with the Army Corps or the state wetland agency before undertaking any activity that might require wetland permit approval. Although "after-the-fact" permits may be granted, failure to secure necessary permits in advance may end up costing the developer huge sums of money in penalties and litigation. Moreover, when ordered to cease and desist from completing a project already underway, to restore a wetland site to its previous condition, a developer's financial loss can be enormous.

SECTION 404 PERMIT APPLICATIONS

Under Section 404(a) of the Clean Water Act, the Army Corps is authorized to issue permits for the discharge of dredged or fill material into waters of the United States, which includes wetlands.[1] The Army Corps also may issue "nationwide permits" for certain activities undertaken in wetland areas that are deemed to have minimal environmental impacts.[2] Although the Army Corps' field personnel are responsible for making the initial decision to grant or deny permits, the EPA is responsible for formulating Section 404(b)(1) guidelines used by the Army Corps to make the permit decisions.[3] The EPA is also empowered to veto or overrule the granting of permits by the Army Corps.[4] However, notwithstanding this veto authority, EPA has rarely overruled an Army Corps decision to issue a permit.[5]

In fiscal year 1994, over 48,000 people applied to the Army Corps for a Section 404 permit. Eight-two percent of these applications were covered by general permits which were issued in an average time of 16 days. Less than 10 percent of the applications were subject to the more detailed individual evaluation—which took an average of 127 days. Only 358, or 0.7 percent, of the permits were denied. Thus, almost all individuals who applied for a Section 404 permit in 1994 received their permits, and the average time for a decision was 27 days. In addition, general permits cover an estimated 50,000 activities that do not require any notification to the Army Corps.

The Army Corps regulations set forth extensive procedures for the permit process.[6] The application form must describe the purpose, scope, and need for the proposed activity, its location, and the names and addresses of adjoining property owners. Following submission of a permit application for activity in a wetland area, the Army Corps must decide whether to grant the permit and, if granted, whether any conditions should be placed on the permit.[7] In evaluating a permit application, the Army Corps is required to consider the recommendations of the Fish and Wildlife Service and the National Marine Fishery Service.[8] Comments and objections from certain state agencies must also be considered. Although various state and federal agencies may object to a permit application, the Army Corps may decide to issue a permit over the objections of other agencies.[9] However, if a state objects to issuance of a permit application because of inconsistency with a federally approved Coastal Zone Management Program (CMP),[10] the Army Corps cannot issue the permit unless the state's consistency objection is overruled by the Secretary of the Interior, or until the applicant modifies the proposal so that it is consistent with the goals of the state CMP.[11] Further, even if the Army Corps issues a permit, the applicant may need to secure additional state and local wetland permit approvals.

Application Form

Applicants for Section 404 permits may obtain copies of the permit application form[12] from the local Army Corps district office where application will be submitted.[13] The permit form is also reproduced in the regulations as Appendix A to 33 C.F.R. 325. Still, it is best to contact the appropriate local district office because some districts require the use of application forms that contain slight variations from the standard form in order to facilitate local coordination with other federal, state, or local agencies.

The applicable regulations describing the contents of the permit application are found at 33 C.F.R. 325.1(d). Generally speaking, an application is deemed complete and ready for consideration "when sufficient information is received to issue a public notice."[14] Submission of the following information will satisfy this requirement:[15]

1. A complete description of the proposed activity, including necessary drawings, sketches, or plans sufficient for a public notice (detailed engineering plans and specifications are not required). Three maps must be submitted: (a) a vicinity map (a road map, or U.S. Geological Survey topographic map, scale 1:24,000); (b) a plan view that shows the development as it would appear if one were looking straight down on it from above, and that indicates water bodies (names, water levels, depths, and dimensions), dimensions of the activity, and various other details; and (c) an elevation or cross-section view that is a scale drawing of the project that shows side, front, and rear views.
2. The location, purpose, and need for the proposed activity.
3. Scheduling of the activity.
4. The names and addresses of adjacent property owners.
5. The location and dimensions of adjacent structures.
6. A list of authorizations required by other federal, interstate, state, or local agencies for the work,

including a list of all approvals already received and denials already made.
7. If the proposed activity involves dredging, the applicant must include a description of the type, composition, and quantity of the material to be dredged, the method of dredging, and the site and plans for disposal of the dredged material.
8. If the proposed activity involves the discharge of dredged or fill material or the transportation of dredged material for the purpose of disposing of it in ocean waters, the application must include the source of the material, the purpose of the discharge, a description of the type, composition and quantity of the material, the method of transportation and disposal of the material, and the location of the disposal site.[16]
9. If the proposed activity involves the construction of a filled area or pile or float-supported platform, the project description must include the use of, and specific structures to be erected on, the fill or platform.
10. Signature. The application must be signed by the person who desires to undertake the activity or by a duly authorized agent.[17]

In addition, the regulations require that "[a]ll activities which the applicant plans to undertake which are reasonably related to the same project and for which a [Army Corps] permit would be required, should be included in the same permit application. District engineers should reject, as incomplete, any permit application that fails to comply with this requirement."[18] There has been considerable disagreement as to what constitutes "reasonably related" projects.[19]

Finally, the Army Corps has discretion to require submission of additional information by the applicant as may be necessary to make a public interest determination. Additional information may include environmental data and information on alternate methods and sites that may be necessary to comply with required environmental documentation.[20]

Exemptions

Section 404(f)(1) of the Clean Water Act[21] lists several kinds of activities that are exempt from the requirement for a Section 404 dredge and fill permit. No permit is required for discharges:

- From normal farming, silviculture, and ranching activities such as plowing, seeding, cultivating, minor drainage, harvesting for the production of food, fiber, and forest products, or upland soil and water conservation practices.
- For the purpose of maintenance ... of currently serviceable structures such as dikes, dams, levees, groins, riprap, breakwaters, causeways, ...
- For the purpose of construction or maintenance of farm or stock ponds or irrigation ditches, or the maintenance of drainage ditches.
- For the purpose of construction of temporary sedimentation basins on a construction site ...
- For the purpose of construction or maintenance of farm roads or forest roads, or temporary roads for moving mining equipment.
- Resulting from any activity with respect to which a state has an approved [statewide water quality plan under 33 U.S.C. § 1288(b)(4)].

The Section 404(f)(1) exemptions are limited by the Section 404(f)(2) "recapture clause," which makes the exemptions inapplicable if the purpose of the activity is to bring navigable waters into a use to which they were not previously subject, or where the flow of water is impaired. Courts have construed narrowly the reach of Section 404(f)(1) exemptions based on the Section 404(f)(2) recapture clause.

PERMIT APPLICATION PROCESS

Upon receipt of a Section 404 permit application, the district engineer must immediately assign it a number for identification purposes, and advise the applicant of receipt of the application and assignment of the identification number.[22] Within 15 days of receipt of an application, the district engineer must review the application and either: (1) advise the applicant that the application is complete and issue a public notice, or (2) advise the applicant that additional information is necessary for a complete application.[23]

The Corps is also required to evaluate each permit application to determine if it meets the requirements for a nationwide permit, or would meet those requirements after reasonable modification or conditions.[24] If the district engineer determines that an application meets the nationwide permit criteria, then the applicant must be so informed.

Army Corps Action on Permit Applications

The Corps can respond in several ways to a Section 404 permit application. First, a determination is made whether the Corps has jurisdiction over the wetland in question. Second, the Corps may determine that a public hearing is required, during which time any party wishing to make an oral statement regarding the permit application has an opportunity to do so.[25] Third, the Corps may determine that the project will not degrade wetlands in a manner that would prohibit a Section 404 permit and issue the permit. A fourth alternative response is the issuance of a General or "Nationwide" permit, or determination that the project meets any of several statutory exemptions to the requirement for a Section 404 permit. Fifth, the Corps may issue the permit while requiring project modifications and/or mitigation. Finally, the Corps may determine that the project is unacceptable under Section 404, and reject the application.

The regulations instruct the district engineer to render a decision on all applications within 60 days after receipt, but this time limit is rarely met because of the time required for compliance with other regulations and statutes,[26] understaffing in Corps offices, and other reasons.

Public Notice

Corps regulations contain specific requirements for the contents of the public notice, as detailed in 33 CFR 325.3. In general, the contents of the public notice must "include sufficient information to give a clear understanding of the nature and magnitude of the activity to generate meaningful comment."[27]

In general, the Corps attempts to make knowledge of the application available as widely as practicable. Under Corps regulations, public notices are to be distributed to the public in general by placing in post offices "or other appropriate public places in the vicinity of the site of the proposed work ...."[28] Notices are sent specifically to the applicant, adjacent property owners, appropriate local officials and state agencies, Indian tribes, and to concerned federal agencies. Notices are also sent to concerned business interests, environmental organizations, state and regional clearinghouses for such information, and local news media. In addition, the Corps will send a notice to "all parties who have specifically requested copies of public notices...."[29]

The notice should include the following information:[30]

1. Applicable statutory authority or authorities.
2. Name and address of the applicant.
3. Name or title, address and telephone number of the Army Corps employee from whom additional information concerning the application may be obtained.
4. Location of the proposed activity.
5. Brief description of the proposed activity, its purpose and intended use, so as to provide sufficient information concerning the nature of the activity to generate meaningful comments.
6. A plan and elevation drawing showing the general and specific site location and character of all proposed activities, including the size relationship of the proposed structures to the size of the impacted waterway and depth of water in the area.
7. A list of other government authorizations obtained or requested by the applicant, including required certifications relative to water quality, coastal zone management, or marine sanctuaries.
8. If appropriate, a statement that the activity is a categorical exclusion for purposes of NEPA.
9. A statement of the district engineer's current knowledge on historic properties.

10. A statement of the district engineer's current knowledge on endangered species.
11. A statement on evaluation factors.[31]
12. Any other available information which may assist interested parties in evaluating the likely impact of the proposed activity, if any, on factors affecting the public interest.
13. The comment period.
14. A statement that any person may request, in writing, within the comment period specified in the notice, that a public hearing be held to consider the application. Requests for public hearings shall state, with particularity, the reasons for holding a public hearing.

Further, if the proposed activity would occur in the territorial seas or ocean waters, the notice must contain a description of the activity's relationship to the baseline from which the territorial sea is measured.[32] If the proposed activity involves ocean dumping, additional relevant information must be contained in the public notice.[33]

Each public notice contains a time limit for receipt of comments by the local district office. Generally, the comment period should not be for more than 30 days, nor for less than fifteen days from the date of the notice.[34] Comments received after that date need not be considered by the Corps in subsequent deliberations. The district engineer may issue a supplemental, revised, or corrected public notice at his discretion if he feels that there has been a change in the application or application data that would affect the public's view of the proposal,[35] and time limits may be extended for this and other reasons.[36]

Public Comment

The district engineer must "consider all comments received in response to the public notice in his subsequent actions on the permit application."[37] Any interested person or organization may make comments on a Section 404 permit application. The district engineer acknowledges receipt of comments "if appropriate," and will make them a part of the administrative record of the application.[38] If the comments received by the Corps indicate that the views of the applicant are necessary in order to conduct a public interest determination on a particular issue, then the applicant will be given the opportunity to furnish his views on the issue.[39]

At the "earliest practicable time," the Army Corps will supply copies of substantive comments to the applicant for his information. These comments may be supplied in the form of summaries, the actual letters (or portions of them), or representative comments. The applicant is then given the choice to contact the objectors if he so chooses to resolve conflicts regarding the application.[40]

Public Hearing

The regulations specify that "any person" may request, in writing, a public hearing on a permit application within the time period specified in the public notice for comments. The written request must specify with particularity the reasons for holding a public hearing. Following such a request, the district engineer may attempt to resolve the issues informally (usually by meeting with the applicant and the person requesting the hearing). Otherwise, the district engineer must grant the request for the public hearing, or make a determination in writing that "the issues raised are insubstantial or there is otherwise no valid interest to be served by a hearing."[41] In practice, public hearings are seldom granted except for large or very controversial projects.

Permit Decision

Once the district engineer has considered all the information on the permit application (including all public comments and hearings), he is required to issue a statement of findings (SOF), or issue a record of decision (ROD) in those cases where an environmental impact statement has been prepared pursuant to NEPA.[42] The SOF or ROD must include the district engineer's views on the effects of the proposed project on "the public interest," including compliance with all aspects of the Section 404(b)(1) Guidelines and the conclusions of the district engineer.[43] The district engineer must normally accept the decisions of local and state governing bodies on zoning and land use issues,[44] or he must include in the SOF or ROD an explanation of why national issues should override local or state decisions.[45]

When reaching a decision whether to grant or deny a permit application, Army Corps regulations mandate a careful public interest review:

"The decision whether to issue a permit will be based on an evaluation of the probable impacts, including cumulative impacts, of the proposed activity and its intended use on the public interest. Evaluation of the probable impact ... on the public interest requires a careful weighing of all those factors which become relevant in each particular case. The benefits which reasonably may be expected to accrue from the proposal must be balanced against its reasonably foreseeable detriments."[46]

This general balancing process determines whether a permit will be issued, and what kinds of conditions may be required.[47] Among the factors to be considered are conservation, economics, aesthetics, general environmental concerns, fish and wildlife values, water quality, and public welfare.[48]

If the final decision is to deny the permit, the applicant is advised in writing of the reasons for the denial. If the final decision is to issue the permit and a standard individual permit form is used, the issuing official forwards the permit to the applicant for signature accepting the conditions of the permit. "Final action on the permit application is the signature on the letter notifying the applicant of the denial of the permit or signature of the issuing official on the authorizing document."[49]

The duration of a Section 404 permit generally depends on the nature of the permitted activity. Permits for permanent structures are usually indefinite with no expiration date. However, where a structure or project is temporary in nature, the permit will be of limited duration with a definite expiration date.[50] Permits automatically expire on the expiration date specified on the permit unless they are modified, suspended, or revoked.[51]

GENERAL AND NATIONWIDE PERMITS

Section 404(e) of the Clean Water Act authorizes the Army Corps to issue "general" permits on a state, regional, and nationwide basis for certain types of activities that are similar in nature and will have only minimal individual and cumulative environmental impacts.[52] In general, an activity covered by a general permit does not require submission of a Section 404 permit application as long as the permitee complies with the conditions of the general permit.[53] However, some general permits do require a pre-notification procedure before construction can be commenced.[54]

The most significant general permits are called "nationwide" permits (NWPs).[55] Nationwide permits are issued by Army Corps headquarters in Washington, D.C., and as the name implies, these permits apply to all areas of the country. The Army Corps has issued over 25 nationwide permits which are listed and described in Appendix A to 33 C.F.R. Part 330. The following is a listing of some of these nationwide permits:

NWP 1: Construction of aids to navigation and regulatory markers.
NWP 5: Scientific measurement devices.
NWP 12: Utility line backfill and bedding.
NWP 18: Minor discharges that do not exceed 25 cubic yards.
NWP 20: Oil spill cleanup activities.
NWP 26: Discharges of dredged or fill material into headwaters or isolated waters.

The most controversial nationwide permit is NWP 26, which exempts from the permit process any discharges of dredged or fill materials into "headwaters and isolated waters," provided: (1) the discharge does not cause the loss of more than ten acres of waters; (2) the Corps district is notified of the discharge and loss; and (3) the discharge is part of a single and complete project. Nationwide Permit 26 applies to wetlands above the headwaters, as well as the water bodies to which they are adjacent.

Nationwide permits contain a number of general conditions that apply to all nationwide permits.[56] Many of these conditions relate to environmental controls and maintenance associated with the permitted activities. It is important to note that nationwide permits also require compliance with the Endangered Species Act and the consistency requirements of the Coastal Zone Management Act.[57] District engineers may suspend, modify, or revoke use of nationwide permits if individual or cumulative impacts are more than minimal, or when the activity is contrary to the public interest.[58]

Two or more nationwide permits can be combined to authorize a "single and complete project,"[59] but the same nationwide permit may not be used more than once for a single and complete project.[60] For projects that combine individual permits with nationwide permits, the applicant may proceed with the parts of the project covered by a nationwide permit while awaiting review of the individual permit.[61]

On July 27, 1995, the Army Corps issued a new nationwide general permit (NWP) under Section 404 of the Clean Water Act and Section 10 of the Rivers and Harbors Act for single-family residential housing activities. This NWP permit was issued in direct response to the Clinton Administration's Wetlands Plan.[62] This NWP has been developed to reduce the regulatory burden on small landowners proposing to build or expand a single-family home while simultaneously maintaining environmental safeguards. This NWP seeks to strike a balance by allowing a landowner to build or expand a home with minimal regulatory oversight while protecting the aquatic resource through specific limitations.[63]

REMEDIES FOR PERMIT DENIALS

No mechanism exists for administrative appeal to the Army Corps, nor is there any right to an adjudicatory hearing for Section 404 permit denials like there is for denial of other types of environmental permits. Still, a permittee or other party who is adversely impacted by an Army Corps wetland permit decision is not without any legal remedy. After the Army Corps rules on a federal wetland permit application, a final decision may be subject to judicial review under the Administrative Procedure Act.[64] Further, in some cases, parties opposing the approval of a permit may have standing to institute a "citizen suit" under the Clean Water Act, National Environmental Policy Act or other environmental law. However, permit applicants must be aware that judicial review is usually an uphill battle because in reviewing the Army Corps decision, the court is bound by a "substantial evidence" standard. Under this standard, the court may set aside the permit decision only if it finds that the Army Corps action is arbitrary, capricious, an abuse of discretion, or otherwise not in accordance with law.[65] The courts are bound by the administrative record and may not admit new evidence unless the record is so scant that it makes judicial review virtually impossible.[66] In other cases, applicants who have been denied a permit may challenge the Army Corps decision in federal court on constitutional grounds. For example, regulatory takings actions have frequently been brought in federal court to challenge permit denials.[67]

ENDNOTES

1. 33 U.S.C. § 1344(a). The Army Corps regulations governing individual permits are found at 33 C.F.R. Part 323.

2. 33 U.S.C. § 1344(e). Army Corps regulations governing the nationwide permit program are found at 33 C.F.R. Part 330.

3. EPA, "Clean Water Act Section 404(b)(1) Guidelines," 55 Fed. Reg. 9210 (Feb. 7, 1990), *codified at* 40 C.F.R. § 230.

4. 33 U.S.C. § 1344(b)-(c).

5. As of February 1995, the EPA had completed only 11 veto actions out of an estimated 150,000 permit applications received by the Army Corps since the regulations went into effect in October 1979.

6. 33 C.F.R. Parts 325, 323, 320.

7. 33 C.F.R. § 320.4 lists the criteria for evaluating a permit application.

8. 33 C.F.R. § 320.4(c).

9. 33 C.F.R. § 325.

10. 16 U.S.C. § 1456(c)(3)(A).

11. 16 U.S.C. § 1456(d).

12. ENG Form 4345, OMB Approval No. OMB 49-R0420; see 33 C.F.R. § 325.1(c).

13. Appendix B provides a listing of the local Army Corps district offices.

14. 33 C.F.R. § 325.1(d)(9).

15. 33 C.F.R. § 325.1(d)(1).

16. State certification under Section 401 of the Clean Water Act is required for such discharges. 33 C.F.R. § 325.1(d)(4).

17. If the applicant is represented by an agent (e.g., a contractor, consultant, or attorney), that information must be included with the application. 33 C.F.R. § 325.1(d)(7).

18. 33 C.F.R. § 325.1(d)(2).

19. See *Russo Development Corp v. Thomas*, 735 F. Supp. 631 (D.N.J. 1989).

20. 33 C.F.R. § 325.1(e).

21. 33 U.S.C. § 1344(f)(1).

22. 33 C.F.R. § 325.2(a)(1).

23. 33 C.F.R. § 325.2(a)(2).

24. 33 C.F.R. § 330.2(f).

25. 33 C.F.R. § 325.2(a)(5). Procedures for determining the need for a public hearing are found at 33 C.F.R. Part 327.

26. 33 C.F.R. § 325.2(d)(3).

27. 33 C.F.R. § 325.3(a).

28. 33 C.F.R. § 325.3(d)(1).

29. *Id.*

30. 33 C.F.R. § 325.3(a)(1)-(17).

31. *See* 33 C.F.R. § 325.3 (c) for the list of evaluation factors.

32. 33 C.F.R. § 325.3(a)(7).

33. This information is listed at 33 C.F.R. § 325.3(a)(17)(i)-(vii).

34. 33 C.F.R. § 325.2(d)(2).

35. 33 C.F.R. § 325.2(a)(2).

36. 33 C.F.R. § 325.2(d)(2).

37. 33 C.F.R. § 325.2(a)(3).

38. *Id.*

39. *Id.* The applicant will be given a reasonable time to respond to requests of the district engineer, not to exceed 30 days. 33 C.F.R. § 325.2(d)(5).

40. 33 C.F.R. § 325.2(a)(3).

41. 33 C.F.R. § 327.4(b).

42. 33 C.F.R. § 325.2(a)(6).

43. *Id.*

44. 33 C.F.R. § 320.4(j)(2).

45. 33 C.F.R. § 325.2(a)(6).

46. 33 C.F.R. § 320.4(a).

47. *See* 33 C.F.R. § 325.4 regarding imposition of permit conditions.

48. *See* 33 C.F.R. § 320.4(a).

49. 33 C.F.R. § 325.2(a)(7).

50. 33 C.F.R. § 325.6(b).

51. 33 C.F.R. § 325.6(a). Guidelines on permit modification, suspension, and revocation are found at 33 C.F.R. § 325.7.

52. 33 U.S.C. § 1344(e)(1).

53. 33 C.F.R. § 320.1(c).

54. 33 C.F.R. §§ 320.1(c) and 330.6(a).

55. Corps regulations governing the nationwide permit program are found at 33 C.F.R. § 330.

56. These are listed at Appendix A (C) to 33 C.F.R. Part 330.

57. *See* 33 C.F.R. § 330.4(d).

58. 33 C.F.R. §§ 330.1(d), 330.4(e), and 330.5. The Army Corps may suspend, modify, or revoke use of a' nationwide permit without providing a hearing. *O'Connor v. Corps of Engineers*, 801 F. Supp. 185 (N.D.Ind. 1992).

59. 33 C.F.R. § 330.2(i).

60. 33 C.F.R. § 330.6(c).

61. 33 C.F.R. § 330.6(d).

62. *See* discussion of the Clinton Administration's Wetlands Plan in Chapter 1.

63. The nationwide permit for single-family housing activities became effective on September 25, 1995. The NWP will remain in effect for 5 years from this date unless it is revoked, modified, or reissued earlier.

64. 5 U.S.C. § 701-706.

65. 5 U.S.C. § 706(2)(a). *See also Avoyelles Sportsmen's League, Inc. v. Marsh*, 715 F.2d 897 (5th Cir. 1983).

66. *See Friends of the Earth v. Hintz*, 800 F.2d 822 (9th Cir. 1986).

67. *See Loveladies Harbor, Inc. v. United States*, 28 F.3d 1171 (Fed. Cir. 1994).

Chapter 5

Wetland Mitigation Compliance

INTRODUCTION

Development project approvals in wetland areas typically require some form of "mitigation" to restore or replace wetland values that will be adversely impacted by the proposed activity. When reviewing applications for Section 404 dredge and fill permits in wetland areas, the Army Corps must apply mitigation guidelines[1] which require that the permit applicant sequentially avoid, minimize, and compensate for wetland impacts.

Mitigation compliance can be a complex and difficult process. Developers are often required to readjust lot lines, redirect stormwater or other runoff, or completely relocate a development project in order to protect important wetland values. But if the permit applicant can devise a plan for mitigating the development impacts on wetlands which results in "no-net-loss" of wetlands then, generally speaking, the project is allowed. This chapter examines and explains how to comply with the mitigation requirements for dredge and fill permits issued under Section 404 of the Clean Water Act.

WETLAND MITIGATION POLICY

Wetland mitigation is a key component of the federal government's "no-net-loss" policy.[2] Yet, mitigation is not specifically mentioned in Section 404 of the Clean Water Act, the provision governing wetland dredge and fill permits.[3] Instead, the mitigation requirement is found in other federal laws, most notably the National Environmental Policy Act (NEPA)[4] and the Fish and Wildlife Coordination Act,[5] which require mitigation for all federal actions that adversely affect the environment. Issuance of a Section 404 dredge and fill permit is the kind of federal agency action that will trigger NEPA's mitigation requirements.

The Council on Environmental Quality (CEQ) adopted regulations implementing NEPA in 1978.[6] The CEQ regulations, which spell out the procedures required by federal agencies to implement NEPA, included mitigation measures. The regulations defined "mitigation" to include:

- Avoiding environmental impacts altogether by not taking an action (or part of an action) that might lead to environmental degradation.
- Minimizing impacts by limiting the degree or magnitude of the action and its implementation.
- Rectifying the impact by repairing, rehabilitating, or restoring the affected environment.
- Reducing or eliminating the impact over time by preservation and maintenance operations during the life of the action.
- Compensating for the impact by replacing or providing substitute resources or environments.

The Army Corps took a somewhat more restrictive view of mitigation than did the CEQ, regarding compensatory mitigation as a last step after attempts at avoidance, minimizing impact, and repairing damage had failed. Current mitigation policies administered by the Army Corps under its Section 404 regulations state that:

"Mitigation is an important aspect of the review and balancing process on many Department of Army permit applications. Consideration of mitigation will occur throughout the permit application review process and includes avoiding, minimizing, rectifying, reducing, or compensating for resource losses. Losses will be avoided to the extent practicable. Compensation may occur on-site or at an off-site location."[7]

Table 5-1 is a listing of various documents that set mitigation policy.

Table 5-1. Government Policy on Mitigation

1.	Army Corps, EPA, NRCS, FWS, NOAA, "Federal Guidance for the Establishment, Use, and Operation of Mitigation Banks", 60 Fed. Reg. 58605 (Nov. 28, 1995).
2.	EPA/Army Corps, Memorandum to the Field: Appropriate Level of Analysis Required for Evaluating Compliance With the Section 404(b)(1) Guidelines Alternatives Requirements (Aug. 23, 1993).
3.	EPA/Army Corps, Memorandum to the Field: Establishment and Use of Wetland Mitigation Banks in the Clean Water Act Section 404 Regulatory Program (Aug. 23, 1993).
4.	Environmental Protection Agency, Section 404(b)(1) Guidelines (40 CFR part 230). Guidelines for Specification of Disposal Sites for Dredged or Fill Material.
5.	Department of the Army, Section 404 Permit Regulations (33 CFR parts 320-330). Policies for Evaluating Permit Applications to Discharge Dredged or Fill Material.
6.	Memorandum of Agreement between the Environmental Protection Agency and the Department of the Army Concerning the Determination of Mitigation under the Clean Water Act Section 404 (b)(1) Guidelines (Feb. 6, 1990).
7.	Fish and Wildlife Service Mitigation Policy, 46 Fed. Reg. 7644 (Jan. 23, 1981).
8.	National Marine Fisheries Service Habitat Conservation Policy, 48 Fed. Reg. 53142 (1983).

STATE LAW MITIGATION REQUIREMENTS

At least twenty states have wetland management laws and regulations. These state programs generally require permits for activities impacting wetland areas, which are similar to the Section 404 permits issued by the Army Corps. Two states, Michigan and New Jersey, have assumed responsibility for administering the federal Section 404 permit program. Some states have effectively taken partial assumption of the federal wetland permitting program through the Army Corps' issuance of general permits. For example, the Army Corps has issued a five-year general permit to the State of Oregon for wetland restoration and enhancement projects.[8]

In addition, many state wetland laws include mitigation requirements in their regulatory schemes. For example, Maryland's law requires that applicants "take all necessary steps to first avoid significant impairment and then minimize losses of nontidal wetlands.[9] Further, at least nine states have laws expressly authorizing wetland mitigation banks.[10] Others address mitigation banking through regulatory guidance or regulations.[11]

A thorough review of these state wetland laws and regulations cannot be provided here. Applicants for permits to carry out development activities are well advised to contact their state environmental agencies for guidance on state-specific wetland regulations. Appendix C provides a listing of state wetland agency offices.

CORPS/EPA 404(b)(1) MITIGATION GUIDELINES

When the Army Corps reviews applications for dredge and fill activities, it must consider substantive criteria developed by the EPA. Pursuant to Section 404(b)(1) of the CWA,[12] the EPA has issued Guidelines that the Army Corps must use to evaluate the environmental impacts of proposed activities on wetlands.[13] These Section 404(b)(1) Guidelines are a critical component of the federal wetland permit process. The guidelines protect wetlands by prohibiting discharges that have significant adverse effects on human health or welfare, recreation, aesthetics, economics, aquatic ecosystems, and wildlife dependent on aquatic ecosystems.[14] In terms of mitigation requirements, the Guidelines require that the permit applicant undertake all appropriate and practicable steps to minimize any potential harm to the aquatic ecosystem. The Army Corps evaluates permit applications according to a sequencing of mitigation options. The preferred mitigation option is avoidance of impacts, followed by minimization of impacts, and finally, appropriate and practicable compensation for unavoidable impacts. The EPA and Army Corps further clarified this sequencing methodology in a joint Memorandum of Agreement (MOA) issued in February 1990, which is discussed below.

The Guidelines further mandate that "no discharge of dredged or fill material shall be permitted if there is a practicable alternative to the proposed discharge which would have less adverse impact on the aquatic ecosystem."[15] Consideration must be given to whether the proposed discharge is the least environmentally damaging "practicable" alternative. With non-water-dependent projects, there is a presumption that a practicable alternative exists unless the permit applicant can demonstrate otherwise.

An alternative is considered "practicable" if it is available and capable of being performed after taking into consideration cost, existing technology, and logistics in light of overall project goals. This standard for evaluating practicable alternatives has been the subject of considerable strife between permit applicants, the Army Corps, and the EPA. The scope and degree of analysis necessary to fulfill the practicable alternatives requirement is far from clear. As a result, several courts have been called upon to interpret the meaning of the "practicable alternatives" language.[16] In addition, the agencies have found it necessary to issue further clarifications on the proper method for analyzing practicable alternatives.[17] A detailed discussion of the practicable alternatives is provided on page 97.

The Guidelines also prohibit the Army Corps from issuing Section 404 permits if the proposed discharge would result in a violation of other environmental laws or regulations or cause or contribute, either individually or collectively, to significant degradation of wetlands or other waters of the United States.[18]

EPA/CORPS MITIGATION MOA

Due to various conflicts between the EPA and Army Corps over interpretation of the Section 404(b)(1) guidelines, including the "practicable alternatives" provision, the two agencies issued a joint Memorandum of Agreement in 1990 (1990 MOA) concerning the determination of mitigation measures under Section 404(b)(1).[19]

Under the 1990 MOA, during the evaluation process of a Section 404 permit application, "[t]he Corps ... first makes a determination that potential impacts have been avoided to the maximum extent practicable; remaining unavoidable impacts will then be mitigated to the extent appropriate and practicable by requiring steps to minimize impacts and, finally, compensate for aquatic resource values." This sequencing requirement condenses the CEQ mitigation definition into three phases (avoidance, minimization, compensation) and is consistent with the Section 404(b)(1) Guidelines. In determining if proposed mitigation is "appropriate and practicable," the 1990 MOA further provides that "such [mitigation] measures should be appropriate to the scope and degree of those impacts[20] and practicable in terms of cost, existing technology, and logistics in light of overall project purposes."[21]

SEQUENCING REQUIREMENT

The 1990 MOA formalized a three-step sequencing requirement for determining appropriate mitigation of project impacts: avoidance, minimization, and compensatory mitigation. The first step, avoidance, is synonymous with the "practicable alternatives" analysis of the Section 404(b)(1) Guidelines.[22] The second step, minimization, requires that permit applicants make changes to project design that will reduce impacts to wetlands. The third step, compensation, requires replacement of wetlands that are degraded or destroyed by unavoidable impacts. This sequencing methodology applies to all individual permits, regardless of the type or ecological value of the wetlands adversely affected by project impacts. The 1990 MOA does, however, provide for some deviations from the sequencing requirement where the requirements have been incorporated in a Army Corps or EPA comprehensive plan, such as a Special Area Management Plan (SAMP), or where necessary to avoid environmental harm, or where the EPA and Army Corps agree that a proposed discharge "can reasonably be expected to result in environmental gain or insignificant environmental losses."

Avoidance

The 1990 MOA interprets the Section 404(b)(1) Guidelines to mean that the primary focus of the mitigation alternatives analysis should be on "avoidance of impacts." The Corps must determine that impacts have been avoided "to the maximum extent practicable" before it issues a permit. Permits are not to be issued if there is a "practicable alternative ... which would have less adverse impact on the aquatic ecosystem, so long as the alternative does not have other significant adverse environmental consequences."[23]

Minimization

In the event that impacts cannot be avoided, the 1990 MOA requires minimization of any unavoidable impacts on the aquatic ecosystem. "Appropriate and practicable" steps must be taken to minimize potential adverse impacts through project modifications and permit conditions.[24] The Section 404(b)(1) Guidelines describe several means for minimizing impacts, including the following measures:

- Locating and confining the discharge to minimize smothering of organisms;[25]
- Designing the discharge to avoid a disruption of periodic water inundation patterns.[26]
- Selecting a site that has been used previously for dredged material discharge.[27]
- Selecting a site at which the substrate is composed of material similar to that being discharged, such as sand on sand or mud on mud.[28]
- Designing to prevent the creation of standing water in an area of normally fluctuating water levels, and preventing the drainage of areas subject to such fluctuation.[29]

The "minimization" requirement focuses on the care that an applicant should take when designing and implementing any mitigation project so as to minimize adverse environmental impacts to the maximum extent practicable.

Compensatory Mitigation

The last step, and least preferred mitigation option, is compensation for unavoidable adverse environmental impacts. If impacts still remain after all appropriate and practicable avoidance and minimization measures have been taken, then compensatory mitigation is required. The 1990

MOA describes compensatory actions as "restoration of existing degraded wetlands or creation of man-made wetlands." This means that wetland restoration and creation are only to be considered after exhaustion of all appropriate and practicable avoidance and minimization measures. The 1990 MOA indicates a preference for restoration over compensation: "There is continued uncertainty regarding the success of wetland creation or other habitat development. Therefore, in determining the nature and extent of habitat development of this type, careful consideration should be given to its likelihood of success. Because the likelihood of success is greater and the impacts to potentially valuable uplands are reduced, restoration should be the first option considered."

The 1990 MOA shows a strong preference for on-site compensatory mitigation. Compensatory actions should be undertaken, when practicable, in areas adjacent or contiguous to the discharge site. If on-site compensatory mitigation is not practicable, off-site compensatory mitigation should be undertaken "in the same geographical area if practicable (*i.e.*, in close physical proximity and, to the extent possible, the same watershed)." The preference for on-site compensatory mitigation is consistent with Army Corps and EPA policies. Army Corps policy permits mitigation to occur on-site (*i.e.*, restoring those wetlands located on the project site which are degraded by the project or by previous actions), or off-site (either the purchase of wetlands at another site, or creation of new wetlands at a site where none exist), although there is a strong preference for on-site mitigation.

In deciding if compensatory mitigation is acceptable, the Army Corps and EPA consider the functional values that will be lost as a result of the proposed project. Scientific techniques, such as the Habitat Evaluation Procedures (HEP) developed by the FWS, and the Wetland Evaluation Technique (WET), are used to determine the value of wetlands that will be impacted, as well as those which will replace them.[30]

The 1990 MOA also indicates a preference for "in-kind" over "out-of-kind" compensatory mitigation. Compensatory mitigation should be designed, to the maximum extent possible, to replace lost wetland values with functionally equivalent wetland values. In most instances, this means replacing the impacted wetland with the same type of wetland (*i.e.*, replacing a salt marsh with a salt marsh). Mitigation must provide "at a minimum, one for one functional replacement (*i.e.*, no net loss of values)." The MOA specifically authorizes the use of "approved" mitigation banks as an acceptable form of compensatory mitigation.[31]

Exceptions to Sequencing Requirement

The 1990 MOA specifically recognizes two limited exceptions to the mitigation sequencing requirement. First, it may be necessary to deviate from the normal sequence when the Army Corps and EPA agree that a proposed discharge is necessary to avoid environmental harm. The 1990 MOA gives the examples of such deviations "to protect a natural aquatic community from saltwater intrusion, chemical contamination, or other deleterious physical or chemical impacts." A second exception to sequencing occurs when the Army Corps and EPA agree "that the proposed discharge can reasonably be expected to result in environmental gain or insignificant environmental losses."

There is an additional implied exception. In discussing one-for-one replacement of functional values, the 1990 MOA recognizes that this minimum requirement "may not be appropriate and practicable, and thus may not be relevant in all cases." In a controversial footnote, the 1990 MOA further explains:

"For example, there are certain areas where, due to hydrological conditions, the technology for restoration or creation of wetlands may not be available at present, or may otherwise be impracticable. In addition, avoidance, minimization, and compensatory mitigation may not be practicable where there is a high proportion of land which is wetlands."[32] For the latter statement, EPA has given the example that the creation of tundra or permafrost in Alaska is not technically feasible at this time, such that mitigation may not be practicable. The degree to which this exception applies to other situations is the subject of current discussions within the Army Corps and EPA.

PRACTICABLE ALTERNATIVES TEST

One of the most important aspects of the Section 404(b)(1) Guidelines is the "practicable alternatives" requirement. The Guidelines create a presumption against filling wetlands by prohibiting the discharge of dredged or fill material into waters where "a practicable alternative to the proposed discharge [exists] which would have less adverse impact on the aquatic ecosystem, so long as the alternative does not have other significant adverse environmental consequences."[33] It also provides that a practicable alternative may include "an area not presently owned by the applicant which could reasonably be obtained, utilized, expanded, or managed in order to fulfill the basic purpose of the proposed activity."[34] It further provides that, "unless clearly demonstrated otherwise", practicable alternatives are (1) "presumed to be available", and (2) "presumed to have less adverse impact on the aquatic ecosystem."[35] Thus, an applicant must rebut both of these presumptions in order to obtain a permit.

EPA/Corps 1993 Memorandum to the Field

On August 23, 1993, the EPA and Army Corps released a joint Memorandum to the Field which provides additional guidance for completing the practicable alternatives analysis.[36] The memorandum helps to clarify the appropriate level of analysis required to fulfill the practicable alternatives requirement of the Section 404(b)(1) guidelines.[37] The memorandum describes the flexibility afforded by the Guidelines to make regulatory decisions based on the relative severity of the environmental impact of proposed discharges of dredged or fill material into waters of the United States, including wetlands.

The preamble to the Section 404(b)(1) Guidelines makes it clear that some flexibility is inherent in the evaluation of practicable alternatives.[38] Still, the record must contain sufficient information to show that the proposed activity complies with the Guidelines.[39] The amount of information required generally depends on the severity of impact on the environment and the scope/cost of the proposed project.[40] The Guidelines state that the level of analysis required will vary with the nature of the proposed activity:

"Although all requirements in Section 230.10 must be met, the compliance evaluation procedures will vary to reflect the seriousness of the potential for adverse impacts on the aquatic ecosystems posed by specific dredged or fill material discharge activities."[41] The section on "adaptability" in the Guidelines addresses further the analysis required for minor activities. Section 230.6(9) states that the Guidelines "allow evaluation and documentation for a variety of activities, ranging from those with large, complex impacts on the aquatic environment to those for which the impact is likely to be innocuous. It is unlikely that the Guidelines will apply in their entirety to any one activity, no matter how complex. It is anticipated that substantial numbers of permit applications will be for minor, routine activities that have little, if any, potential for significant degradation of the aquatic environment. It generally is not intended or expected that extensive testing, evaluation, or analysis will be needed to make findings of compliance in such routine cases."[42]

These provisions indicate that the Guidelines afford flexibility to adjust the degree of the alternatives review for projects that would only have minor impacts. The 1993 Memorandum to the Field gives several examples of minor impacts, including projects that:

- Are small in size and cause little direct impact.
- Have little potential for secondary or cumulative impacts.
- Cause only temporary impacts.

The Memorandum states that it is inappropriate for the agencies to consider compensatory mitigation in determining whether a proposed discharge will cause only minor impacts for purposes of the alternatives analysis required by Section 230.10(a) of the Guidelines.

The Memorandum provides several "rules of thumb" for Army Corps and EPA field personnel to consider when evaluating projects with the potential for creating only minor impacts on the aquatic environment. These guidelines, however, only apply to application of the practicable alternatives analysis to minor projects. Projects that may cause more than minor impacts to the aquatic environment, either individually or cumulatively must be subjected to a proportionately more detailed review to determine compliance with the Section 404(b)(1) Guidelines. Projects with substantial impacts must be thoroughly evaluated during the standard permit review process.

First, the Memorandum recognized that minor projects should not ordinarily cause or contribute to significant degradation of the aquatic environment, either individually or cumulatively. Therefore, as a general rule, it should not be necessary to conduct or require completion of detailed analyses to determine compliance with Section 230.10(c) of the Guidelines.

Second, the Memorandum states that the Guidelines do not require an elaborate search for practicable alternatives if it is reasonably anticipated that there are only minor differences between the environmental impacts of the proposed activity and potentially practicable alternatives. The Memorandum indicates that it is usually more sensible first to examine whether potential alternatives would result in no identifiable or discernible difference in impact on the aquatic environment.[43] Since the Guidelines only prohibit discharges when a practicable alternative exists which would have "less adverse impact on the aquatic ecosystem,"[44] this approach may limit (or in some instances eliminate altogether) the number of alternatives that have to be evaluated for practicability. Because evaluating practicability is generally the more difficult aspect of the alternatives analysis, this approach should save time and effort for both the applicant and the regulatory agencies. When it is determined that there is no identifiable or discernible difference in adverse impact on the environment between the applicant's proposed alternative and all other practicable alternatives, then the applicant's alternative is considered as satisfying the requirements of Section 230.10(a) of the Guidelines.

The Memorandum further clarifies that even where a practicable alternative exists that would have less adverse impact on the aquatic ecosystem, the Guidelines allow it to be rejected if it would have "other significant adverse environmental consequences."[45] As explained in the preamble to the Guidelines, this allows for consideration of "evidence of damages to other ecosystems in deciding whether there is a 'better' alternative." Hence, in applying the alternatives analysis required by the Guidelines, it is not appropriate to select an alternative where minor impacts on the aquatic environment are avoided at the cost of substantial impacts to other natural environmental values.

In cases of negligible impacts (*e.g.*, small discharges to construct individual driveways), it may be possible to conclude that no alternative location could result in less adverse impact on the aquatic environment within the meaning of the Guidelines. In such cases, the Memorandum explains that it may not be necessary to conduct an off-site alternatives analysis but instead only requires any practicable on-site minimization.

Finally, the Memorandum clarifies the relationship between the scope of alternatives analysis and the scope and cost of the project. The Guidelines define practicable alternatives as those alternatives that are "available and capable of being done after taking into consideration cost, existing technology, and logistics in light of overall project purposes."[46] The Memorandum explains how the overall scope and cost of the project should be considered when evaluating practicable alternatives. Generally, as the scope and cost of the project increase, the level of alternatives analysis should also increase.

The preamble to the Guidelines indicates that "[i]f an alleged alternative is unreasonably expensive to the applicant, the alternative is not 'practicable.'"[47] The Memorandum emphasizes that the determination of what constitutes an unreasonable expense should generally be considered in light of whether the project cost is substantially greater than the costs normally associated with the particular type of project. The Memorandum cautions that it is not the applicant's financial status that is the primary consideration, but rather characteristics of the project and what constitutes a reasonable expense for that type of project.

EPA/Corps 1995 Memorandum Regarding Small Landowners

On March 6, 1995, the EPA and Army Corps issued a Memorandum to the Field regarding permit flexibility for small landowners. The Memorandum recognizes a presumption that alternatives located on property not presently owned by the applicant are not practicable for discharges of dredged or fill material affecting up to two acres of non-tidal wetlands for the construction or expansion of a home or farm building, or the expansion of a small business.

This presumption specifically applies to those activities not otherwise covered by a general permit[48] involving discharges of dredged or fill material affecting up to two acres into jurisdictional wetlands for:

- The construction or expansion of a single-family home and attendant features, such as a driveway, garage, storage shed, or septic field.

- The construction or expansion of a barn, or other farm building.
- The expansion of a small business facility.

The requirement of the Section 404(b)(1) Guidelines to appropriately and practicably minimize and compensate for any adverse environmental impact of such activities nevertheless remain in effect.

The Memorandum recognized that for such small projects that would solely expand an existing structure, the basic project purpose is so tied to the existing structures owned by the applicant, that it would be highly unusual that the project could be located practicably on other sites not owned by the applicant.

In the Memorandum, the agencies do, however, explain that the presumption that is being afforded small landowners may be rebutted in certain situations. For example, a more thorough review of practicable alternatives may be warranted for individual sites comprising a subdivision of homes, if a real estate developer subdivided a large, contiguous wetlands parcel into numerous parcels.

Illustrative Cases

In a 1994 case, *National Wildlife Federation v. Whistler*,[49] the Eighth Circuit Court of Appeals dismissed a challenge to the Army Corps of Engineers' issuance of a dredge and fill permit that permitted conversion of 14.5 acres of wetlands to deep water habitat to provide a residential development with boat access to the Missouri River. In affirming the Corps decision under the "arbitrary and capricious" standard of judicial review, the court concluded that the Corps decision to issue the permit met the requirements of the Clean Water Act Section 404(b)(1) Guidelines, including sufficient evaluation of the impacts of the proposed activity on the public interest. The court found that the Corps gave ample consideration to "practicable alternatives" and that the approved plan to enhance 20 acres of off-site wetlands provided adequate wetland mitigation.

The National Wildlife Federation (NWF) brought an action in federal district court seeking to suspend the Corps' issuance of a dredge and fill permit to the Turnbow Development Corporation (Turnbow) which had secured permission to fill wetlands adjacent to its residential development. The Corps had issued the permit pursuant to Section 10 of the Rivers and Harbors Act, 33 U.S.C. Section 403, and Section 404(b) of the Clean Water Act, 33 U.S.C. Section 1344(b), conditioning its approval on fulfillment of forty-two conditions, including the required enhancement of a 20-acre wetland mitigation area. The district court upheld the Corps decision to issue the permit, and the Eighth Circuit in the instant case upheld this determination.

Turnbow owned a planned housing development near Bismarck, North Dakota, located on uplands on the east side of the Missouri River. The permit allowed Turnbow to provide these lots with boat access to the Missouri River by re-opening an old river channel adjacent to the planned development, thereby destroying the channel's existing wetlands. The project called for removal of an earthen roadway, dredging and widening of the old river channel, widening of the connection of the old channel to the Missouri River, and replacement of 200 feet of bank stabilization on the Missouri River. In total, approximately 14.5 acres of wetlands would be converted to deep water habitat.

As required by 33 C.F.R. Section 325.2-.3, the Corps gave public notice of the application and solicited comments from several state and federal agencies. These agencies suggested that the Corps condition the permit on a mitigation plan to offset the loss of wetlands. Thus, Turnbow responded with a plan to enhance an existing 20-acre wetland area by providing it with year-round water and saturated soil conditions.

After additional public notice and comment, the Corps issued an environmental assessment and decision document containing the agency's determination that the permit should be issued. The Corps concluded that the project's purpose was to provide boat access to the Missouri River from Turnbow's planned development. Given this purpose, the Corps considered the project water-dependent and site-specific. No other alternative, the Corps stated, would serve Turnbow's purpose, since "A boat access area located elsewhere would not be functional for the applicant's needs." The Corps concluded that the permit did not conflict with the public interest and satisfied the Clean Water Act Section 404(b)(1) guidelines.

On appeal, the NWF argued that the Corps had failed to perform an adequate alternatives analysis, as required by 40 C.F.R. § 230.10, before issuing the permit. In particular, the NWF contended that the Corps completely failed to consider the feasibility of a nearby public boat ramp as a means of water access to residents of the development. The Corps responded that it had properly conducted an alternatives analysis, specifically considering and rejecting several categories of response: (1) no action; (2) reduction of the scope of dredging; and (3) use of other sites. Applying the deferential standard of review applicable to agency actions, the court ruled that it could not find that the Corps' decision that no practicable alternatives existed was arbitrary and capricious. The court also found from its review of the record that the Corps did, in fact, consider the boat ramp as one possible alternative, but had properly dismissed it as inadequate.

In this case, the Corps concluded—and the court gave deference to this conclusion—that Turnbow's proposal to dredge the wetlands adjacent to the residential development site was a "water-dependent" project. The Corps' characterization of the project as "water-dependent" turned out to be dispositive of the NWF's challenge. The NWF pointed to cases in which courts rejected attempts by developers to build housing developments and adjacent docks on wetlands. The Eighth Circuit, however, distinguished these cases from the instant case because they involved projects that were defined as "water-dependent." Thus, the courts in those cases applied the regulatory presumption that practicable alternatives existed.

The Court said that a determination of a project's purpose is "central to evaluating practicable alternatives." The NWF characterized the Turnbow project as the building of a residential development with boat access. The Corps, however, characterized the project as solely limited to boat access. The Corps, accordingly, limited its alternatives analysis to the boat access area. The court agreed with the Corps' characterization of the project's purpose because the residential area was located entirely on uplands, thus, deeming it proper to exclude that area from consideration as part of the project for which the permit applied.

The location of Turnbow's residential dwellings on adjacent uplands distinguished it from other cases where the developers sought to build residential units on wetlands. The court stated that "[i]n those cases, the developers could have presumably relocated the entire developments to other locations". Here, the court agreed with the Corps' finding that

Turnbow's residential development could proceed on the upland area even if the Corps denied the dredge and fill permit for the boat access.

Still, the court offered some important words of caution to developers, stating that:

> In light of these findings, and after conducting a thorough review, the Corps accepted Turnbow's characterization of the overall project as encompassing two severable projects, a conclusion that is not without support. 'Obviously, an applicant cannot define a project in order to preclude the existence of any alternative sites and thus make what is practicable appear impracticable.' The cumulative destruction of our nation's wetlands that would result if developers were permitted to artificially constrain the Corps' alternatives analysis by defining the projects' purpose in an overly narrow manner would frustrate the statute and its accompanying regulatory scheme. We do not believe the case before us raises these concerns.[50]

In a 1995 case, *Dare County Bd. of Educ. v. Sakaria*,[51] a North Carolina court held that it was within a county board of education's eminent domain powers to condemn a privately-owned site to mitigate wetland impacts associated with development of new school athletic facilities. The court found that the board possessed state statutory authority to condemn property necessary for construction of school facilities and did not abuse its discretion in deciding to use the condemned property only for wetlands mitigation, despite evidence that alternative sites were available which the board did not consider.

The County Board of Education owns 12.5 acres of land located west of the Cape Hatteras School's campus, which is situated on the Pamlico Sound side of Hatteras Island. The Board planned to use its 12.5 acre lot, which contains 3.1 acres of wetlands, to expand the School's athletic facilities. In June 1988, the North Carolina Division of Coastal Management denied the Board's requests for a dredge and fill permit and water quality certification to make the 12.5 acre tract suitable for building athletic fields because its proposal would result in an unacceptable loss of wetlands. In 1992, a second permit application by the Board was denied by both the state Division of Coastal Management and the Division of Environmental Management after the coastal wetlands were realigned.

Consequently, the Board adopted a resolution in February 1993, approving condemnation of six privately-owned lots and submitted a proposal involving these lots to the Army Corps of Engineers. Under this proposal, defendants' lots 5 and 6 would be used only as a source of fill and for wetlands mitigation. This proposal received a conditional permit from the Corps. Thereafter, the Board filed actions in Dare County Superior Court to condemn the six lots. The court conducted a bench trial on the issue of plaintiff's authority to condemn defendants' property.

At trial, the court heard evidence from a member of the Board who testified that after Coastal Management denied a permit to use the 12.5 acres for additional facilities, the Board "formed an ad hoc committee" to look for available and suitable properties that were within "five miles of the facility. The properties considered by the ad hoc committee were unavailable because they either did not meet the criteria necessary for school facilities, were deemed an Area of Environmental Concern, consisted of federal property belonging to the National Park Service, or were rejected by the various federal and state agencies having jurisdiction over the wetlands.

The evidence showed that in order for the Board to obtain a permit from the Army Corps, it had to mitigate damages to wetlands. Under the Board's proposal, of the 1.8 acres necessary to satisfy the requirement of wetlands mitigation, approximately a half an acre of lots 5 and 6 would be used, with property owned by the Board supplying the remaining 1.3 acres necessary for mitigation.

Significantly, the Board's witness indicated that the ad hoc committee had looked for complete sites and, thus, had not searched "for alternatives to find a half acre that can be offered for mitigation." The Board member testified that there were numerous parcels within the County that would contain a half acre of property that could be used to satisfy the mitigation requirement, but because the federal and state regulatory agencies had indicated that on-site mitigation was preferred over off-site mitigation, and would increase its chances of obtaining a permit, the committee looked for on-site, in-kind mitigation.

An environmental consultant for the committee offered similar supporting testimony. The consultant testified that forty-one sites were considered by the ad hoc committee. They first were reviewed as sites for the athletic facilities, and subsequently reviewed again as sites for mitigation. None of the sites, however, were appropriate for various reasons, including distance, expense, unsuitability, or unavailability.

He also testified that the Board advanced its proposal involving lots 5 and 6 to meet the Army Corps' requirements "to minimize wetland impacts and then to adequately mitigate under their sequence of preference" and to comply with applicable regulations.

Based on this testimony, the trial court concluded that the Board had authority to condemn the lots since this property was necessary for the construction of the proposed school facilities. The trial court also concluded that the Board's authority to use portions of the property for wetlands mitigation was implied under this condemnation authority since this action was necessary for approval of the proposal to construct the facilities. The North Carolina appellate court affirmed these findings.

Relying on the evidence in the trial court record, the appellate court concluded that the Board had not abused its discretion, finding that although the Board was aware that off-site mitigation was permitted and there were other potential mitigation sites, the Army Corps and state Division of Coastal Management clearly gave off-site mitigation a lower preference than on-site mitigation, had rejected all of the off-site mitigations proffered by the Board, and encouraged the proposal involving lots 5 and 6, which would provide on-site mitigation. Thus, although there were alternate sites available that the Board did not consider, the court found that the evidence failed to show that the Board had acted in an arbitrary and capricious manner in deciding to condemn lots 5 and 6 to satisfy the wetland mitigation necessary for construction of its athletic facilities.

ACHIEVING MITIGATION COMPLIANCE

Mitigation compliance is a complex and difficult process. All applicants for Section 404 permits are encouraged to arrange preapplication meetings with the Army Corps, other federal agencies, and state and local governmental authorities. Such meetings are crucial to applicants because they provide a background in specific application procedures which may vary from site to site, and often indicate to the applicant what specific mitigation procedures, monitoring requirements, etc. may be considered acceptable. Failure to arrange a preapplication meeting often results in unnecessary expenditures of time, effort, and finances.

Virtually all mitigation actions require some form of monitoring by the applicant and the Army Corps during the construction phase, as well as once the mitigation is in place. Compensatory mitigation techniques with high levels of scientific uncertainty will require long-term monitoring, reporting, and possible remediation actions. Monitoring is to be directed toward determining whether permit conditions are being met, and whether the purposes of the mitigation are actually being achieved. If permittees are found to be in non-compliance, the Army Corps will notify them, request a corrected plan, attempt to resolve the violation, then issue an order demanding compliance. If permittees fail to comply with the order, then the Army Corps may suspend or revoke the permit,[52] and/or recommend legal action, which includes both civil and criminal penalties.[53]

ENDNOTES

1. Clean Water Act § 404(b)(1), 33 U.S.C. § 1344(b)(1).

2. *See* White House Office of Environmental Policy, *Protecting America's Wetlands: A Fair, Flexible, and Effective Approach*, (Aug. 24, 1993).

3. 33 U.S.C. § 1344.

4. 42 U.S.C. § 4321 *et seq.*

5. 16 U.S.C. § 661-667e. The Act requires that the Army Corps "consult" with the FWS and consider ompensating for habitat loss, but it does not require the Army Corps to adopt those recommendations.

6. 40 C.F.R. § 1508.20.

7. 33 C.F.R. § 320.4(r)(1).

8. *See* General Permit for Wetland Restoration and Enhancement Projects Within the State of Oregon, Permit No. 95-003 issued on April 10, 1995.

9. Md. Nat. Res. Code Ann. § 8-1209.

10. *See, e.g.,* Colo. Rev. Stat. § 37-85.5-101 to -111; La. Rev. Stat. § 49-214.41; Or. Rev. Stat. § 196.600 to .665.

11. *See, e.g.,* Minnesota Department of Transportation, *Guidelines for Implementation of Wetland Habitat Mitigation Banking,* Technical Memorandum No. 87-28-Env-2 (June 18, 1987).

12. Clean Water Act § 404(b)(1), 33 U.S.C. § 1344(b)(1).

13. The Guidelines are binding regulations and are codified at 40 C.F.R. § 230.

14. 40 C.F.R. § 230.10(c).

15. 40 C.F.R. § 230.10(a).

16. *See, e.g., National Wildlife Federation v. Whistler,* 1994 WL 284468 (8th Cir. June 29, 1994); *Bersani v. EPA,* 674 F. Supp. 405 (N.D.N.Y. 1987), *aff'd,* 850 F.2d 36 (2nd Cir. 1988), cert. denied, 489 U.S. 1089 (1989).

17. *See* EPA/Army Corps, *Memorandum to the Field: Appropriate Level of Analysis Required for Evaluating Compliance With the Section 404(b)(1) Guidelines Alternatives Requirements* (Aug. 23, 1993).

18. *See* 40 C.F.R. § 230.10 (c) and (d).

19. Army Corps/EPA, *Section 404(b)(1) Guidelines Mitigation MOA* (Feb. 7, 1990). *See also* EPA/Army Corps, *Memorandum to the Field: Appropriate Level of Analysis Required for Evaluating Compliance With the Section 404(b)(1) Guidelines Alternatives Requirements* (Aug. 23, 1993).

20. Thus, "appropriate" mitigation refers to the ecological value of the affected wetland.

21. Again, this language mirrors the Guidelines. "Practicable" is defined in the 404(b)(1) Guidelines at 40 C.F.R. § 230.3(q) and requires consideration of "cost, existing technology, and logistics in light of overall project purposes."

22. *See* further discussion of the practicable alternatives test on page 97.

23. 40 C.F.R. § 230.10(a).

24. 1990 MOA at 3; 40 C.F.R. § 230.10.

25. 40 C.F.R. § 230.70(a).

26. 40 C.F.R. § 230.70(b).

27. 40 C.F.R. § 230.70(c).

28. 40 C.F.R. § 230.70(d).

29. 40 C.F.R. § 230.70(f).

30. *See* further discussion on page 114.

31. *See* Chapter 6.

32. 1990 MOA at 5, footnote 7.

33. 40 C.F.R. § 230.10(a).

34. 40 C.F.R. § 230.10(a)(2).

35. 40 C.F.R. § 230.10(a)(3).

36. EPA/Army Corps, *Memorandum to the Field: Appropriate Level of Analysis Required for Evaluating Compliance With the Section 404(b)(1) Guidelines Alternatives Requirements* (Aug. 23, 1993).

37. 40 C.F.R. § 230.10(a).

38. The preamble states: "Of course, as the regulation itself makes clear, a certain amount of flexibility is still intended. For example, while the ultimate conditions of compliance are 'regulatory,' the Guidelines allow some room for judgment in determining what must be done to arrive at a conclusion that those conditions have or have not been met." 45 Fed. Reg. 85336 (Dec. 24, 1980).

39. The burden of proof to demonstrate compliance with the Guidelines rests with the applicant; where insufficient information is provided to determine compliance, the Guidelines require that no permit can be issued. 40 C.F.R. § 230.12(a)(3)(iv).

40. 40 C.F.R. § 230.6 states that "[t]he level of documentation should reflect the significance and complexity of the discharge activity."

41. 40 C.F.R. § 230.10.

42. 40 C.F.R. § 230.6.

43. In certain instances, however, it may be easier to examine practicability first. Some projects may be so site-specific (*e.g.*, erosion control, bridge replacement) that no off-site alternative could be practicable. In such cases, the alternatives analysis may appropriately be limited to on-site options.

44. 40 C.F.R. § 230.10(a).

45. *Id.*

46. 40 C.F.R. § 230.10(a)(2).

47. 45 Fed. Reg. 85343 (Dec. 24, 1980).

48. Many activities related to the construction or expansion of a home, farm, or business are already covered by a general permit. For example, in July 1995, the Army Corps issued a nationwide general permit authorizing discharges related to development of single-family housing. 60 Fed. Reg. 38650 (July 27, 1995).

49. *National Wildlife Federation v. Whistler*, 1994 WL 284468 (8th Cir. June 29, 1994).

50. 1994 WL 284468 at *4 (citations omitted).

51. *Dare County Bd. of Educ. v. Sakaria*, 456 S.E.2d 842 (N.C. App. 1995).

52. *See* 33 C.F.R. § 325.7 (c) for procedures.

53. 33 C.F.R. § 326.5.

Chapter 6

Wetland Mitigation Options

INTRODUCTION

Mitigation options must be evaluated in light of the regulations discussed in Chapter 5, the nature of the impacted wetland, and the options available to mitigate a particular project's impacts. This chapter examines different types of wetland mitigation measures that may be undertaken to minimize adverse environmental impacts and secure development permit approvals.

MITIGATION CATEGORIES

Army Corps regulations place mitigation measures into three basic categories.[1] The first category refers to minor project modifications designed to minimize adverse project impacts. Minor project modifications are those that are considered feasible to the applicant and that, if adopted, will result in a project that generally meets the applicant's purpose and need. Such modifications can include reductions in scope and size; changes in construction methods, materials, or timing; and operation and maintenance practices or other similar modifications that reflect a sensitivity to environmental quality within the context of the work proposed. For example, erosion control features could be required on a fill project to reduce sedimentation impacts or a pier could be reoriented to minimize navigational problems even though those projects may satisfy all legal requirements and the public interest review test without such modifications.

The second category refers to mitigation measures necessary satisfy the legal requirements of the Section 404(b)(1) Guidelines.[2]

The third category refers to any additional measures that may be required as a result of the public interest review process. The Army Corps may only require such additional measures necessary to ensure that the project is not "contrary to the public interest." Thus, an applicant seeking to attack the Army Corps' mitigation requirements imposed according to this public interest review justification carries a heavy burden of challenging the rather vague and all-inclusive notion of "the public interest."

KINDS OF WETLANDS LOSSES REQUIRING MITIGATION

The Army Corps' Section 404 regulations are fairly straightforward with respect to the kinds of wetlands losses for which mitigation is required:

> "All compensatory mitigation will be for significant resource losses which are specifically identifiable, reasonably likely to occur, and of importance to the human or aquatic environment. Also, all mitigation will be directly related to the impacts of the proposal, appropriate to the scope and degree of those impacts, and reasonably enforceable."[3]

In other words, if wetland degradation is considered minor, insignificant, unimportant, or speculative, mitigation requirements will not be triggered. Further, the Army Corps cannot require mitigation that is unrelated to the impacts that will result from the project itself (*i.e.*, a developer cannot be forced to provide mitigation for a project unrelated to the one for which the Section 404 permit is granted).

FUNCTIONAL VALUE ANALYSIS

Many questions remain regarding mitigation. Should the unit of mitigative compensation be defined in terms of area (*i.e.*, acre for acre) or in terms of environmental function? If the latter, which functional losses should be mitigated? If mitigation is conducted off-site, how far away is allowable? Should the federal government encourage "mitigation banking," a form of off-site mitigation where credits are accrued by restoring or protecting other areas to offset damage that would result from a project? These questions essentially focus on the functional value of the impacted wetland and how this value should figure in the mitigation equation. Considerable debate has centered on the appropriate functional value analysis. Several techniques have been developed for evaluating the functional value of the impacted wetland and the determination of an equivalent value of replacement wetlands. The two most common are the Habitat Evaluation Procedures (HEP) developed by the U.S. Fish and Wildlife Service (FWS), and the Wetland Evaluation Technique (WET), developed jointly by the Army Corps and the Federal Highway Administration.[4]

The U.S. Fish and Wildlife Service (FWS) plays an important advisory role in regard to Section 404 permits and compensatory mitigation under the Fish and Wildlife Coordination Act,[5] NAPA,[6] and the Endangered Species Act.[7] The FWS focuses its policy specifically on the "value" of the affected wetlands, and recommends: (1) that damage to the most valued resources be avoided; and (2) that the degree of mitigation correspond to the value and scarcity of the habitat at risk.[8] In general, the Army Corps is deferential to FWS recommendations, which tend to focus more precisely on impacts to fish and wildlife habitat than does the Army Corps.

The National Marine Fisheries Service (NFS) also comments on potential damage to fisheries. The NFS typically becomes involved early in the planning process in order to resolve potential conflicts and minimize adverse effects on marine resources and habitats. NFS will recommend mitigation measures for "essential public interest projects" when practical alternatives are unavailable, and recommend habitat enhancement measures.[9]

The FWS has formulated procedures for evaluating the functional values for fish and wildlife habitat in wetlands. The most frequently used methodology is the Habitat Evaluation Procedures (HEP), which utilizes standard computer models to relate biological requirements and tolerances for certain indicator species to environmental variables as they occur on the subject property, such as water depth and quality, flooding periodicity, vegetation density and type, and soil type. The HEP then provides numerical values for habitat suitability, which can be used as objective measures of the relative "quality" of wetland functional values.[10]

The first version of HEP was released in 1976 (HEP76) and a revision was released in 1980 (HEP80). The latter version is in more common use today. Proper use of HEP requires a relatively high scientific skill level, and formal training from the FWS. The HEP analysis is site-specific so the analyst must first define the study area. Then, the analyst must delineate the different land covers in the selected area. Once the area has been selected and the cover types have been identified, the analyst must select the evaluation species. This process involves a consideration of those species that might be found in a wetland and selection of those species that have a "high public interest, economic value, or both," or that give a "broader ecological perspective of an area.[11] The project objectives usually will determine which species are most appropriate for the HEP analysis. The effectiveness of the HEP analysis can be improved by selecting species that are most sensitive to human interference, that are critical parts of the wetland ecosystem, or that are representative of a class of species with similar habitat preferences.

Most mitigation banks use some version of the HEP to assess the functional values of wetlands offered as replacement for impacted wetlands. The HEP calculates the suitability of a wetland ecosystem as habitat through the use of a Habitat Suitability Index (HSI) model for each indicator species selected. The HSI compares the ecological information gathered by the analyst for the impacted wetland and the compensatory wetland to arrive at the optimum habitat for the indicator species. The HSI for each species is the percentage of the optimum habitat support provided by the land cover in question. This index is then multiplied by the number of acres that fall within a distinct vegetation cover type to calculate the number of habitat units (HUs) available as credits. The total number of bank credits is the total of the HUs of all cover types in the bank. HUs are used as the currency for the mitigation bank. A developer who destroys 100 HUs at a project site must acquire at least 100 HUs produced at the bank.

Due to the narrow function-specific analysis of HEP, other types of wetland assessment methodologies have emerged to evaluate a wider range of functional values. The Wetland Evaluation Technique (WET), developed by the Federal Highway Administration and the Army Corps, has frequently been used to evaluate the appropriate mitigation for project impacts to wetlands. The WET originally came into use in 1983

(WET1.0). The technique underwent extensive modifications and was released as WET2.0 in 1987. WET1.0 was formulated as a method for evaluating a broad range of observable wetland functions. This technique required the analyst to gather information on some 80 different wetland characteristics or "indicators." Once the indicators are collected, WET1.0 combines the indicators into three ratings for each of the following eleven different wetland functions:

1. Groundwater recharge.
2. Groundwater discharge.
3. Flood-flow storage and desynchronization.
4. Shoreline anchoring and dissipation of erosive forces.
5. Sediment trapping.
6. Nutrient retention and removal.
7. Food chain support.
8. Fisheries habitat.
9. Wildlife habitat.
10. Active recreation.
11. Passive recreation and heritage value.

Three ratings are given to each of these functions: (1) effectiveness; (2) opportunity; and (3) social significance. "Effectiveness" refers to whether the wetland can perform the function. "Opportunity" refers to whether the wetland has the opportunity to be effective. "Social significance" refers to the importance of the function to society. The analyst takes each function and applies the three ratings to arrive at a qualitative value ("low," "moderate," or "high" value) for each function. For example, under the first function, groundwater recharge, the rating could be high for effectiveness, moderate for opportunity, and low for social significance. The qualitative value indicates the probability that the wetland supplies that aspect of the function. Although in wide use by wetland managers, use of the WET has often been criticized for its failure to recognize differences in wetland types and its inability to take regional differences into account. Because the WET employs a broad type of analysis, HEP and other narrowly focused assessment methodologies are sometimes used in conjunction with the WET. For example, the HEP might be used to complete a more detailed habitat assessment.

SPECIFIC TYPES OF MITIGATION

A wide range of mitigation measures have been allowed by the Army Corps, including:

- Increased public access to the area.
- Acquisition of other wetlands to provide enhanced protection, or acquisition with a management commitment.
- Restoration or creation of wetlands, either as general compensation or as replacement for a specific habitat type.
- Indemnification or direct monetary payment for lost wetland values.
- Mitigation banking (compensatory off-site wetlands restoration or creation).

Most federal agencies and most states no longer permit the first two approaches unless the goal of increased public access is compensation for lost public recreational opportunities, or the acquisition includes enhancement or assurance of proper management to compensate for lost wetland values.

ALTERNATIVES FOR COMPENSATORY MITIGATION

For purposes of the Section 404 permit program, compensatory mitigation refers to the restoration, creation, enhancement, or in exceptional circumstances, preservation of wetlands and/or other aquatic resources expressly for the purpose of compensating for unavoidable adverse impacts which remain after all appropriate and practicable avoidable and minimization has been achieved. Table 6-1 summarizes these alternatives for compensatory mitigation.

Preservation refers to the protection of ecologically important wetlands or other aquatic resources in perpetuity through the implementation of appropriate legal and physical mechanisms. Preservation may include protection of upland areas adjacent to wetlands as necessary to ensure protection and/or enhancement of the aquatic ecosystem. Preservation has been the most controversial type of mitigation. Generally speaking, preservation only arises as an acceptable method of compensatory mitigation in the context of wetland mitigation banking. Awarding credits for preservation is discouraged because it does not replace lost wetland values and functions; it results in a "net loss" of wetlands. Of 46 existing mitigation banks, only two are "preservation" banks.[12] Acceptance of preservation as a mitigation method usually requires the establishment of monitoring and maintenance programs to guarantee the continued quality of the preserved wetland.

Table 6-1. Compensatory Mitigation Options

Preservation or Exchange	Purchase of a parcel of land containing a valuable wetland, which is then placed in public ownership with provisions for long-term protection and/or management (this may take the form of "conservation easements" or other devices). The exchange for a wetland area which will be damaged by a project for another wetland (typically of larger size and higher wetland values), which is placed in long-term protection.
Enhancement	A wetland in which some functions have been degraded (or lost) is "repaired," such that the degraded (or lost) wetland functions are again available.[13]
Restoration	A former wetland with few (or no) remaining wetland functions is restored to a form in which specific functions (perhaps all) are available.
Creation	A wetland is created where none previously existed. The goal is usually to create specific wetland functions.[14]

Enhancement involves activities conducted in existing wetlands or other aquatic resources to achieve specific management objectives or provide conditions which previously did not exist, and which increase one or more aquatic functions. Enhancement may involve trade-offs between aquatic resource structure, functions, and values; a positive change in one function may result in negative effects to other functions. Enhancement has been criticized as a mitigation method because of the danger that new functions or stimulation of particular functions over others may not be ecologically sound. For example, in some cases, enhancements may focus on management of preferred wildlife species which may not adequately compensate for losses of diverse wetland functions. It also may result in loss of certain functions performed prior to enhancement, such as habitat for non-preferred species.

Restoration refers to the re-establishment of previously existing wetland or other aquatic resource character and function(s) at a site where they have ceased to exist, or exist only in a substantially degraded state. Restoration of previously existing wetlands is the preferred mitigation method of all federal and most state mitigation policies. This is primarily due to the uncertainty associated with wetland creation and concern over the ecological wisdom of enhancement. The National Research Council has concluded that funding priority should be given to restoration over creation because restoration has a superior chance of success.[15]

Creation refers to the establishment of a wetland or other aquatic resource where one did not formerly exist. The goal is to replace a wetland by creating another of comparable size and function.

Of course, the particular type of mitigation required for a specific project will depend on the nature of the project, location of the project site, the quantity and quality *(i.e.* functional value) of the wetlands that will be damaged or destroyed.

The amount of land involved in mitigation raises an important issue. In most cases, the only time a 1:1 mitigation ratio (mitigated acres: impacted wetland acres) is permitted is when the mitigation is offered up front and there is no risk of lost wetland values. More typical exchange ratios are 1.5:1 for wetland restoration, 2:1 for creation, and 3:1 for enhancement. Draft guidelines for mitigation banking issued by EPA Region IV in 1992 give the following compensation ratios: 2:1 for restoration, 3:1 for creation, 4:1 for enhancement, and 10:1 for preservation.

ENSURING MITIGATION PROJECT SUCCESS

The ultimate success of a wetland mitigation project depends on the proper siting, design, construction, and monitoring of the mitigation site. Improper design of the site hydrology is the most common cause of failure. If a site's elevations are incorrectly surveyed or constructed, the project is likely to suffer from hydrologic conditions which will not adequately sustain wetland vegetation. Further, sites that require active manipulation to maintain wet conditions are susceptible to problems, such as insufficient availability of water supplies or malfunctioning pumping equipment. Site selection difficulties may arise from failure to consider surrounding land uses. Mitigation sites without upland buffer areas or that are surrounded by impervious surfaces can themselves quickly convert to uplands. Inappropriate plant selection or improper planting depths can also cause startup failures, as can the failure to import soil amendments where on-site soils are inadequate for plant establishment. Other common factors that inhibit the success of a mitigation project include vandalism, natural disasters, off-site activities, accumulation of debris, and invasion of nuisance plants. Mitigation projects that are designed by qualified biologists, engineers, and other environmental professionals are more likely to succeed. Further, ongoing maintenance can help to prevent mitigation project failures.

WETLAND RESTORATION AND CREATION CHECKLIST

For sites where restoration or creation has been approved as the acceptable form of compensatory mitigation, a number of issues must be evaluated to carry out an effective and successful mitigation plan. Many relevant concerns are outlined in the following checklist.[16] Further, Chapter 8 provides several helpful case studies which detail the process of wetland restoration and creation.

1. What functions will be addressed at the restored or created wetland?
    - ☐ Education and research
    - ☐ Erosion control
    - ☐ Fish and shellfish habitat
    - ☐ Flood conveyance
    - ☐ Flood storage
    - ☐ Food production
    - ☐ Historic, cultural, and archaeological resources
    - ☐ Open space and aesthetic values
    - ☐ Recreation
    - ☐ Sediment control

☐ Threatened, endangered species habitat
☐ Timber production
☐ Water quality
☐ Water supply
☐ Wildlife habitat
☐ Other _____

2. Have the following baseline data needs been addressed?
   Yes ☐ No ☐ Soils
   Yes ☐ No ☐ Water budget
   Yes ☐ No ☐ Water quality
   Yes ☐ No ☐ Existing vegetation
   Yes ☐ No ☐ Existing fish and wildlife
   Yes ☐ No ☐ Landscape context
   Yes ☐ No ☐ Wetland complex
   Yes ☐ No ☐ Aesthetic quality
   Yes ☐ No ☐ Other needs _____

3. Are there limiting factors and constraints to restoring, enhancing, or creating the wetlands?
   Yes ☐ No ☐

4. Are there related opportunities?
   Yes ☐ No ☐
   List related opportunities:
   _____
   _____
   _____

5. Has the land user made decisions and examined alternatives for the planned wetland?
   Yes ☐ No ☐

6. Are structures needed to restore or create the wetland and meet objectives?
   Yes ☐ No ☐

7. Can a natural colonization of vegetation occur at the wetland?
    Yes ☐ No ☐
    Is there an acceptable seedbank in the existing soil at the site?
    Yes ☐ No ☐
    Are there available plant material sources from nearby or adjacent wetlands that will be transported to the site by wind, waves, currents, or animals?
    Yes ☐ No ☐
    Will the wetland be created on non-hydric soil where seedbanks and other plant material do not exist?
    Yes ☐ No ☐

8. Will planting be required to meet wetland objectives?
    Yes ☐ No ☐
    Will wind and wave actions cause moderate-to-high wave energy conditions?
    Yes ☐ No ☐
    Do you need to bypass early successional stages of wetland establishment and hasten development?
    Yes ☐ No ☐
    Are conditions suitable for application of soil-bioengineering planting methods?
    Yes ☐ No ☐
    Will there be a problem of invading nuisance plant species that will compete with desired plant species?
    Yes ☐ No ☐
    Will selected plant species be compatible with surrounding landscape?
    Yes ☐ No ☐
    Are vegetated buffers, transition zones, or fences needed to protect the establishing wetland from human disturbance, excess sedimentation, pollutants, and/or intensive grazing pressures?
    Yes ☐ No ☐

9. Will the desired plant species adapt to wetland site conditions and the selected location?
    Yes ☐ No ☐

Will they adapt to expected water depths, flood frequencies, fluctuating water levels?
Yes ☐ No ☐
Will they adapt to expected water quality, salinity, acidity, alkalinity?
Yes ☐ No ☐
Will they adapt to high velocity conditions?
Yes ☐ No ☐
Will they adapt to standing water conditions?
Yes ☐ No ☐
Are they compatible with planned landscape features, aesthetics, and other functions?
Yes ☐ No ☐

10. Is there adequate water supply for the wetland?
Yes ☐ No ☐
Is too much water available, requiring a water control structure to prevent the wetland from drowning?
Yes ☐ No ☐
Are water rights assured?
Yes ☐ No ☐
Are there existing water quality problems that may limit the success of wetland restoration or enhancement activities?
Yes ☐ No ☐

11. Will soil amendments (fertilizers, lime, microbial enhancers) and mulch be required for adequate plant establishment?
Yes ☐ No ☐
Are substrate materials generally infertile, cobble, gravel, or sand?
Yes ☐ No ☐
Are substrate materials generally fertile clayey, silty, and loamy textures?
Yes ☐ No ☐
Have soil analyses been taken to determine soil amendment needs?
Yes ☐ No ☐

12. Are plant materials of desired species available and of good quality?
    Yes ☐ No ☐
    Can enough seeds, transplants, and other propagates of appropriate size be obtained at the appropriate time for wetland planting?
    Yes ☐ No ☐
    Will handling, storing, and stockpiling of plant materials be necessary before the wetland is completed?
    Yes ☐ No ☐
    Are plant material costs within budget?
    Yes ☐ No ☐
    Are adapted plant materials released by the Natural Resource Conservation Service and available from commercial sources?
    Yes ☐ No ☐

13. Has the land user been consulted about:
    Yes ☐ No ☐ Cropping/herbicide history
    Yes ☐ No ☐ Current and past land uses
    Yes ☐ No ☐ Ability to carry out engineering work, including avoiding compacting of soils in areas not to be disturbed
    Yes ☐ No ☐ Ability to carry out planting work
    Yes ☐ No ☐ Willingness to conduct simple monitoring of wetland progress
    Yes ☐ No ☐ Willingness to carry out mid-course corrections and active wetland management
    Yes ☐ No ☐ Landscape context
    Yes ☐ No ☐ Wetland complex
    Yes ☐ No ☐ Management

14. Has a conservation plan been developed and decisions been documented?
    Yes ☐ No ☐

15. Has landowner been advised about needed permits?
    Yes ☐ No ☐

ENDNOTES

1. 33 C.F.R. § 320.4(r)(1).

2. Some of these mitigation measures are enumerated at 40 C.F.R. § 230.70 through 40 C.F.R § 230.77 (Subpart H of the 404(b)(1) Guidelines).

3. 33 C.F.R. § 320(r)(2).

4. *See* Adams et al., "Wetland Evaluation Technique (WET)", in *U.S. Army Corps of Engineers Technical Report Y-87 (1987)*.

5. 16 U.S.C. §§ 661-666.

6. 42 U.S.C. §§ 4321, 4363.

7. 16 U.S.C. § 1531 *et seq*.

8. "Fish and Wildlife Service Mitigation Policy," 46 Fed. Reg. 7644 (Jan. 23, 1981).

9. "National Marine Fisheries Service Habitat Conservation Policy," 48 Fed. Reg. 53142 (1983).

10. *See* Adams, "Criteria for Created or Restored Wetlands." In: D. Hook et. al (eds.) *The Ecology and Management of Wetlands, Vol. 2: Management, Use, and Value of Wetlands* (Timber Press 1988).

11. Fish and Wildlife Service, *Habitat Evaluation Procedures Manual*, 102 ESM (1980).

12. *See* Environmental Law Institute, *Wetland Mitigation Banking* (1993), at p. 55.

13. *See National Wildlife Federation v. Whistler*, 1994 WL 284468 (8th Cir., June 29, 1994).

14. *See* Kruczynski, "Options to Be Considered in Preparation and Evaluation of Mitigation Plans." In: J. Kusler and M. Kentula (ed's.) *Wetland Creation and Restoration: The Status of the Science* (Island Press 1990).

15. National Research Council Report, *Restoration of Aquatic Ecosystems: Science, Technology, and Public Policy,* National Academy of Science, Washington, D.C. (1991).

16. This checklist was adapted from *The Oregon Wetlands Conservation Guide*, Oregon Wetlands Conservation Alliance (1995).

Chapter 7

Wetland Mitigation Banking

INTRODUCTION

A relatively new approach to mitigation, known as mitigation banking, may provide an effective means of ameliorating development impacts while promoting the government's no-net-loss policy.[1] Mitigation banking is a flexible method for balancing the competing needs of private developers and government regulators. Essentially, the concept combines the mitigation needs of many permit applicants into one large off-site area. This area is developed as a wetland mitigation bank to compensate for wetland impacts from numerous development projects.

Wetland mitigation banks can be a cost-effective means of balancing development needs and environmental protection goals. Permit applicants should experience savings in both time and money because mitigation costs and procedures are identifiable at the outset. Most mitigation banking projects are for large projects so they experience the cost savings associated with economies of scale. Larger mitigation banking projects also should tend to favor fish and wildlife because entire ecosystems are protected. Finally, wetland restoration and enhancement (as opposed to creation) involves already-functioning wetlands, so that uncertainty about success of mitigation actions should be reduced.

CONCEPT OF MITIGATION BANKING

Mitigation banking is generally defined as off-site wetland restoration, creation, enhancement, and in exceptional circumstances, preservation undertaken expressly for the purpose of mitigating unavoidable adverse wetland losses in advance of development actions. It can be used by permittees when compensatory mitigation cannot be achieved at the development site or is not as environmentally beneficial. For purposes of the Section 404 permit program, use of a mitigation bank may only be authorized when impacts are unavoidable.

The objective of a mitigation bank is to provide for the replacement of the chemical, physical, and biological functions of wetlands and other aquatic resources which are lost as a result of authorized impacts. Using appropriate methods, the newly established functions are quantified as mitigation "credits" which are available for use by the bank sponsor or by other parties to compensate for adverse impacts (*i.e.*, "debits").

Mitigation banking typically involves the consolidation of scattered needs for wetland mitigation into one large contiguous site. Ideally, mitigation banks are constructed and functioning in advance of development impacts, and are seen as a way of reducing uncertainty in the Section 404 permit program by having established compensatory mitigation credit available to a permittee. By consolidating compensation requirements, banks can more effectively replace lost wetland functions within a watershed, as well as provide economies of scale related to the planning, implementation, monitoring, and management of wetlands.

The Clinton Administration's comprehensive package of improvements to federal wetlands programs, released in August 1993, included support for the use of mitigation banks within environmentally sound limits as a means for compensating for authorized wetland impacts. At that same time, EPA and the Department of the Army have issued guidance clarifying the role of mitigation banks in the Section 404 permit program and providing general guidelines for their establishment and use.[2]

The U.S. Fish and Wildlife Service (FWS) first developed the concept of mitigation banking in the early 1980s in an attempt to increase the effectiveness of wetlands mitigation while reducing the costs to the regulated community.[3] Some commentators have described mitigation banking as "the most promising solution to the loss of wetlands during development."[4]

Mitigation banking is considered an acceptable form of compensatory mitigation under the 1990 Army Corps/EPA Memorandum of Agreement (1990 MOA) concerning the determination of mitigation measures under

Clean Water Act Section 404(b)(1).[5] When a mitigation bank has been approved by the Army Corps and EPA as mitigation for a specific identified project, use of the bank for those projects is considered to be meeting the requirements for compensatory mitigation regardless of the practicability of other forms of compensatory mitigation.[6] It should be cautioned, however, that simple purchase or "preservation" of existing wetlands will be accepted as compensatory mitigation only in exceptional circumstances.

How Mitigation Banking Works

Mitigation banking basically involves the sale of mitigation credits to permit applicants who are seeking off-site mitigation to offset on-site development activities. Units of restored, created, enhanced or preserved wetlands at the mitigation bank are expressed as "credits" which may subsequently be withdrawn to offset "debits" incurred at a project development site. Credits and debits are the terms used to designate the units of trade (*i.e.*, currency) in mitigation banking. Credits represent the accrual or attainment of aquatic functions at a bank; debits represent the loss of aquatic functions at an impact or project site. Credits are debited from a bank when they are used to offset aquatic resource impacts.

Mitigation credits have been defined as "the unit of wetland value that is recognized as the basis for comparing the destroyed wetland to the banked wetland offered in compensation. Credits are expressed in units such as acres, habitat units, or numbers."[7] The credit value is used to determine the price a permit applicant must pay to the bank to satisfy its mitigation requirements. The dollar cost of mitigation credits to a third party is determined by the bank sponsor. For example, if a permittee is allowed to satisfy its mitigation obligations through the purchase of credits from a mitigation bank, the permittee comes to a mitigation bank to draw down credit for a specific impact. The number of acres or units charged to the permittee will depend on the quality of the wetlands impacted by the project and the quality of the replacement wetlands constructed at the bank site.

Functional Value Assessment

The number of credits available for withdrawal (*i.e.*, debiting) should generally be commensurate with the level of aquatic functions attained at a bank at the time of debiting. The level of function may be determined through the application of performance standards tailored to the specific restoration, creation, or enhancement activity at the bank site or through the use of an appropriate functional assessment methodology.

The number of credits received from a particular wetland bank is based on wetland values as determined by various evaluation techniques, such as the Habitat Evaluation Procedures (HEP) developed by the FWS, and the Wetland Evaluation Technique (WET), developed jointly by the Army Corps and the Federal Highway Administration. The most frequently used procedure is HEP, which utilizes standard computer models to relate biological requirements and tolerances for certain indicator species to environmental variables as they occur on the subject property, such as water depth and quality, flooding periodicity, vegetation density and type, and soil type. The HEP then provides numerical values for habitat suitability, which can be used as objective measures of the relative "quality" of wetland functional values.[8]

Credits in the Florida Wetlandsbank are determined by using an Integrated Functional Index (IFI) system for evaluating the ecological characteristics of the impacted site and the bank site. This system calculates the Integrated Functional Units (IFUs) that are lost from impacts at the project site and then establishes the number of IFUs that need to be created in the bank to compensate for these impacts.[9]

The range of functions to be assessed will depend upon the assessment methodology approved for use by the mitigation bank. The same methodology should be used to assess both credits in the bank and debits at the project site. If an appropriate functional assessment methodology is impractical to employ, credits and debits can be based on simple indices (*e.g.*, acres) of various classes of wetlands and/or other aquatic resources. Regardless of the method employed, credits should be based on the difference between site conditions under the with- and without-bank scenarios. The bank sponsor should be responsible for assessing the development of the bank and submitting appropriate documentation of such assessments to the authorizing agency for review. Alternatively, functional assessments may be conducted by a team representing involved resource and regulatory agencies and other appropriate parties.

Timing of Credit Withdrawals

The number of credits available for withdrawal (*i.e.*, debiting) should generally be commensurate with the level of aquatic functions attained at a bank at the time of debiting. The level of function may be determined through the application of performance standards tailored to the specific restoration, creation, or enhancement activity at the bank site or through the use of an appropriate functional assessment methodology.

The success of a mitigation bank with regard to its capacity to establish a healthy and fully functional aquatic system relates directly to both the ecological and financial stability of the bank. Since financial considerations are particularly critical in early stages of bank development, it may be appropriate to allow limited debiting based upon a projected level of aquatic functions at a bank (*e.g.*, 15 percent of the total credits projected for the bank at maturity). However, it is the intent of this policy to ensure that those actions necessary for the long-term viability of a mitigation bank be accomplished prior to any debiting of the bank. In this regard, the following requirements should be satisfied prior to debiting:

- Banking instrument and final mitigation plans have been approved.
- Bank site has been secured.
- Appropriate financial assurances have been established.

In addition, initial physical and biological improvements should be completed within the first full growing season following initial debiting of a bank. The temporal loss of functions associated with the debiting of projected credits may require higher compensation ratios. Further debiting of the bank should not occur until the allocated projected credits have accrued and additional credits have accrued to match proposed debiting.

TYPES OF MITIGATION BANKS

There are three primary types of mitigation banks: single-user, private, and public.[10] A brief summary of each type is provided here.

Single-User Banks

Single-user mitigation banks are developed by a single entity, such as a real estate development company, which uses the bank to fulfill its own mitigation needs. According to a 1993 survey by the Environmental Law Institute, 42 banks were developed by single-users as a means of mitigating development impacts on wetlands.[11]

Private Banks

Private mitigation banks are developed by entrepreneurs who are not wetland permit applicants. They invest their resources to develop a mitigation bank in order to sell credits to permit applicants. Through the end of 1994, only three federally-approved private mitigation banks were in operation in the United States.[12]

For example, Florida Wetlandsbank, a general partnership, is the only private mitigation bank operating in the state of Florida. The mitigation bank is located on 350 acres owned by the City of Pembroke Pines. The property is a highly degraded wetland that is infested with invasive exotic species of plants, predominantly melaleuca trees. The area has no significant wildlife habitat value and no wildlife has been observed inhabiting the site. Florida Wetlandsbank expects to transform the bank site into a high quality wetland by introducing a diverse mixture of habitats, including cypress stands, emergent marshes, forested wetlands, sawgrass prairies, and tree island habitats.[13] The bank is obligated to maintain the newly planted wetlands vegetation for five years. After wetland credits have been sold and the restoration has been completed, the mitigation bankers will return responsibility for the site to the city as a permanent wildlife preserve. The preserve will be protected by a conservation easement and a trust fund will ensure its perpetual maintenance. The City of Pembroke Pines plans to use the site as a wetland education center and wetland park with nature walks, canoeing trails, and picnic areas.

Publicly Owned Banks

Publicly owned mitigation banks are developed with public funds which the government seeks to recoup by selling mitigation credits to permit applicants. Some states charge a mitigation fee to permit applicants and then place the money into a fund for future mitigation activities by the state. One study attacked this "in-lieu fee system" because the revenues collected by the government for a prospective mitigation bank might later be diverted to other uses.[14] Another problem may be that government agencies may not be able to raise the necessary funds to acquire the property and maintain the site.

ADVANTAGES OF MITIGATION BANKING

Mitigation banks can have several advantages over individual mitigation projects, some of which are listed below:[15]

- It may be more advantageous for maintaining the integrity of the aquatic ecosystem to consolidate compensatory mitigation into a single large parcel or contiguous parcels when ecologically appropriate.
- Establishment of a mitigation bank can bring together financial resources, planning, and scientific expertise not practicable to many project-specific compensatory mitigation proposals. This consolidation of resources can increase the potential for the establishment and long-term management of successful mitigation that maximizes opportunities for contributing to biodiversity and/or watershed function.
- Use of mitigation banks may reduce permit processing times for projects that qualify and provide more cost-effective compensatory mitigation opportunities.
- Compensatory mitigation is typically implemented and functioning in advance of project impacts, thereby reducing

- temporal losses of aquatic functions and uncertainty over whether the mitigation will be successful in offsetting project impacts.
- The existence of mitigation banks can contribute towards attainment of the goal for no overall net loss of the nation's wetlands by providing applicants with opportunities to compensate for authorized impacts when mitigation might not otherwise be required.

Mitigation banking has a high degree of intellectual and practical appeal at many levels. To developers and the regulated community in general, mitigation banks offer much greater flexibility than traditional mitigation procedures. By buying or using existing mitigation credits, developers save the time and expense of designing a specific mitigation plan for each project. In addition, the higher success of mitigation banks is due to their larger size, preferable placement, and superior design, combined with the fact that most mitigation credits are only issued after the bank has been certified a success. Finally, because mitigation banks can store credits, the process should save time, money, and create greater certainty for the developer during the permit process.[16]

Another potential advantage of wetland mitigation banking is that it encourages the development of large-scale, cost-effective mitigation sites which include a larger portion of available ecosystems for fish and wildlife. In addition, single, large mitigation banks will reduce the number of mitigation sites, and will also allow more efficient use of limited agency compliance staff.[17]

While there are situations where on-site mitigation may be preferable for maintenance of local species, in many cases greater ecological benefits may be attained by off-site mitigation as part of a large mitigation bank. A 1993 report by the Environmental Law Institute touted the benefits of using large mitigation bank sites:

> "Larger wetland systems are generally more self-sustaining. They can provide habitat for more types of species, a longer and more self-sustaining food chain, more habitat niches, and a wider variety of habitat types—which in turn, can better accommodate ecosystem succession, migration, and change.

Larger sites provide more interior habitat for many species dependent upon such habitat. They may better protect species from inbreeding effects due to isolation of small populations, and may be more resilient to natural disasters because of their larger size, larger seed banks, and more varied habitat."[18]

In addition, smaller projects may ultimately fail due to poor design, poor construction, and poor monitoring. One study for the South Florida Water Management District concluded that out of 100 permitted projects that required mitigation only four met the environmental goals set forth in the permits.[19] Further, in another study of 1,262 permits issued by the Florida Department of Environmental Regulation during the period 1985 to 1990 with requirements for wetland creation, restoration, enhancement, or preservation, only 27 percent of the projects achieved "ecological success," defined as a site that is, or appears likely to become, a functional wetland of the type permitted as a mitigation wetland.[20]

Other common reasons cited for the lack of success of wetland mitigation without the use of a mitigation bank include:

- Inadequate design and engineering of the mitigation site.
- Insufficient agency resources for monitoring of mitigation projects.
- Tendency of permit applicants to attempt to reduce mitigation costs in order to maximize profit from the project.
- Failure of successor property owners to maintain the mitigation site.
- Absence of long-term monitoring and maintenance resources.
- Proponents of mitigation banking believe that the use of mitigation banks can effectively solve the problems associated with traditional on-site mitigation. For example, one commentator cited several ecological benefits of consolidating small mitigation projects into one contiguous bank:

- Banks provide significant water recharge benefits because they contain large, contiguous wetland areas where water is retained which will percolate through the ground into the aquifer. The bank will serve as a retention basin during rainy periods and act as a reservoir during periods of drought.
- Banks provide integrated wetland functions that support a wide variety of wildlife species, including threatened and endangered species.
- Banks have a long-term management plan and the financial means for carrying out the plan.
- It is easier for government regulators to monitor activities at a large consolidated bank as opposed to numerous small mitigation sites.[21]

Tenneco-LaTerre Wetland Mitigation Bank

Most wetland banking projects have, indeed, involved large-scale projects. Perhaps the best known mitigation banking project is the Tenneco-LaTerre wetland mitigation bank in Terrebonne Parish, Louisiana. This project was undertaken in an area within the coastal Mississippi River delta where subsidence and intrusion of salt water was gradually destroying a large freshwater marsh. The Tenneco Company (and its predecessor, the LaTerre Co.) invested over $20 million to construct over 100 weirs, 200 bulkheads and mud dams, and 30 miles of levees, which primarily were designed to protect the integrity of the freshwater marshes.

The Tenneco-LaTerre mitigation bank was established by a 1984 Memorandum of Agreement (MOA) between the Tenneco Company and five government agencies: the FWS, Soil Conservation Service, National Marine Fisheries Service, the Louisiana Department of Natural Resources, and the Louisiana Department of Wildlife and Fisheries. Under the terms of the MOA, Tenneco is required to spend $3 million per year over a 25-year period to preserve and enhance fish and wildlife habitats on approximately 5,000 acres of marsh owned by Tenneco, and another 2,200 acres owned by other parties but which lie within the system of dikes. Tenneco is responsible for maintaining and monitoring the wetlands during this period. In November 1988, American Petrofina acquired mineral rights to the LaTerre site, and assumed management responsibilities of the LaTerre mitigation bank.[22]

In return for its investment in the LaTerre mitigation bank, Tenneco (and Petrofina) have earned nearly 8.5 million Habitat Units (GHUs), which are calculated by multiplying the habitat suitability for a particular species of interest to wildlife managers (scaled from zero to one) times the number of acres protected. These credits may be used to offset mitigation requirements either off-site or on-site, although on-site projects require a 2:1 ratio of credits to debits. Thus far, relatively few of the available credits have been redeemed, and most of these were for dredging of canals to allow drilling equipment to be brought to a site by barge.

DISADVANTAGES OF MITIGATION BANKING

Despite the appeal and potential utility of wetland mitigation banks, there have been critics and problems with the process from the beginning. Many of these are criticisms and problems of mitigation procedures in general, but others are specific to mitigation banking. One such problem is that wetland functions and values tend to be specific to a particular site, in as much as a wetland's relationship to other wetlands, sources of groundwater and surface water, and adjacent upland areas usually determines its values. The "off-site" nature of wetland banks is contrary to the on-site mitigation preference by federal agencies.

Another problem with mitigation banking is that it tends to result in the creation of those wetland types that are the easiest and cheapest to create, namely shrub wetlands and marshes. As a result, the habitat type received in exchange may be quite different from the wetlands that were damaged by the project.

A problem shared by all mitigation projects—which has a particular impact on mitigation banking—is the lack of technical expertise by many individuals involved in both the planning and monitoring of wetland banking projects. No guidelines currently exist to identify the qualifications necessary for an effective designer of mitigation projects, and agencies responsible for monitoring the mitigation banks are usually understaffed and incompletely trained. As a result, mitigation banks are often poorly designed, poorly monitored, and destined for failure from the outset. To make matters worse, mitigation banks are often creatures of complex agreements between private and public interests, and are subject to a variety of federal, state, and local laws, such that design and monitoring require an advanced level of expertise that is often unavailable and always expensive.

Despite the problems and criticisms associated with wetland mitigation banks, several states have seen enough positive attributes to approve use of this mitigation technique in conjunction with various development projects.

ENDNOTES

1. *See* Blaesser, "New Federal Wetlands Policy: The Landowner's Perspective," 46 *Land Use Law & Zoning Digest* 3, 6-8 (Jan. 1994).

2. 60 Fed. Reg. 58605 (Nov. 28, 1995). *See also* EPA/Army Corps, *Memorandum to the Field: Establishment and Use of Wetland Mitigation Banks in the Clean Water Act Section 404 Regulatory Program* (Aug. 23, 1993).

3. *See* Fish and Wildlife Service, *Interim Guidance on Mitigation Banking*, Ecological Service Instructional Memorandum No. 80 (June 1983).

4. *See* Sokolove and Huang, "Privatization of Wetland Mitigation Banking," 7 *Nat. Resources & Env.* 36-38, 68-69 (ABA 1992).

5. *Memorandum of Agreement between the Environmental Protection Agency and the Department of the Army Concerning the Determination of Mitigation under the Clean Water Act Section 404 (b)(1) Guidelines* (February 6, 1990). Detailed discussion of this MOA is provided in Chapter 5.

6. *See* 1990 MOA at 4.

7. *See* discussion of "compensation credit" in Environmental Law Institute, *Wetland Mitigation Banking* (1993), at 77-94.

8. *See also* Environmental Law Institute, *Wetland Mitigation Banking* (1993).

9. *See* Hopen, "Wetlands Mitigation Banking: Giving Entrepreneurs a Chance to Build Better Wetlands," 2 *J. of Envt'l Law & Practice* 32-37 (Nov./Dec. 1994), at 35.

10. *Id.* at 33-34.

11. *See* Environmental Law Institute, *Wetland Mitigation Banking* (1993), at 5. The 218-page report is available for $20.00 by calling (800) 433-5120 or (202) 939-3844.

12. The three private commercial banks that had received federal approval from the Army Corps are: (1) Millhaven Plantation Bank, Georgia; (2) Florida Wetlandsbank; and (3) Land and Water Resources, Illinois.

13. *See* Hopen, "Wetlands Mitigation Banking: Giving Entrepreneurs a Chance to Build Better Wetlands," 2 *J. of Envt'l Law & Practice* 32-37 (Nov./Dec. 1994).

14. *See* Shabman, Scodari, and King, *Expanding Opportunities for Successful Wetland Mitigation: The Private Credit Market Alternative* (Dec. 1993). For an opposing viewpoint, see Marsh and Acker, "Mitigation Banking on a Wider Plane," 14(1) *Nat'l Wetlands Newsletter* 8-9 (1992).

15. *See* 60 Fed. Reg. 12286, 12287 (Mar. 6, 1995).

16. *See* Kusler, "The Mitigation Banking Debate," 14 *Nat'l Wetlands Newsletter* 4 (1992).

17. Lewis, "Why Florida Needs Mitigation Banking," 14 *Nat'l Wetlands Newsletter* 7 (1992).

18. *See* Environmental Law Institute, *Wetland Mitigation Banking* (1993), at 32.

19. Erwin, *An Evaluation of Wetland Mitigation within the South Florida Water Management District: Vol. 1*, Kevin L. Erwin Consulting Geologist, Inc., Fort Myers, FL (1991).

20. Redmond, *Report on Mitigation - Florida State Permitting Efforts*, Florida Dept. of Environmental Regulation (1990).

21. *See* Hopen, "Wetlands Mitigation Banking: Giving Entrepreneurs a Chance to Build Better Wetlands," 2 *J. of Envt'l Law & Practice* 32-37 (Nov./Dec. 1994), at 33.

22. *See* Anderson and DeCaprio, "Banking on the Bayou," 14(1) *Nat'l Wetlands Newsletter* 10 (1992).

Chapter 8

Wetland Mitigation Banking Guidance

INTRODUCTION

On November 28, 1995, the Army Corps of Engineers (Army Corps), the U.S. Environmental Protection Agency (EPA), the Natural Resources Conservation Service (NRCS), the Fish and Wildlife Service (FWS), and the National Marine Fisheries Service (NMFS) issued guidance regarding the establishment, use, and operation of mitigation banks for the purpose of providing compensatory mitigation of adverse impacts to wetlands and other aquatic resources.[1] The purpose of the guidance is to clarify the manner in which mitigation banks might be used to satisfy mitigation requirements associated with the Clean Water Act (CWA) Section 404 permit program and the wetland conservation provisions (*i.e.*, "Swampbuster" provisions) of the Food Security Act (FSA). This chapter examines this new guidance on wetland mitigation banking.[2]

PURPOSE AND SCOPE OF GUIDANCE

Recognizing the potential benefits mitigation banking offers for streamlining the wetland permit evaluation process and providing more effective mitigation for authorized impacts to wetlands, the new guidance jointly issued by the Army Corps, EPA, NRCS, FWS, and the NMFS encourages the establishment and appropriate use of mitigation banks. The guidance document is provided expressly to assist federal agency personnel, mitigation bank sponsors, permit applicants, and others in complying with the mitigation requirements of CWA Section 404, Section

10 of the Rivers and Harbors Act, the wetland conservation provisions (*i.e.*, "Swampbuster" provisions) of the Food Security Act (FSA), and other federal laws and regulations requiring wetland mitigation. The policies and procedures discussed in the new guidance are applicable to the establishment, use, and operation of public mitigation banks, as well as privately-sponsored mitigation banks, including third party banks (*e.g.*, entrepreneurial banks). The basic prerequisites to mitigation bank approval, establishment, and use are examined below.

POLICY CONSIDERATIONS

This wetland mitigation banking guidance applies to all mitigation bank proposals submitted for approval on or after November 28, 1995 and to those in early stages of planning or development. The guidance document does not apply retroactively to mitigation banks that have already received agency approval. While it is recognized that individual mitigation banking proposals may vary, the fundamental precepts of this guidance should apply to all future mitigation banks.

For the purposes of the Section 404 program, and consistent with the CEQ regulations, the Section 404(b)(1) Guidelines, and the Memorandum of Agreement Between the Environmental Protection Agency (EPA) and the Department of the Army Concerning the Determination of Mitigation under the Clean Water Act Section 404(b)(1) Guidelines, mitigation means sequentially avoiding impacts, minimizing impacts, and compensating for remaining unavoidable impacts. Compensatory mitigation, under the Section 404 program, is the restoration, creation, enhancement, or in exceptional circumstances, preservation of wetlands and/or other aquatic resources expressly for the purpose of compensating for unavoidable adverse impacts. A site where wetlands and/or other aquatic resources are restored, created, enhanced, or in exceptional circumstances, preserved expressly for the purpose of providing compensatory mitigation in advance of authorized impacts to similar resources is a mitigation bank.

PLANNING CONSIDERATIONS

Prospectus

Prospective bank sponsors are encouraged to submit a prospectus to the Army Corps or NRCS to initiate the planning and review process by the appropriate agencies (*e.g.*, pre-application coordination). The Army Corps will typically serve as the lead agency for the establishment of mitigation banks. Bank sponsors proposing establishment of mitigation banks solely for the purpose of complying with the "Swampbuster" provisions of the FSA should submit their prospectus to the NRCS.

The purpose of the prospectus is to provide information to the agencies regarding the general need for and technical feasibility of a bank, as well as its potential for providing compensatory mitigation within a particular watershed or other designated geographic area (i.e., bank service area). Formal agency involvement and review is initiated with submittal of a prospectus.

Goal Setting

The overall goal of a mitigation bank should be the establishment or reestablishment of a self-sustaining, functioning aquatic system, which replaces the functions and acreage of wetlands and other aquatic resources anticipated to be adversely affected within a watershed or other designated geographic area. It is desirable to set the particular objectives (*i.e.*, determining the type and character of compensatory mitigation to be developed) for a mitigation bank in advance of site selection. The goal and objectives should be driven by the anticipated mitigation need; the site selection should support achieving the goal and objectives.

Consideration should be given to the ecological suitability of a site for achieving the goal and objectives of a bank, *i.e.*, that it possess the physical, chemical, and biological characteristics to support establishment of the desired aquatic resources and functions. Size and location of the site relative to other ecological features, hydrologic sources (including the availability of water rights), and compatibility with adjacent land uses and watershed management plans are important factors for consideration. It also is important that ecologically significant upland resources, or threatened and endangered species habitats are not compromised in the process of establishing a bank. Other factors for consideration include development trends (*i.e.*, land use changes), habitat status and trends, local or regional goals for the restoration or protection of particular habitat types or functions, water quality and floodplain management goals, and establishment of habitat for species of concern.

Site Selection

Banks may be sited on public or private lands. Cooperative arrangements between public and private entities to use public lands for mitigation banks may be acceptable. In some circumstances, it may be appropriate to site banks on federal, state, tribal, or locally owned resource management areas (*e.g.*, wildlife management areas, national or state forests, public parks, or recreation areas). The siting of banks on such lands may be acceptable if the internal policies of the public agency allow use of its land for such purposes, and the public agency grants approval. Mitigation credits generated by banks of this nature must be based solely on those values in the bank that are supplemental to the public program(s) already planned or in place.

Technical Feasibility

Mitigation banks should be planned and designed to be self-sustaining over time to the extent possible and to pose little risk of failure. The techniques for restoring and creating wetlands and/or other aquatic resources must be carefully selected, since restoration/creation science is constantly evolving. The restoration of historic or substantially degraded wetlands and/or other aquatic resources utilizing proven techniques increases the likelihood of mitigation success and lessens the loss of valuable uplands due to wetland creation. Thus, restoration should be the first option considered when siting a bank.

In general, banks which involve complex hydraulic engineering features and/or questionable water sources (*e.g.*, pumped water systems) are more costly to develop, operate and maintain, and have a higher risk of failure than banks designed to function with little or no human intervention. The former situations should be avoided to the extent possible. The guidance, however, recognizes that in some circumstances, wetlands must be actively managed to ensure their viability and sustainability. Furthermore, long-term maintenance requirements may be necessary and appropriate in some cases.

Role of Preservation

Credit may be given when existing wetlands and/or other aquatic resources are preserved in conjunction with restoration, creation, or enhancement activities, and when it is demonstrated that the preservation will augment the functions of the restored, created, or enhanced aquatic resource. Such augmentation may be reflected in the total number of credits available from the bank. However, the preservation of existing wetlands and/or other aquatic resources in perpetuity may be authorized as the sole basis for generating credits in mitigation banks only under exceptional circumstances. Under such circumstances, preservation may be accomplished through the implementation of appropriate legal mechanisms (*e.g.*, transfer of deed, deed restrictions, conservation easement) to protect wetlands and/or other aquatic resources, accompanied by implementation of appropriate changes in land use or other physical changes as necessary.

Determining whether preservation is appropriate as the sole basis for generating credits at a mitigation bank requires careful judgment regarding a number of factors. Consideration must be given to whether wetlands and/or other aquatic resources proposed for preservation: (1) perform physical or biological functions, the preservation of which is important to the region in which the aquatic resources are located, and (2) are under demonstrable threat of loss or substantial degradation due to human activities that might not otherwise be expected to be restricted. The existence of a demonstrable threat must be based on clear evidence of destructive land use changes which are consistent with local and regional land use trends and are not the consequence of actions under the control of the bank sponsor. The number of mitigation credits available from a bank that is based solely on preservation should be based on the functions that would otherwise be lost or degraded if the aquatic resources were not preserved, and the timing of such loss or degradation. As such, compensation for aquatic resource impacts will generally require a greater number of acres from a preservation bank than from a bank which is based on restoration, creation or enhancement.

Inclusion of Upland Areas

Credit may be given for the inclusion of upland areas occurring within a bank only to the degree that such features increase the overall ecological functioning of the bank. If such features are included as part of a bank, it is important that they receive the same protected status as the rest of the bank and be subject to the same operational procedures and requirements. The presence of upland areas may increase the per-unit value of the aquatic habitat in the bank. Alternatively, limited credit may be given to upland areas protected by the bank to reflect the functions inherently provided by such areas (*e.g.*, nutrient and sediment filtration of stormwater runoff, wildlife habitat diversity) which directly enhance or maintain the integrity of the aquatic ecosystem and that might otherwise be subject to threat of loss or degradation. An appropriate functional assessment methodology should be used to determine the manner and extent to which such features augment the functions of restored, created, or enhanced wetlands and/or other aquatic resources.

Mitigation Banking and Watershed Planning

Mitigation banks should be planned and developed to address resource needs within a particular watershed. Moreover, decisions regarding the location and uses of a mitigation bank, as well as the type of wetlands and/or other aquatic resources to be restored, created, enhanced, or preserved may often be made within the context of ecological objectives set for the watershed. Watershed planning efforts often identify categories of activities having minimal adverse effects on the aquatic ecosystem which could be authorized under a general permit. In order to reduce potential cumulative effects of such activities, it may be appropriate to offset these types of impacts through the use of a mitigation bank established in conjunction with a watershed plan.

ESTABLISHMENT OF MITIGATION BANKS

Mitigation Banking Instruments

All mitigation banks need to have a banking instrument as documentation of agency concurrence on the objectives and administration of the bank. The banking instrument should describe in detail the physical and legal characteristics of the bank, and how the bank will be established and operated. The banking instrument will be signed by the bank sponsor and the concurring regulatory and resource agencies represented on the Mitigation Bank Review Team (MBRT). The bank sponsor is responsible for the preparation of the banking instrument in consultation with the MBRT. The following information should be addressed, as appropriate:

1. Bank goals and objectives.
2. Ownership of bank lands.
3. Bank size and classes of wetlands and/or other aquatic resources proposed for inclusion in the bank.
4. Description of baseline conditions.
5. Geographic service area.
6. Wetland classes or other aquatic resource impacts suitable for compensation.
7. Methods for determining credits and debits.
8. Accounting procedures.
9. Performance standards for determining credit availability and bank success.
10. Reporting protocols and monitoring plan.
11. Contingency and remedial actions and responsibilities.
12. Financial assurances.
13. Compensation ratios.
14. Provisions for long-term management and maintenance.

In cases where initial establishment of the mitigation bank involves a discharge into waters of the United States requiring Section 404 authorization, the banking instrument will be made part of the Army

Corps permit. The permit application to establish a bank will be evaluated by the Corps on its own merits pursuant to Section 404 policies and procedures. As such, preparation of a banking instrument should not alter the normal permit evaluation process timeframes. In cases where the mitigation bank is established pursuant to the FSA, the banking instrument will be included in the plan developed or approved by NRCS and the Fish and Wildlife Service (FWS).

Agency Roles and Coordination

Collectively, the signatory agencies to the banking instrument will comprise the Mitigation Bank Review Team (MBRT). Representatives from the Army Corps, EPA, FWS, NMFS, and NRCS, as appropriate given the projected use for the bank, should typically comprise the MBRT. In addition, it is appropriate for representatives from state, tribal, and local regulatory and resource agencies to participate where an agency has authorities and/or mandates directly affecting or affected by the establishment, use, or operation of a bank. No agency is required to sign a banking instrument; however, in signing a banking instrument, an agency agrees to comply with the terms of that instrument.

The Chair of the MBRT will be the Army Corps, except in cases where the bank is proposed solely for the purpose of complying with the FSA, in which case NRCS will be the MBRT Chair. Either agency may delegate that responsibility to another federal, state, tribal, or local agency, as appropriate. The primary role of the MBRT is to facilitate the establishment of mitigation banks through the development of mitigation banking instruments.

Because of the different authorities and responsibilities of each agency represented on the MBRT, there is a benefit in achieving agreement up front. For this reason, the MBRT will strive to obtain consensus on its actions. The MBRT will review and reach consensus on the banking instrument and final plans for the restoration, creation, enhancement, and/or preservation of wetlands and other aquatic resources. Once the banking instrument has been signed, the MBRT will not typically be involved in the operation of a bank on a project-specific basis. Periodically, the MBRT will review monitoring and accounting reports. In the event a bank sponsor proposes remedial actions, or an agency on the

MBRT considers remedial actions to be necessary, the MBRT will review and reach consensus on the specific remedial measures to be implemented at a bank.

Role of the Bank Sponsor

The bank sponsor is responsible for the preparation of the banking instrument in consultation with the MBRT. The bank sponsor is also responsible for the overall operation and management of the bank in accordance with the terms of the banking instrument, including the preparation and distribution of monitoring reports and accounting statements/ledger.

Dispute Resolution Procedure

The MBRT will work to reach consensus on its actions in accordance with this guidance. It is anticipated that all issues will be resolved by the MBRT in this manner.

Development of the banking instrument. During the development of the banking instrument, if the agency representatives on the MBRT cannot reach consensus on the content of the banking instrument within a reasonable timeframe, or if an agency representative considers that a particular decision raises concern regarding the application of existing policy or procedures, an agency may request the issue be reviewed by a higher level within each agency. If resolution is still not achieved, any agency(ies) may initiate interagency review through written notification to, as appropriate, the Army Corps, EPA, FWS, NMFS, NRCS and other agencies represented on the MBRT. Said notification will describe the issue in sufficient detail and provide recommendations for resolution. Within 20 days, the Army Corps or NRCS (as appropriate), or an appropriate designee, will lead necessary discussions to achieve interagency concurrence on the issue of concern, and forward documentation of the resolution to the MBRT Chair for distribution to the other MBRT member agencies. The bank sponsor may also request that the Army Corps or NCRS review actions taken to develop the banking instrument if the sponsor believes that inadequate progress has been made on the instrument by the MBRT.

Application of the banking instrument. In the event an agency on the MBRT is concerned that a proposed use may not comply with the terms of the banking instrument, that agency may raise the issue to the attention of the Army Corps or NRCS through the permit evaluation process. In order to facilitate timely and effective consideration of agency comments, the Army Corps or NRCS, as appropriate, will advise the MBRT agencies of a proposed use of a bank and initiate discussion as necessary. The Army Corps will fully consider comments provided by the review agencies regarding mitigation as part of the permit evaluation process. The NRCS will consult with FWS in making its decisions pertaining to mitigation. If, in the view of an agency on the MBRT, an issued permit or series of permits reflects a pattern of concern regarding the application of the terms of the banking instrument, that agency may initiate review of the concern by the full MBRT through written notification to the MBRT Chair. The MBRT Chair will convene a meeting of the MBRT, or initiate another appropriate forum for communication, typically within 10 days upon receipt of notification, to resolve concerns. If resolution is not reached, an agency may request that the issue be reviewed by higher levels within each agency. Invoking this dispute resolution procedure to address concerns regarding the application of a banking instrument will not delay any permit decision pending before the authorizing agency *(i.e.*, Army Corps or NRCS).

CRITERIA FOR USE OF A MITIGATION BANK

Project Applicability

All regulated activities may be eligible to use a mitigation bank as compensation for unavoidable impacts to wetlands and/or other aquatic resources in so far as the use complies with the terms of the banking instrument. Mitigation banks established for FSA purposes may be debited only in accordance with the mitigation and replacement provisions of 7 CFR Part 12.

Mitigation banks may also be used to compensate for adverse impacts to wetlands and/or other aquatic resources authorized under other resource protection programs, such as state regulatory programs. In no case may the same credits be used to compensate for more than one activity; however, the same credits may be used to compensate for an activity which requires authorization under more than one program.

Relationship to Mitigation Requirements

All appropriate and practicable steps must be undertaken by the applicant to first avoid and then minimize adverse impacts to aquatic resources, prior to authorization to use a particular mitigation bank. Remaining unavoidable impacts must be compensated to the extent appropriate and practicable. Requirements for compensatory mitigation may be satisfied through the use of mitigation banks when either on-site compensation is not practicable or use of the mitigation bank is environmentally preferable to on-site compensation. Applicants should not expect that establishment of, or participation in, a mitigation bank will ultimately lead to a determination of compliance with applicable mitigation requirements (*i.e.*, Section 404(b)(1) Guidelines or FSA Manual), or as excepting projects from any applicable requirements.

Geographic Limits of Applicability

The service area of a mitigation bank is the designated area (*e.g.*, watershed, county) wherein a bank can reasonably be expected to provide appropriate compensation for impacts to wetlands and/or other aquatic resources. Designation of the service area should be based on consideration of hydrologic, soil, and biotic criteria, and be stipulated in the banking instrument. The geographic extent of a service area should be guided by the cataloging unit of the "Hydrologic Unit Map of the United States" (USGS, 1980) and ecoregion of the "Ecoregions of the United States" (James M. Omernik, EPA, 1986) or section of the "Descriptions of the Ecoregions of the United States" (Robert G. Bailey, USDA, 1980). It may be appropriate to use other hydrologic and biotic classification and mapping systems developed at the state or regional level for the purpose of specifying bank service areas, when such systems compare favorably in their objectives and level of detail. In the interest of integrating banks with other resource management objectives, bank service areas may encompass larger watershed areas if the designation of such areas is supported by local or regional management plans (*e.g.* Special Area Management Plans, Advance Identification), State Wetland Conservation Plans, or other federally sponsored or recognized watershed management plans.

Furthermore, designation of a more inclusive service area may be appropriate for mitigation banks whose primary purpose is to compensate for linear projects that typically involve numerous small impacts in several different watersheds.

Use of a Mitigation Bank vs. On-Site Mitigation

As indicated in the 1990 joint MOA between the EPA and Army Corps, compensatory mitigation should be undertaken in areas adjacent or contiguous to the site of the aquatic resource impacts when practicable and environmentally preferable. The preference for on-site mitigation, however, should not preclude the use of a mitigation bank when there is no practicable opportunity for on-site compensation, or when use of a bank is environmentally preferable to on-site compensation. In making the latter determination, careful consideration must be given to wetland functions, landscape position, affected species populations at the impact and mitigation bank sites, and potential on-site compensation areas. In general, it may be desirable to provide compensation for minor aquatic resource impacts through consolidation in a well-managed bank. There may also be circumstances warranting a combination of on-site and off-site (*i.e.*, bank) mitigation to compensate for losses.

With respect to larger aquatic resource impacts, use of a bank may be appropriate if it is capable of replacing essential physical and/or biological functions of the aquatic resources which are expected to be lost or degraded and is environmentally preferable to on-site compensatory mitigation. Moreover, for projects that might otherwise cause or contribute to significant degradation (40 C.F.R. Part 230.10(c)), a bank may only be used when it is demonstrated that use of the bank will prevent or replace the lost functions that give rise to the significant degradation finding, and where a reasonable assurance of success is provided.

In-Kind vs. Out-of-Kind Mitigation Determinations

In the interest of achieving functional replacement, in-kind compensation of aquatic resource impacts should generally be required. Out-of-kind compensation may be acceptable if it is determined to be practicable and environmentally preferable to in-kind compensation (*e.g.*, of greater ecological value to a particular region). Decisions regarding out-of-kind mitigation are typically made on a case-by-case basis during the permit evaluation process. The banking instrument may identify circumstances in which it is environmentally desirable to allow out-of-kind compensation within the context of a particular mitigation bank. Mitigation banks developed as part of an area-wide management plan to address a specific resource objective (*e.g.*, restoration of a particularly vulnerable or valuable wetland habitat type) may be such an example.

Crediting/Debiting/Accounting Procedures

Credits and debits are the terms used to designate the units of trade (*i.e.*, currency) in mitigation banking. Credits represent the accrual or attainment of aquatic functions at a bank; debits represent the loss of aquatic functions at an impact or project site. Credits are debited from a bank when they are used to offset aquatic resource impacts.

An appropriate functional assessment methodology (*e.g.*, Habitat Evaluation Procedures, hydrogeomorphic approach to wetlands functional assessment) acceptable to all signatories should be used to assess wetland and/or other aquatic resource restoration, creation, and enhancement efforts within a mitigation bank, and to quantify the amount of available credits. The range of functions to be assessed will depend upon the assessment methodology identified in the banking instrument. The same methodology should be used to assess both credits and debits. If an appropriate functional assessment methodology is impractical to employ, credits and debits can be based on simple indices (*e.g.*, acres) of various classes of wetlands and/or other aquatic resources. Regardless of the method employed, credits should be based on the difference between site conditions under the with- and without-bank scenarios.

The bank sponsor should be responsible for assessing the development of the bank and submitting appropriate documentation of such assessments to the authorizing agency(ies) and members of the MBRT for review. Alternatively, functional assessments may be conducted by a team representing involved resource and regulatory agencies and other appropriate parties. Bank sponsors will establish and maintain an accounting system (*i.e.*, ledger) which documents the activity of all mitigation bank accounts. Each time an approved debit/credit transaction occurs at a given bank, the bank sponsor will submit a statement to each member agency of the MBRT. The bank sponsor will also generate an annual ledger report for all mitigation bank accounts for similar distribution.

Credits may be sold to third parties. The cost of mitigation credits to a third party is determined by the bank sponsor.

Timing of Credit Withdrawal

The number of credits available for withdrawal (*i.e.*, debiting) should generally be commensurate with the level of aquatic functions attained at a bank at the time of debiting. The level of function may be determined through the application of performance standards tailored to the specific restoration, creation, or enhancement activity at the bank site or through the use of an appropriate functional assessment methodology.

The success of a mitigation bank with regard to its capacity to establish a healthy and fully functional aquatic system relates directly to both the ecological and financial stability of the bank. Since financial considerations are particularly critical in early stages of bank development, it may be appropriate to allow limited debiting based upon a projected level of aquatic functions at a bank (*e.g.*, 15 percent of the total credits projected for the bank at maturity). However, the policy of the guidance is to ensure that those actions necessary for the long-term viability of a mitigation bank be accomplished prior to any debiting of the bank. In this regard, the following requirements should be satisfied prior to debiting: (1) Banking instrument and final mitigation plans have been approved; (2) bank site has been secured; and (3) appropriate financial assurances have been established. In addition, initial physical and biological improvements should be completed within the first full growing season following initial debiting of a bank. The temporal loss of functions associated with the debiting of projected credits may require higher compensation ratios. Further debiting of the bank should not occur until the allocated projected credits have accrued and additional credits have accrued to match proposed debiting.

Party Responsible for Bank Success

The bank sponsor is responsible for assuring the success of the restoration, creation, enhancement, and preservation activities at the mitigation bank. This responsibility must be clearly documented in the banking instrument and in any authorization approving the use of the bank as compensatory mitigation. Where Army Corps and/or NRCS authorization is necessary to establish the bank, the Army Corps permit or NRCS plan should be conditioned to ensure that provisions of the banking instrument are enforceable by the appropriate agency(ies). In circumstances where establishment of a bank does not require such authorization, the details of the bank should be delineated by the relevant authorizing agency in any permit in which the permittee's mitigation obligations are met through use of the bank. In addition, the bank sponsor should sign such permits for the limited purpose of meeting those mitigation responsibilities, thus confirming that those responsibilities are enforceable against the bank sponsor if necessary.

LONG-TERM MANAGEMENT, MONITORING, AND REMEDIATION

Bank Operational Life

The operational life of a bank refers to the period during which the terms and conditions of the banking instrument are applicable, and signatories of the instrument are responsible for carrying out its provisions. With the exception of arrangements for the long-term management and protection in perpetuity of the bank, the operational life of a mitigation bank terminates at the point when: (1) compensatory mitigation credits have been exhausted or banking activity is voluntarily terminated with written notice by the bank sponsor provided to the Army Corps or NRCS and other members of the MBRT, and (2) it has been determined that the debited bank is functionally mature and/or self-sustaining to the degree specified in the banking instrument.

Long-Term Management and Protection

Mitigation banks should be protected in perpetuity with appropriate real estate arrangements. In exceptional circumstances, real estate arrangements may be approved which dictate finite protection for a bank. However, in no case should finite protection extend for a lesser time than the duration of project impacts for which the bank is being used to provide compensation. All banks must be protected by legal instruments which effectively prevent harmful activities (*i.e.*, incompatible uses)[3] that would jeopardize their continued conservation purpose. Acceptable instruments are deed restrictions, conservation easements, or other enforceable legal mechanisms.

Banking instruments should identify the entity responsible for the management of the bank beyond its operational life as a means to assure the conservation purpose of the bank. The bank sponsor is responsible for securing adequate funds for the operation and maintenance of the bank during its operational life, as well as for management of the bank beyond its operational life, as necessary. Where needed, the acquisition and protection of water rights should be secured by the bank sponsor and documented in the banking instrument.

Monitoring Requirements

The bank sponsor is responsible for monitoring the mitigation bank in accordance with monitoring provisions identified in the banking instrument to determine the level of success and identify problems requiring remedial action. Monitoring provisions need to be set forth in the banking instrument and based on scientifically sound performance standards prescribed for the bank. Monitoring should be conducted at timed intervals appropriate for the particular project type and until such time that the authorizing agency(ies), in consultation with the MBRT, are confident that success is being achieved (*i.e.*, performance standards are attained).

Annual monitoring reports should be submitted to the authorizing agency(ies) which is responsible for distribution to the other members of the MBRT, in accordance with the terms specified in the banking instrument.

Remedial Action

The banking instrument should stipulate the procedures for identifying and implementing remedial measures at a bank, or any portion thereof. Remedial measures should be based on information contained in the monitoring reports (*i.e.*, the attainment of prescribed performance standards), as well as site inspections. The need for remediation will be determined by the authorizing agency(ies) in consultation with the MBRT and bank sponsor.

Financial Assurances

The bank sponsor is responsible for securing sufficient funds to cover contingency actions in the event of bank default or failure. Accordingly, banks that pose a greater risk of failure and that have already had credits debited, should have comparatively higher financial sureties in place, than those where the likelihood of success is more certain. In addition, the bank sponsor is responsible for securing adequate funding to monitor and maintain the bank throughout its operational life, as well as beyond the operational life if not self-sustaining. Total funding requirements should reflect realistic cost estimates for monitoring, long-term maintenance, contingency, and remedial actions.

Financial assurances may be in the form of performance bonds, irrevocable trusts, escrow accounts, casualty insurance, or other approved instruments. Such assurances may be phased-out or reduced, once it has been demonstrated that the bank is functionally mature and/or self-sustaining (in accordance with performance standards).

ENDNOTES

1. *See* 60 Fed. Reg. 58605 (Nov. 28, 1995).

2. *See also* EPA/Army Corps, *Memorandum to the Field: Establishment and Use of Wetland Mitigation Banks in the Clean Water Act Section 404 Regulatory Program* (Aug. 23, 1993).

3. For example, certain silvicultural practices (*e.g.,* clear cutting and/or harvests on short-term rotations) may be incompatible with the objectives of a mitigation bank. In contrast, silvicultural practices such as long-term rotations, selective cutting, maintenance of vegetation diversity, and undisturbed buffers are more likely to be considered a compatible use.

Chapter 9

Wetland Mitigation Case Studies

by James A. Schmid, Ph.D.

INTRODUCTION

This chapter provides four case studies which illustrate specific instances where compensatory mitigation was required for permit approvals to fill wetlands. These cases demonstrate how replacement wetlands were sited, designed, and constructed as mitigation for project impacts. The elements of successful mitigation are the same for each project although the details of the implementation necessarily differ in each case.

As explained in Chapter 5, applicants for dredge and fill permits must mitigate impacts to wetlands that will result from construction activities. Although they must first try to avoid and minimize all impacts as much as possible, some project impacts are unavoidable. These remaining "unavoidable" impacts may require "compensatory" mitigation to offset impacts to wetlands located in the vicinity of the project site. Four types of compensatory alternatives are available, in order of preference accorded them by regulatory authorities: restoration, creation, enhancement, and preservation. The first option, and the one most preferred by regulators, is restoration of previously existing wetlands at a site where they have ceased to exist, or exist only in a substantially degraded state. The second option is to create replacement wetlands from dry land. The new wetlands can be created on-site or off-site, but generally regulators prefer that they be located as near to the site of the unavoidable loss as practicable. The third option is to enhance wetland values and functions in existing wetlands that currently are considered to be impaired or degraded, often as a result of past human intervention. The fourth option is preservation, whereby wetland mitigation is credited for significant efforts to preserve existing ecosystems in their natural state. However, because the net extent of wetlands decreases and no new functions are introduced, preservation has been criticized and seldom has been accepted as a mitigation technique.

Determining which of these alternatives is appropriate for a specific project, whether used separately or in combination, depends on many case-specific and localized considerations. Where no practicable site is available nearby for wetland restoration, creation, or enhancement, it has increasingly become possible to purchase mitigation credits in regional mitigation banks or to contribute cash or land to agencies charged with wetland creation.

CASE STUDY 1: CREATION OF FRESHWATER WETLAND

The first example of a wetland mitigation project recounts the expansion of a major industrial wastewater treatment plant. This project illustrates the successful creation of a relatively small, new wetland from dry land. It is typical of instances where mitigation is necessary for unavoidable impacts.

Project Site

The industrial plant site occupies a 1,500-acre tract of industrial land in the coastal plain of southern New Jersey along the estuary of the Delaware River. This entire landholding has been much disturbed over some 80 years of industrial use and abandonment, and today forms a mosaic of freshwater wetlands and uplands. Intensive, ongoing uses (*e.g.*, manufacturing and research) are clustered in one section of the plant site; other parts of the property are devoted to landfills and dredged spoil disposal.

The remainder of the industrial complex presently consists of hundreds of acres of vacant open space within a security fence. These greenbelt lands form a complex of wetlands with scattered uplands. Much of the wetland supports deciduous forest, and extensive areas consist of herbaceous marsh. More than 250 species of plants typical of the

Delaware River floodplain have been recorded within the plant site, and it receives intensive use by migratory waterfowl and other wildlife. The fencing and tight security of the entire industrial facility contribute to the value of the vacant sections of the property as a wildlife refuge.

The wastewater treatment plant serves major on-site manufacturing and waste disposal enterprises. Capable of handling more than 100 million gallons of effluent daily, the treatment plant consisted of a 24-acre complex of facilities prior to its upgrading during the mid-1980s. Additional clarifiers were needed to upgrade the level of waste treatment and, thus, to help maintain water quality standards in the Delaware River.

The only practicable site for the new structures, which would occupy 9.7 acres, was a mostly upland tract adjacent to the existing wastewater treatment plant. The expansion site had been disturbed during the initial construction of the treatment plant some 15 years prior to the expansion project, but site preparation was not completed at that time. The expanded facilities could not avoid an area that had become, in the interim, an excavated, intermittent, 1.7-acre pond, together with about 0.5 acre of forested and herbaceous wetland with a very localized drainage area. The extent of the affected wetlands was determined using the 1987 Army Corps wetland delineation manual.

Functional Value of Impacted Wetland

The wetland at the fill site exhibited relatively modest environmental values. It encompassed 0.2 acre of marsh and 0.3 acre of deciduous forest. The site of the authorized construction (wetlands and uplands) was found to support about 70 species of plants typical of the Delaware River floodplain. Many of these species were facultative hydrophytes capable of growing in both wet and dry habitats. The disturbed uplands exhibited an array of non-native and invasive weeds.

Young red maples and black gums (typically 3 inches dbh) were the principal trees of the wetland forest and the adjacent uplands. Shrubs and woody vines were relatively sparse, and the ground cover of Japanese honeysuckle reflected the historic disturbance of the area. In the forest, herbs were generally sparse, probably in response to overgrazing by white-tailed deer. A distinct browse line was quite noticeable on the woody vegetation at the maximum height reachable by the deer. The small area of marsh supported chiefly hollow Joe-Pye-weed, sedges, rushes, and grasses. Shrubs along the edge of the marsh included northern bayberry, marsh-elder, and common buttonbush. Wildlife common to the vicinity made some use of the habitat.

Mitigation as a Condition of Permit Approval

The work in waters and wetlands required an individual permit pursuant to Section 404 of the Clean Water Act. Permit conditions required preparation and implementation of a mitigation plan to offset the unavoidable loss of wetlands. Mitigation was also required by the New Jersey Department of Environmental Protection pursuant to a stream encroachment permit for work in a regulated floodplain. The Army Corps of Engineers mandated creation of 1.4 acres of new wetlands from uplands as mitigation. As is typical in New Jersey, work on a mitigation plan began after the permits were issued.

Selection of Mitigation Site

Given the size of the surrounding property and its history of industrial use and abandonment, attention was focused on-site within the industrial facility for a place suitable for the creation of a 1.4-acre replacement wetland. (No off-site mitigation bank was available for consideration at the time, had there been no on-site alternatives.) Several uplands of sufficient size to accommodate the replacement wetland were identified on-site. The site selected was judged to be ideal both because of its location adjacent to existing wetlands several hundred acres in extent and in consequence of its remoteness from existing and foreseeable future industrial activities.

The vacant upland was located about 3,000 feet from the fill site, adjacent to an extensive complex of forested wetlands, marshes, and open water. Its limits were established through delineation of the adjacent wetlands by using the 1987 Army Corps manual. The mitigation site supported a stand of scrubby young red maple and white poplar trees surrounding the foundation and other remains of an old industrial building accessed by a gravel road. Openings between the stands of trees supported grasses and a few shrubs. The existing upland habitat value of the mitigation area was deemed to be low. The site was buffered from industrial operations by intervening deciduous forest.

The probability for successful installation of a functioning wetland was deemed high, because it would be possible to match the elevations of the adjacent wetlands after the building remains and fill were removed. The site was considered possibly to have been a wetland before its industrial development some 75 years prior to this wetland creation project, and the seasonal high water table was known to be near the surface in the adjacent wetlands. Thus, it was considered virtually certain that wetland hydrology could be secured in the new wetland.

Submission of Mitigation Plan

A formal mitigation plan was drawn up and submitted to the federal and state agencies. Agency comments were considered in developing the final plan. The primary objective of the mitigation plan was to replace the wildlife habitat that would be lost, by establishing a new wetland habitat of diverse structure and vegetation. The plan included drawings showing the site location, its existing topography, a proposed grading plan, cross-sections of the proposed topography, a proposed planting plan, and ground-level photographs. A narrative set forth the rationale for the mitigation, described the work necessary to implement the plans, proposed a schedule for the work, and described post-construction monitoring that would record and report the establishment of the new wetland plant community.

Mitigation Project Design

The conversion of the upland to wetland required removal of three to five feet of concrete and soil material to reach the elevation of the adjacent wetland forest. Five small depressions were designed, ranging from two to four feet lower in elevation than the general wetland surface. The deepest of the depressions were expected to intersect the permanent local water table, thus providing small areas of open water year-round. The shallower depressions and the pond margins were expected to support marsh vegetation. It was assumed that water elevations in the depressions would vary from season to season and from year to year. The remainder of the new wetland was expected to support a mixture of planted and volunteer herbs and shrubs with a few trees around the outer margins. The plantings were to consist of a mixed stand of herbs and shrubs, with the long-term expectation that trees may invade to make most of the wetland into a forest.

Within the wetlands of the surrounding industrial complex, shrub-covered wetlands are not abundant, so a particular goal was to install numerous shrubs in the new wetland. The objective was to establish a diverse new vegetation on the land surface rapidly and then allow it to grow on its own without further maintenance.

Attainment of the wildlife habitat function was considered to be achievable and not in conflict with other wetland functions. Other functions were judged to be insignificant here. Excavation of the land surface did increase the flood storage potential of the floodplain site, but this function was not considered important because the property already is isolated from normal and high water levels in the Delaware River by dikes and tide gates. The additional storage volume provided during 100-year storms was judged inconsequential in comparison to the volume of the nearby Atlantic Ocean. Likewise, water quality was not a significant design consideration. Virtually all runoff from the mitigation area is captured on-site in its ponds and depressions. The key water quality functions are being provided by the wastewater treatment plant. The remote location of the new wetland within the secure industrial plant renders it virtually inaccessible to people.

Implementation of Mitigation Plan

The small trees covering the site were chipped and stockpiled for use as mulch. Stumps were collected and placed in two piles to serve as hibernacula, that is, as winter habitat for reptiles. The meager topsoil that was available was stockpiled and spread across the site after excavation. The entire mitigation area was surrounded with a 12-foot tall, chain-link fence to prevent rapid destruction of the plantings by the abundant white-tailed deer. Silt fencing was installed surrounding the excavation site in accordance with the approved soil erosion and sediment control plan. The building rubble and excess subsoil materials were conveyed to an on-site landfill within the industrial complex.

Site preparation began in late August and was completed in October. The deeper depressions exhibited open water as soon as they were dug. The first volunteer narrow-leaf cat-tail seedlings were observed within about three weeks of the creation of the new ponded areas. Accordingly, no effort was made to plant cat-tails, although they had been on the list of species planned for propagation. The cat-tails spread vigorously in the shallow marsh depression over the next couple of seasons. Presumably the seeds were brought in by local waterfowl. Muskrat consumption of the cat-tails began soon after they became established.

More than 1,500 potted shrubs and trees were planted in November. Shrubs included species already present in the surrounding wetlands, such as silky dogwood, southern arrow-wood, common buttonbush, false indigo-bush, crimson-eyed rose-mallow, and American elderberry. A few individuals of the locally common trees were planted, such as red maple, pin oak, and black willow. Other shrubs and trees not reported on-site, but typical of regional wetlands, also were planted to ensure an array of wildlife food sources: black chokeberry, common winter berry, Maryland wild sensitive-plant, steeplebush, Virginia sweet spire, eastern red-cedar, Atlantic white-cedar, red mulberry, swamp white oak, willow oak, and slippery elm. Wood chips stockpiled on-site were used to mulch the woody plantings, and several truckloads of municipal leaf compost were used to supplement the wood chips. A fertilizer tablet was supplied to each of the potted plants at the time it was set out. The shrubs were planted in randomized clumps.

About 300 potted herbs were planted individually, such as harlequin blueflag, swamp loosestrife, wool-grass, and narrow burr-reed. (Such native wetland plants have become increasingly available commercially during the past decade.) In addition, about 10 pounds of seed mix collected from wild marshes during the summer also were spread as soon as the woody plantings had been made in the autumn. The mix contained species such as sallow sedge, blunt spike-rush, purple-leaf willow-herb, Atlantic manna grass, Canadian rush, smartweeds, tearthumbs, wool-grass, and soft-stem bulrush.

Post-Construction Monitoring

Monitoring of the new wetland proceeded for the next three annual growing seasons, as mandated by permit conditions, with written, annual reports to the responsible agencies. Very little maintenance was performed during the years of wetland establishment. Individuals of non-native tree-of-heaven growing near the wetland were cut to reduce the chance of their seedlings becoming established in the newly planted site. Scattered common reed plants were noticed on the margins of the marsh depressions during the third and fourth growing seasons, so they were sprayed individually using a backpack sprayer in early September of those years. No massive invasion of common reed was experienced, and this species is expected to remain an insignificant component of the flora of the new wetland. Some sprouts of white poplar around the margins of the wetland were pulled by hand. In general, the target plants appeared to be outcompeting the unwanted plants, and no massive intervention was warranted.

For the final monitoring report, a survey of the vegetation was made during August of the third growing season. The living plants were deemed to cover 90 percent of the land surface, with only a few areas where the wood chips were not hidden by dense greenery. The total number of species recorded was 140. The overwhelming preponderance of the vegetation consisted of native hydrophytes, with only minimal invasion by undesirable exotics deemed capable of sustained persistence.

About 82 percent of the kinds of plants observed in the mitigation area are listed as hydrophytes by the National Wetland Inventory, with half of the recorded species classed as facultative (FAC) or wetter in the northeast region. The dominant species were plants of very wet habitats (obligate and wet facultative species), such as cat-tail, sallow sedge, common rush, purple-leaf willowherb, American elderberry, silver maple, black gum, green ash, swamp white oak, pin oak, and black willow. Tall pussy willow and black willow had become 10 feet tall; many false indigo-bush were six feet tall and fruiting heavily. The slower growing green ash and swamp white oak, although only four feet tall, were obviously vigorous. Many shrubs displayed basal sprouts even though there had been no pruning, and none were "top-heavy". Volunteer recruitment seedlings of pin oak, black gum, sweet-gum, red maple, black cherry, and southern arrow-wood appeared healthy.

American water-plantain and blunt spike-rush were vigorous beneath the cat-tails around the ponds. Sallow sedge and common rush were the premier dominants of the seasonally saturated wetlands, where, along with wool-grass and sweet wood-reed, they are expected to outcompete weedy oldfield herbs. Substantial populations of seven species of sedge and three species of smartweed were observed. Most of the shrubs and herbs were fruiting heavily, providing abundant food for birds and other wildlife.

Mortality of the woody plantings over the three years of monitoring was less than 10 percent. The initial planting of Atlantic white-cedar was not successful, and all of the individuals died out during the second growing season. A new planting of 30 potted white-cedars was made in the spring of the third season. Several of these white-cedars have survived for three additional seasons, have increased several feet in height, and appear healthy.

Success of the Mitigation Project

The success of wetland creation at this mitigation site was confirmed during field visits within or after the third growing season by representatives of the New Jersey Department of Environmental Protection and the U.S. Fish and Wildlife Service. The objectives laid out in the mitigation plan were achieved. Target grades were appropriate. A water supply was assured for hydrologic support of the wetland. Species planted were suitable. The diversity of plants is high. The target vegetation continues to flourish. The wetland habitat that was created is being used by waterfowl and other birds, reptiles, amphibians, insects, and small mammals. No future monitoring is anticipated.

This mitigation project was a success because the created wetland was:

- Sited properly, adjacent to existing wetlands.
- Designed by professionals familiar with the surrounding ecosystem.
- Graded in accordance with the approved plans to provide the requisite hydrology.

- Planted with suitable native plants.
- Protected from interference by people and browsing mammals during the early years of its establishment.

The new wetland can be expected to persist indefinitely. From the experience at this mitigation site it was concluded that the number of woody plants installed (one per 30 square feet on average) could be reduced somewhat at comparable sites in the future without adverse effects.

CASE STUDY 2: CREATION OF TIDAL WETLAND

The second example of wetland mitigation involves the creation of a brackish tidal marsh along a backbarrier estuary. The mitigation was small and typifies requirements in the highly regulated coastal zone. It also illustrates the kinds of problems that can beset mitigation efforts in areas densely settled by people.

Background and Setting

In this case, the mitigation was required as compensation for dredging along the shoreline of an artificial lagoon near Barnegat Bay in coastal New Jersey. The dredging had been performed during the construction of a residential subdivision whose sponsor later went bankrupt. In order for the bank to sell the remaining three acres of property for completion of the approved development, it was necessary to secure approval after-the-fact for the dredging.

The unauthorized dredging had removed about 2,500 square feet of previously dredged, intertidal shallows adjacent to a bulkhead to enable small boats to access the bulkhead. About 10 to 15 percent of the shallows may have supported common reed marsh. As mitigation, the regulatory agencies required the establishment of new tidal marsh at a 2:1 acreage ratio for the entire disturbed area. Both federal and state approvals were required to legalize the dredging and to authorize four proposed small, private docks and moorings. The state enforcement staffers were the regulators primarily concerned with the mitigation design and implementation.

Design/Implementation of Mitigation Plan

Several alternative concepts for the mitigation were considered. Restoration of shallows and marsh in-situ was not desired by the landowner, because it would limit boat access to the lagoon from the adjacent waterfront homesites. Offshore docks could not be utilized because the lagoon was not wide enough to accommodate the boats without conflict with existing moorings on the opposite shoreline.

Alternate locations for a new marsh were available on-site along an undeveloped peninsula next to the bulkhead and docks. Several configurations were discussed with the state regulators, each of which would entail the replacement of fill previously dredged from the lagoon shoreline in order to provide a suitable substrate for new fringe marsh. The new marsh would offer a measure of protection to the eroding shoreline of the lagoon. The most practicable of three such configurations was proposed to the state in a formal review of alternatives with text and conceptual graphics showing details of the proposed marsh construction.

Upon further review, the state regulators then decided that the new marsh should be constructed, not by returning fill to the dredged lagoon, but by excavation of upland within the peninsula (a concept that they previously had rejected). The landowner was agreeable, inasmuch as the on-land construction was deemed to be much simpler to accomplish than returning fill to the lagoon. The site of the excavation was to be an old berm where several feet of fill had been placed many years before. The long, narrow cut was to be connected to tidal flow at two locations, with an intervening, wooded upland left in place for shoreline stabilization.

The target elevation and the plantings were modeled on a natural marsh about 500 feet away across the lagoon. That marsh supports primarily saltwater cord grass and narrow-leaf cat-tail, with patches of common reed. The state regulators mandated saltwater cord grass and salt-meadow cord grass for the new marsh, with a fringe of highbush blueberry shrubs around the margin.

The area was excavated in December using a conventional backhoe. Commercially grown, peat-potted cord grass acclimated to the measured salinity of the local estuary was planted in mid-April, and nursery-grown blueberry shrubs were installed in early May. During the first growing season no mortality was experienced among the shrubs, and the saltwater

172 / WETLAND MITIGATION

cord grass culms grew three feet tall. No predation by waterfowl or other wildlife was experienced. The adequacy of the design and implementation of the project was confirmed.

Human Disturbance of Mitigation Site

In part of the new marsh, however, survival of the plantings was significantly impaired by the vandalism performed by local youths. Several of the grass rootstocks were pulled within two weeks of planting, and others were pulled throughout the season. Minor earthwork using hand tools to manipulate tidal flows began in the winter and proceeded throughout the growing season, denuding the tidal inlets of their planted vegetation. A large treehouse was built adjacent to the marsh, and miscellaneous debris repeatedly was discarded into the new wetland. Obviously, the new marsh was an attractive playsite.

Fencing was not considered to be an effective means of protecting the new marsh. No replacement of the pulled plantings was deemed warranted prior to construction and occupation of the adjacent homes, at which time unauthorized entry onto the property would be expected to decline. However carefully designed and built, newly planted wetlands cannot withstand deliberate destruction by humans.

CASE STUDY 3: PAYMENT OF FEE IN-LIEU OF MITIGATION

The third case study illustrates how a fee payment in-lieu of mitigation may be accepted by regulators in those situations where no mitigation site is found to be available. This case involves the construction of major petroleum product pipelines which had to cross 500 feet of a wetland along a tidal tributary of the Delaware River. Three hundred linear feet of the pipeline crossing at the tributary were constructed beneath the tributary's tidal marsh using directional drilling, the same technique that was used to install the lines beneath the Delaware River itself. This technique minimizes the impact of pipeline construction on wetlands by installing the pipes beneath the surface, without the need to open and backfill a trench. At the edge of the tidal marsh, however, a 0.4-acre wetland supporting a red maple forest required disturbance. In the applications for state and federal permits for the project, restoration of all the wetland forest was anticipated after the pipeline was installed.

As is typical of individual freshwater wetland permits in New Jersey, the restoration was conditioned to begin prior to the authorized wetland disturbance and to be completed concurrent with the rest of the construction project. During construction the permittee found it would be necessary to maintain 0.25 acre of forested wetland as permanent right-of-way devoid of trees, and requested a permit modification. (The temporarily disturbed, 0.4 acre of wetland forest still was to be restored.) The state required mitigation for the 0.25 acre of wetland to be permanently disrupted for pipeline maintenance.

The permittee examined its landholdings and could not identify a practicable site for creation of replacement wetlands in the vicinity. The permittee also did not find adjacent landowners willing to sell a small parcel of land for wetland creation or enhancement nearby. The permittee's request to contribute cash to the state in lieu of actual mitigation was supported by the Department of Environmental Protection, which concurred that there were no practicable on-site or nearby alternatives for the mitigation.

Hence the permittee proposed a cash donation to the New Jersey Wetlands Mitigation Council. For several years the Council has been accumulating funds in an escrow account. The funds are to be used to support wetland creation and restoration in New Jersey.

Pursuant to state statute, the amount of a cash contribution to the Council for wetland mitigation in New Jersey is to be based on the lesser of the cost of providing a replacement wetland of equal ecological value and of at least equivalent acreage through either the creation of a new wetland or the enhancement of an existing wetland that has experienced past degradation. The permittee's design consultants calculated the amount of the contribution in several ways. The lowest of their estimates was accepted by the Council as the basis for a cash payment. The elements included in the calculations for the pipeline mitigation cost are of interest, inasmuch as they offer the most clearly articulated basis for a cash donation approved to date in New Jersey. They show a typical breakdown of construction costs incurred when creating new wetlands or enhancing existing, degraded wetlands. At the time, the New Jersey Department of Environmental Protection required wetland creation at a 2:1 acreage ratio and enhancement at a 3:1 acreage ratio; currrently both are required at 2:1.

Calculation of Fee Payment

The elements used by the permittee's consultants to derive the cost estimates for wetland creation were based on a number of assumptions regarding a hypothetical, but realistic, mitigation project. The requisite land acquisition would have to be one acre to accommodate the new wetland, a construction staging and soil stockpile area, and long-term access easement close to some part of the pipeline right-of-way. The average existing surface elevation in the new wetland would have to be lowered by one foot to achieve the necessary wetness. After the topsoil was removed and stockpiled, the new wetland would be graded to provide a new surface one third below, one third at, and one third above the water table. After 1.5 feet of subsoil on average have been removed from the site, 0.5 foot of new topsoil would be imported, mixed with the original topsoil, and spread across the newly shaped surface. No significant grading would be required for an access road. Erosion control would consist of a silt fence and temporary basin for dewatering activities. Topsoil would be available within a three-mile radius of the wetland. To create a forested wetland, trees would be planted on 15-foot centers.

Cost Estimate #1

The permittee's cost breakdown for construction of 0.5 acre of replacement wetland consists of land, design, construction, monitoring, and bonding components. As usual, earthwork accounts for the largest share of the total, even given the assumption that a site where only one foot of surface lowering is required can be secured.

Creation Item	**1995 Dollars**
Site Acquisition (1 acre)	5,852
Closing Costs (land survey)	1,600
Subtotal, Land	7,452 (14%)
Site Tests (soil depth, water table)	
5 @ 130	650

Soil Tests (agronomic analyses)	
4 @ 258	1,032
Topographic Survey (32 hr @ 54)	1,728
Layout (60 hr @ 50)	3,000
Specifications (24 hr @ 60)	1,440
Borrow Areas (24 hr @ 60)	1,440
Planting Design (16 hr @ 50)	800
Erosion Control (16 hr @ 80)	1,280
Meeting with State Regulators (12 hr @ 60)	720
Subtotal, Design	12,090 (22%)
Mobilization (land survey)	1,500
Construction Survey (4 hr @ 90)	360
Erosion Control (400 ft @ 4)	1,600
Clearing, Grubbing (0.5 ac @ 3,000)	1,500
Stockpile Topsoil (200 c.y. @ 5)	1,000
Export Excess Material (600 c.y. @ 8)	4,800
Site Dewatering (3 day @ 200)	600
Final Site Grading (600 c.y. @ 1.75)	1,050
Purchase, Place Topsoil (1,300 sq. yd. @ 6)	7,800
On-site Supervision (24 hr @ 60)	1,440
Tree Planting (100 @ 45)	4,500
Wetland Grass Planting (5,000 s.f. @ .20)	1,000
30-day Maintenance (32 hr @ 30)	960
Subtotal, Construction	28,110 (51%)
Monthly Monitoring (6 visits, 4 hr @ 75)	1,800
Annual Inspection, Report (5 @ 640)	3,200
Annual Maintenance (5 @ 360)	1,800
Subtotal, Monitoring & Maintenance	6,800 (12%)
Construction Bond (@ 1.2%)	337
Maintenance Bond (@ 0.4%)	112
Subtotal, Bonding	449 (1%)
Total, 0.5-Acre Wetland Creation	54,901 (100%)

The cost of $55,000 to create half an acre of new wetlands is realistic in terms of this author's experience on other projects in the Delaware Valley. It is premised on a very modest, one-foot deep lowering of the mitigation area surface, and sites needing so little alteration may be hard to obtain. Per-acre costs typically decline somewhat as the size of the wetland creation project increases because of economies of scale in design and supervision of the work. Per-acre wetland mitigation costs for highway projects in the mid-Atlantic states have often exceeded $110,000 per acre, and the success of the mitigation has not been closely correlated with cost.

Cost Estimate #2

The pipeline permittee also estimated the cost of enhancing degraded wetlands. In a scenario similar to that of the creation just described, the elements were broken out as follows, assuming the availability of a degraded wetland cleared of trees and filled one foot deep, to be enhanced by removal of fill and replanting:

Enhancement Item	**1995 Dollars**
Site Acquisition	7,800
Closing Costs	1,125
Subtotal, Land	8,925 (27%)
Environmental Design	1,500
Environmental Analysis, Report	1,200
Engineering Design	3,375
Soil Erosion Permit Fee	300
Subtotal, Design and Permit	6,375 (19.3%)
Excavation	3,000
Grading	750
Stabilization (seeding)	1,530
Tree Planting (144 @ 45)	6,480
Environmental Supervision (21 d @ 150)	3,150
Subtotal, Construction	14,910 (45%)
Annual Maintenance, Monitoring	2,400
Subtotal, Monitoring	2,400 (7.2%)
Construction Bond (1.1%)	360
Maintenance Bond (0.4%)	150
Subtotal, Performance Bonds	510 (1.5%)
Total, 0.75 Acre Wetland Enhancement	33,120 (100%)

Cost Estimate #3

An alternate calculation of enhancement cost was provided by the permittee, based on typical New Jersey wetland real estate values and the average cost per acre to enhance forested wetlands as reported in a recent survey of mitigation projects compiled at the University of Maryland. This calculation was broken down as follows:

Enhancement Item	**1995 Dollars**
Land (0.75 ac @ 2,600)	1,950 (3%)
Enhancement (0.75 ac @ 77,900)	58,425 (97%)
Total, 0.75-Acre Wetland Enhancement	60,375 (100%)

The permittee's offer of $33,120, based on the lowest calculated cost of 3:1 wetland enhancement, was accepted by the New Jersey Wetland Mitigation Council. The cash donation also satisfied the federal wetland permit issued by the Army Corps of Engineers. The Corps did not require any other form of mitigation for the 0.25 acre of forested wetland converted into maintained pipeline right-of-way.

As a percentage of a major pipeline project's construction cost, the cash contribution for the small amount of wetland mitigation required here was a minor cost element. In the context of a small construction project, however, such mitigation costs can be prohibitive when combined with the associated costs of securing the necessary permits.

Pennsylvania Mitigation Guidelines Concerning Cash Contributions

Recognizing the difficulty and expense posed by mitigation for small acreages of wetland losses, the Commonwealth of Pennsylvania recently established a fee schedule for cash contributions. As in New Jersey, the permittee in Pennsylvania is expected to avoid and minimize wetland impacts insofar as possible. Where unavoidable impacts are more than 0.05 acre but do not exceed 0.5 acre, the compensatory mitigation fee is assessed at rates equivalent to $5,000 to $18,000 per acre of wetlands disturbed. The higher rates apply as the impacts become larger within the allowable range. Impacts smaller than 0.05 acre are not required to be mitigated, and impacts larger than 0.5 acre at present cannot be mitigated by cash contribution. The permittee is supposed to provide on-site mitigation if feasible, before resorting to a cash contribution.

Thus, were the 0.25-acre pipeline impact on wetlands to occur in Pennsylvania today, the required compensation would be $2,500. Although land values in rural Pennsylvania typically are lower than those in New Jersey, it remains to be seen whether sufficient compensatory mitigation can be constructed by the state using only the revenues generated by the mitigation fee schedule to meet the state's regulatory goal of 1:1 replacement for each permitted loss. There is no mechanism to assure that the state's mitigation will be sited in the same watersheds where the construction impacts are located. It is not clear that the construction permit mitigation fees will significantly expand wetland improvements that were already being undertaken by other programs. New Jersey also currently lacks plans for specific wetland replacement using its more realistic escrow funds generated by wetland permittees.

Pennsylvania also recently established a voluntary registry for landowners who would like to see wetlands created on their property. Their names are to be passed along to permittees who need sites for mitigation. Terms for purchase or conservation easement on the land for a mitigation area must be negotiated by the permittee with the landowner. It is not known whether landowners seeking wetlands and permittees seeking mitigation will coincide geographically, but the registry is a simple and positive step.

CASE STUDY 4: WETLAND MITIGATION BANK

The fourth case study describes the establishment of a wetland mitigation bank through preservation of an existing ecosystem, rather than through the more common physical intervention used to restore, create, or enhance wetlands. Opportunities for preservation banks are expected to prove limited, although this particular bank was deemed appropriate by environmental groups and by regulators. This was the first major wetland mitigation bank to secure final approval in New Jersey. It was not initiated by any specific construction project that needed mitigation.

Background

Unlike project specific plans for compensatory mitigation, wetland mitigation banks typically are not motivated by any particular construction project. Bank sponsors do, however, look to construction projects for sales of the credits they amass. In sharp contrast to the one-time needs of construction project sponsors for mitigation that they can implement quickly, monitor for a few years, and then forget, the managers of mitigation banks must have a long-term horizon focused on the bank itself. Bank credit is not fully awarded until a bank has been established successfully.

In this case, a large tract of uplands and wetlands had been acquired thirty years earlier for future use as a wellfield for an industrial facility, but its water supply proved to be unnecessary and was never utilized. Recognizing that the property already exhibited extraordinary environmental value, the owner decided to enhance the value of the land as a corporate asset by making it into a mitigation bank fully protected against future development, rather than opening it to subdivision and development. A more typical course for mitigation bank establishment involves securing the permit for a bank, then creating new wetlands and/or enhancing degraded wetlands to establish the bank's credit (in advance of using the credit), and finally marketing the credit to permittees who need off-site mitigation. The specific characteristics of this particular bank warranted preservation.

Location and Description of Bank Site

A conceptual proposal was prepared and submitted to the New Jersey Department of Environmental Protection and to the New Jersey Wetlands Mitigation Council. These agencies are charged with implementing the mitigation bank provisions of the New Jersey Freshwater Wetlands Protection Act of 1987.

The plan identified the location and nature of the land proposed for the bank, its history, zoning, and likely future uses in the absence of bank establishment. It laid out a rationale for the bank, articulating its targeted benefits, long-term ownership, and compatibility with open space preservation efforts in the surrounding vicinity.

The land consists of more than 1,000 acres along three miles of the upper Maurice River and its tributaries. The Maurice River is a designated wild and scenic waterway in southwestern New Jersey that discharges to Delaware Bay. The location is a rural area in the Pine Barrens of the Outer Coastal Plain but outside the regulatory boundary of the Pinelands National Reserve. The watershed is within the Delaware Bayshore Ecosystem, one of the few areas nationwide selected by The Nature Conservancy for its "Last Great Places" land acquisition efforts. The wetlands of the Maurice River drainage have been designated as "priority wetlands" by the U.S. Environmental Protection Agency, rendering them ineligible for certain statewide general fill permits.

The surrounding region long had a very small proportion of its land in public open space, although recent and ongoing efforts have increased the nearby holdings both of conservation organizations and of state agencies using Green Acres bond funds. The subject land is near the center of a major Environmentally Sensitive Planning Area corridor established by the 1992 State Development and Redevelopment Plan.

The property itself consists of two large tracts of virtually unbroken, nearly impenetrable, forest and marsh averaging about 0.5 to 1 mile wide along the River. Nearly half of the property is wetland, situated in the lower elevations closest to the waterway. The outer margins are uplands. The wild ecosystems have recovered to a considerable extent from uses such as logging and cranberry cultivation in the distant past, and are in as near to pristine condition as any lands in New Jersey. The uplands support typical Pine Barrens pitch pine and mixed oak forests that have not burned in recent decades. The wetlands are home to Atlantic white-cedar stands as well as typical, red maple-dominated, deciduous forest. The habitats generally are suitable for rare and protected species of plants and animals, but no populations of endangered species were confirmed as dwelling there. A small part of manmade Willow Grove Lake is included in the bank.

The ongoing construction of new residential subdivisions adjacent to the bank property bore clear testimony to the stimulus for development posed by recent expressway construction. Large farms nearby recently had been acquired by residential developers. At present, more than half of the bank property is afforded some measure of state and/or federal regulatory protection as wetlands, other waters, or wetland fringe transition areas. Were the bank land to have been sold on the open market, the conversion of most of its uplands into rural-fringe suburbia was nearly inevitable.

The development of these uplands would necessarily bring degradation to the adjacent wetlands. Obviously, development would result in the fragmentation of the large, unbroken upland forest corridor next to the wetlands, reducing the habitat value of the wetlands for creatures accustomed to moving back and forth between wetlands and uplands. The uplands serve to buffer the wetlands from human activities. The coarse sands of the Outer Coastal Plain, however, offer minimal buffering to the waterway from any pollutants released into the soil. Hence, waterborne pollutants from the uplands next to the wetlands can travel virtually unimpaired to the Maurice River itself. These concerns motivated keen interest on the part of the agencies and conservation interests in the permanent protection of the land in its current state and thus in the potential designation of the property as a bank.

Bank Establishment

The wetlands and uplands proposed for the Maurice River bank were considered to be already at maximal ecological value, and no alteration was considered appropriate. Any credit allocated to the bank for use in mitigating wetland damage elsewhere would derive from the execution of a conservation easement formally precluding future development of the land and guaranteeing its permanent preservation.

The technical question arose as to how much mitigation credit would be allowed for the bank. In New Jersey, mitigation by creation of replacement wetlands is required at an acreage ratio of two acres created for each acre of authorized fill. Mitigation by enhancement of existing, degraded wetlands at the time was required at an acreage ratio of at least three acres enhanced for each acre of authorized fill. There are no clear acreage ratios for preservation as a means of wetland mitigation, but a discount is required in recognition of the fact that no new wetland values are being added to offset those lost. (Permanently deed-restricted wetlands are not subject to future changes in environmental laws or regulatory policy and, thus, are more stringently protected than wetlands unprotected by enforceable deed restrictions.)

Available federal agency guidance suggested that mitigation credit might be allowed at ratios of 10:1 to 25:1 for preservation of ecologically important wetlands. The few prior New Jersey wetland preservation cases (not associated with mitigation banks) had included preservation of wetlands at ratios of as much as 200:1 for small fills. The Maurice River bank calculation was complicated by the presence of both uplands and wetlands within the bank lands.

Upon recommendation of the Department of Environmental Protection, the New Jersey Wetlands Mitigation Council approved 40 acres of fill as the credit for the Maurice River mitigation bank, approximately a ratio of 25:1 for the property as a whole. The service area for the bank is limited to the Delaware River drainage basin. The bank owner must account to the state annually for any credits allocated to permittees who need to mitigate for wetland disturbance.

The bank itself was implemented by execution of a conservation easement, which was duly recorded against the deed for the land. Both the bank credits and the land itself were donated to The Nature Conservancy, which expects to hold the property for the foreseeable future. The new owner has the options of: (1) marketing the credits to raise funds for its conservation projects, (2) exchanging credits for parcels of land elsewhere that it deems important for conservation, (3) using the credits as incentives to influence the location or design of future construction projects by others within the service area, and (4) retiring the credits unused.

ACHIEVING SUCCESSFUL WETLAND MITIGATION

Looking back over a quarter of a century of work in wetlands, chiefly in those of the mid-Atlantic states, the author can offer some observations regarding the replacement of wetlands when mitigation is required by permit conditions.

Many kinds of wetlands can be replaced, if it is deemed essential that the land they occupy be used for purposes other than open space supporting wild ecosystems. The organisms that dwell in wetlands often demonstrate a remarkable ability to become established and develop after a relatively limited, short-term period of human intervention during which the physical parameters of a new wetland are established.

Many wetlands have flourished in the wake of disruptions and perturbations, both natural and man-made. Examples come readily to mind. Both changes in sea level and storms frequently disrupt coastlines by shifting dunes and by eroding and depositing sediments. Most tidal marsh species are precisely adjusted to the small differences in elevation that govern their tide-related fluxes of nutrients and oxygen. They are able to spread into open areas with suitable water regimes.

Inland, vast landscapes across the continent were plowed by glacial ice only a few thousand years ago. Once the ice melted, they had to be recolonized by plants and animals. Ever since the Amerindians came to North America, fire and other human interventions have been disrupting the biota of its wetlands as well as its uplands. Geomorphic processes such as oxbow cutoffs in floodplains shift the limits of wetlands and uplands, as do the activities of beavers. Nearly half the kinds of plants typically found in the wetlands of mid-Atlantic states can thrive in uplands as well as on sites where drainage is impeded (these are known as facultative hydrophytes). Even many of the obligate hydrophytes virtually always found in wetlands can tolerate the long dry periods that characterize wetland margins in dry years. In those regions where precipitation deficits are more common than surpluses, the inhabitants of scarce, protected, wetland oases must be able to survive cycles of drought. At best, their moisture is variable from year to year and decade to decade. Where wetlands dominate the landscape, sources for recolonizing plants and animals are never far from disturbed sites.

Some wetlands are scarce and are associated with uncommon environmental settings. One example would be oligotrophic bogs nourished only by rainwater on rare types of rocks. Another would be wetlands supporting old-growth trees of great age, which would take centuries to replicate. Such wetlands are less likely to be replaced successfully, and are best avoided altogether.

No natural ecosystems, however, whether wetland or upland, could survive the historic onslaught of urban and suburban land uses brought to North America by the Europeans, nor their agricultural practices in rural areas. Most wetland forests today at minimum show the effects of timber harvest for several centuries. Their communities of plants and animals have been able to tolerate human activities and to disperse into disturbed habitats. Otherwise, they would not have survived this long.

Hence, when necessary, it is possible today to relocate and restore many of the wetland ecosystems that have survived past disruptions. Regulatory agencies charged with protecting wetlands have recognized this fact for years, and occasionally have required that new wetlands be created by those needing to convert wetlands into other uses. Permittees have agreed to undertake wetland replacement when accepting conditional permit approvals. This enterprise is conceived as a short-term intervention aimed at jump-starting a new ecosystem, which then can maintain itself.

Past Efforts at Mitigation

In practice, however, the results of efforts to create new wetlands often have been disappointing. Some promised mitigation is never initiated, and the burden then shifts to the responsible regulatory agency to secure compliance with permit conditions. Inadequate attention may have been given during design to critical issues such as siting of the wetland or grading to achieve the essential hydrology. Opportunities for site adjustment may not have been incorporated into project design in cases of hydrologic uncertainty. Approved plans for mitigation may have been discarded or replaced after the permit was approved, with dramatic consequences for the viability of the proposed wetland. The unplanned deposit of sediment or rubbish may have reduced the values that the replacement wetland otherwise could provide.

Regulatory agencies have begun to learn that the primary attention of many permittees is focused on their own construction projects rather than the replacement wetlands they are required to provide as compensation to the public. The cost of wetland permits and mitigation always reduces the profit realized by permittees from new construction in wetlands. The priorities of regulators generally lie in processing new applications rather than scrutinizing compliance with the conditions of past approvals. This focus makes them even less likely than permittees to follow up and ensure the success of required mitigation.

There is a strong incentive for permittees to make cash contributions whenever possible. It is simpler to pay for mitigation implemented by an agency or by purchasing credit in a mitigation bank run by an entrepreneur focused on the wetland, rather than to undertake and supervise the design, construction, and monitoring of a new wetland for years and bear the risk of mitigation failure during the monitoring period. Hence, in theory, the cash purchase of mitigation from an agency or bank should command a premium as compared with the permittee's own wetland creation or enhancement, considering the convenience and absence of risk for the permittee.

Agencies, unlike permittees, typically prefer on-site mitigation, if space exists where wetlands can be replaced close to a fill site. Permittees are even more reluctant to purchase off-site land nearby for the purpose of wetland mitigation than to undertake mitigation on-site. It is more difficult for permittees and their consultants to find practicable sites suitable for wetland creation or enhancement than merely to compile a basis for dismissing off-site alternatives as a precondition for making a cash payment to a mitigation fund or bank. To date, wetland regulatory agencies have not required public notice of a permittee's need for localized mitigation sites or established a disclosure mechanism for landowners or realtors to learn when mitigation lands are being sought. Hence, project-specific searches for wetland mitigation sites often end in failure. No strong commitment to local mitigation has become established, and the growing availability of mitigation banks is unlikely to foster localized mitigation.

Detailed plans and specifications for wetland construction can be prepared by qualified professionals who understand wetland ecosystems. Performance bonds can be mandated that provide the financial means for agencies to complete successful mitigation projects if the work should be abandoned by permittees. Wetland construction and planting can be supervised by qualified personnel. Explicit performance standards can make clear in advance what conditions are acceptable in created wetlands. Successful wetland creation requires a willingness by permittees to comply with good management practices and a commitment by regulatory agencies to oversee compliance. It also requires adequate funding.

The promise of achieving successful wetland mitigation through the use of mitigation banks has received considerable attention during the past few years. Banks can be located where new wetlands most appropriately can be constructed, even though this may be at some distance from the sites of specific, unavoidable wetland impacts. Mitigation banks are run by land managers whose long-term incentive rests in the success of their wetland creation or enhancement efforts. If the promised values are not achieved, the credits are not allocated and cannot be sold to permittees.

Mitigation is Attainable

If permittees, regulators, politicians, and the public at large want successful wetland mitigation, it can be attained. Practical measures for wetland design and follow-up reporting significantly increase the likelihood that promised mitigation will be attempted and will achieve the objective of replacing lost wetland values. Improvements in the system have been slow and incremental, not glamorous, as agency after agency amends its regulations to ensure that promised mitigation is actually delivered. Native wetland plants for use in mitigation projects have become readily available commercially during the past fifteen years. Over time, increasing technical success can be expected from the design community.

Mitigation can be implemented successfully for many types of wetlands, if properly funded, planned, implemented, supervised, and monitored. The mitigation can be provided on-site, off-site, or in banks, as appropriate to each project. Wetland mitigation is not inexpensive, and its cost will remain an incentive for designers to recognize and avoid wetland incursions in many construction projects. But when expanding human populations and the need for new construction necessitate unavoidable incursions into wetlands, it is possible to maintain wetland values by relocating many kinds of wetland ecosystems. If wetland acreage is deliberately increased as a part of the permit process, it is possible that a net benefit ultimately may result.

Appendix A

U.S. EPA Wetland Offices

U.S. EPA OFFICE OF WETLANDS, OCEANS, AND WATERSHEDS (OWOW)

U.S. Environmental Protection Agency
Office of Water
Office of Wetlands, Oceans, and Watersheds
401 M Street, S.W.
Washington, DC 20460

>   Robert H. Wayland, III, Director
>   David G. Davis, Deputy Director
>   (202) 260-7166

U.S. Environmental Protection Agency
Wetlands Division (4502F)
401 M Street, S.W.
Washington, DC 20460

>   John Meagher, Director
>   Gregory E. Peck, Acting Deputy Director
>   (202) 260-7791
>   (202) 260-2356 (FAX)

Wetlands and Aquatic Resources Regulatory Branch
    Hazel A. Groman, Acting Chief
    (202) 260-1799
    (202) 260-7546 (FAX)

Wetlands Strategies and State Programs Branch
    Phil Oshida, Chief
    (202) 260-9043
    (202) 260-8000 (FAX)

EPA Wetlands Information Hotline
    (800) 832-7828

EPA REGIONAL WETLANDS CONTACTS

Region I: CT, MA, ME, NH, RI, VT

Douglas Thompson, Chief
Wetlands Protection Section (WWP-1900)
U.S. EPA - Region I
John F. Kennedy Federal Building
Boston, MA 02203-1911
    (617) 565-4421
    (617) 565-4940 (FAX)

Region II: NJ, NY, PR, VI

Daniel Montella, Chief
Wetlands Section (2WM-MWP)
U.S. EPA - Region II
26 Federal Plaza - Room 837
New York, NY 10278
    (212) 264-5170
    (212) 264-4690 (FAX)

Region III: DE, MD, PA, VA, WV

Barbara D'Angelo, Chief
Wetlands Protection Section (3ES42)
U.S. EPA - Region III
841 Chestnut Street
Philadelphia, PA 19107
   (215) 597-9301
   (215) 597-1850 (FAX)

Region IV: AL, FL, GA, KY, MS, NC, SC, TN

Tom Welborn, Chief
Wetlands Regulatory Section
U.S. EPA - Region IV
345 Courtland Street, N.E.
Atlanta, GA 30365
   (404) 347-4015
   (404) 347-3269 (FAX)

Region V: IL, IN, MI, MN, OH, WI

Douglas Ehorn, Chief
Wetlands and Watersheds Section (WQW-16J)
U.S. EPA - Region V
77 West Jackson Boulevard
Chicago, IL 60604
   (312) 886-0243
   (312) 886-7804 (FAX)

Region VI: AR, LA, NM, OK, TX

Beverly Ethridge, Chief
Wetlands Protection Section (6E-FT)
U.S. EPA - Region VI
1445 Ross Avenue - Suite 900
Dallas, TX 75202
   (214) 655-2263
   (214) 655-7446 (FAX)

Region VII: IA, KS, MO, NE

Gerry Shimek, Acting Chief
Wetlands Protection Section (ENRV)
U.S. EPA - Region VII
726 Minnesota Avenue
Kansas City, KS 66101
   (913) 551 -7540
   (913) 551-7863 (FAX)

Region VIII: CO, MT, ND, SD, UT, WY

Gene Reetz, Chief
Wetlands Protection Section (8WM-WQ)
U.S. EPA - Region VIII
999 18th Street
500 Denver Place
Denver, CO 80202-2405
   (303) 293-1570
   (303) 391-6957 (FAX)

Region IX: AZ, CA, HI, NV, Pacific Islands

Stephanie Wilson
Watersheds Protection Branch (W-7-4)
75 Hawthorne Street
San Francisco, CA 94105
   (415) 744-1968
   (415) 744-1078 (FAX)

Region X: AK, ID, OR, WA

William Riley, Chief
Wetlands Section (WD-128)
U.S. EPA - Region X
1200 6th Avenue
Seattle, WA 98101
   (206) 553-1412
   (206) 553-1775 (FAX)

Appendix B

Army Corps of Engineers Offices

U.S. ARMY CORPS OF ENGINEERS HEADQUARTERS

Michael L. Davis
Chief, Regulatory Branch (CECW-OR)
U.S. Army Corps of Engineers
20 Massachusetts Avenue, NW
Washington, DC 20314-1000
    (202) 272-1782
    (202) 504-5069 (FAX)

U.S. ARMY CORPS OF ENGINEERS DIVISION AND DISTRICT OFFICES

Please note that some states are within the jurisdiction of more than one divisional office because Corps' divisions are organized by watershed area and not by state boundary.

Lower Mississippi Valley Division

Arkansas, Illinois, Kentucky, Louisiana, Mississippi, Missouri, Tennessee

Susan Hampton
U.S. Army Corps of Engineers
Lower Mississippi Valley Division
(CELMV-CO-R)
P.O. Box 80
Vicksburg, MS 39180-0080
    (601) 634-5821

Memphis District

Larry D. Watson
U.S. Army Corps of Engineers
Memphis District (CELMM-CO-R)
B-202 Clifford Davis Federal Building
Memphis, TN 38103-1894
 (901) 544-3471

New Orleans District

Ronald J. Ventola
U.S. Army Corps of Engineers
New Orleans District (CELMN-OD-R)
P.O. Box 60267
New Orleans, LA 70160-0267
 (504) 862-225

St. Louis District

Michael Brazier
U.S. Army Corps of Engineers
St. Louis District (CELMS-OD-R)
1222 Spruce Street
St. Louis, MO 63103-2833
 (314) 331-8575

Vicksburg District

E. Guynes
U.S. Army Corps of Engineers
Vicksburg District (CELMK-OD-F)
2101 N. Frontage Road
Vicksburg, MS 39180-5191
 (601) 631-5276

Missouri River Division

Colorado, Iowa, Kansas, Missouri, Montana, Nebraska, North Dakota, South Dakota, Wyoming

Mores V. Bergman
U.S. Army Corps of Engineers
Missouri River Division
12565 W. Center Road
Omaha, NE 68144
    (402) 697-2533

Kansas City District

Mel Jewett
U.S. Army Corps of Engineers
Kansas City District (CEMRK-OD-R)
700 Federal Building
Kansas City, MO 64106-2896
    (816) 426-3545

Omaha District

John Morton
U.S. Army Corps of Engineers
Omaha District (CEMRO-OP-N)
215 North 17th Street
Omaha, NE 68102-4978
    (402) 221-4133

New England Division

Connecticut, Maine, Massachusetts, New Hampshire, Rhode Island, Vermont

William R. Lawless
U.S. Army Corps of Engineers
New England Division (CNEED-OD-P)
424 Trapelo Road
Waltham, MA 02254-9149
    (617) 647-8057

North Atlantic Division

Delaware, Maryland, New York, Pennsylvania, Vermont, Virginia, West Virginia

Lenny Kotkiewicz
U.S. Army Corps of Engineers
North Atlantic Division (CENAD-CO-OP)
90 Church Street
New York, NY 10007-9998
 (212) 264-7535

Baltimore District

Donald W. Roeseke
U.S. Army Corps of Engineers
Baltimore District (CENAB-OP-PN)
P.O. Box 1715
Baltimore, MD 31203-1715
 (410) 962-3670

New York District

Joseph Seebode
U.S. Army Corps of Engineers
New York District (CENAN-PL-E)
26 Federal Plaza
New York, NY 10278-0090
 (212) 264-3996

Norfolk District

William H. Poore, Jr.
U.S. Army Corps of Engineers
Norfolk District (CENAO-OP-N)
803 Front Street
Norfolk, VA 23510-1096
 (804) 441-7068

Philadelphia District

Frank Cianfrani
U.S. Army Corps of Engineers
Philadelphia District (CENAP-OP-N)
Wanamaker Building
100 Penn Square East
Philadelphia, PA 19107-3390
   (215) 656-6725

North Central Division

Illinois, Indiana, Iowa, Michigan, Minnesota, Missouri, North Dakota, Ohio, South Dakota, Wisconsin

Dr. Michael Loesch
U.S. Army Corps of Engineers
North Central Division (CENCD-CO-MO)
111 N. Canal Street, 12th FL
Chicago, IL 60606
   (312) 353-7762

Buffalo District

Paul G. Leuchner
U.S. Army Corps of Engineers
Buffalo District
1776 Niagara Street
Buffalo, NY 14207-3199
   (716) 879-4313

Chicago District

Mitchell Isoe
U.S. Army Corps of Engineers
Chicago District (CENCC-CO)
111 N. Canal Street, 6th FL
Chicago, IL 60606
   (312) 886-3555 or (312) 353-6428

Detroit District

Gary R. Mannesto
U.S. Army Corps of Engineers
Detroit District (CENCE-CO-OR)
P.O. Box 1027
Detroit, MI 48231-1027
   (313) 226-2432

Rock Island District

Steven J. Vander Horn
U.S. Army Corps of Engineers
Rock Island District (CENCR-OD-R)
P.O. Box 2004
Clock Tower Building
Rock Island, IL 61204-2004
   (309) 794-5370

St. Paul District

Ben Wopat
U.S. Army Corps of Engineers
St. Paul District (CENCS-SO-PO)
1421 USPO & Custom House
190 Fifth Street East
St. Paul, MN 55101-1638
   (612) 290-5376

North Pacific Division

Alaska, Idaho, Montana, Nevada, Oregon, Washington, Wyoming

Laura Kemp
U.S. Army Corps of Engineers
North Pacific Division (CENPD-CO-R)
P.O. Box 2870
Portland, OR 97208-2870
   (503) 326-3780

Alaska District

Robert K. Oja, Regulatory Branch
U.S. Army Corps of Engineers
Alaska District (CENPA-CO-NF)
P.O. Box 898
Anchorage, AK 99506-0898
   (907) 753-2712

Portland District

Burt Paynter
U.S. Army Corps of Engineers
Portland District (CENPP-OP-PN)
P.O. Box 2946
Portland, OR 97208-2946
   (503) 326-7146

Seattle District

Tom Mueller
U.S. Army Corps of Engineers
Seattle District (CENPS-OP-PO)
P.O. Box 3755
Seattle, WA 98124-2255
   (206) 764-6695

Walla Walla District

Brad Daly
U.S. Army Corps of Engineers
Walla Walla District (CENPW-OP-RM)
City-County Airport
Walla Walla, WA 99362-9265
   (509) 522-6720

Ohio River Division

Alabama, Georgia, Illinois, Indiana, Kentucky, North Carolina, Ohio, Pennsylvania, Tennessee, Virginia, West Virginia

Rodney Woods
U.S. Army Corps of Engineers
Ohio River Division (CEORD-CO-OR)
P.O. Box 1159
Cincinnati, OH 45201-1159
   (513) 684-6212

Huntington District

Mike Gheen
U.S. Army Corps of Engineers
Huntington District (CEORH-OR-F)
502 8th Street
Huntington, WV 25701-2070
   (304) 529-5487

Louisville District

William Christman
U.S. Army Corps of Engineers
Louisville District (CEORH-OR-R)
P.O. Box 59
Louisville, KY 40201-0059
   (502) 582-6461

Nashville District

Joseph R. Castleman
U.S. Army Corps of Engineers
Nashville District (CEORN-OR-R)
P.O. Box 1070
Nashville, TN 37202-1070
   (615) 736-5181

Pittsburgh District

E. Raymond Beringer
U.S. Army Corps of Engineers
Pittsburgh District (CEORP-OR-R)
1000 Liberty Avenue
Pittsburgh, PA 15222-4186
   (412) 644-6872

Pacific Ocean Division

Hawaii District

Mike Lee
U.S. Army Corps of Engineers
Pacific Ocean Division (CEPOD-CO-O)
Building 230
Fort Shafter, HI 96858-5440
   (808) 438-9258

South Atlantic Division

Virginia, North Carolina, South Carolina, Georgia, Florida, Alabama, Mississippi, Tennessee, Puerto Rico, U.S. Virgin Islands

James M. Kelly
U.S. Army Corps of Engineers
South Atlantic Division (CESAD-CO-R)
Room 313
77 Forsythe Street, S.W.
Atlanta, GA 30335-6801
   (404) 331-2778

Charleston District

Clarence H. Ham
U.S. Army Corps of Engineers
Charleston District (CESAC-CO-M)
P.O. Box 919
Charleston, SC 29402-0919
   (803) 727-4604

Jacksonville District

Dr. John Hall
U.S. Army Corps of Engineers
Jacksonville District (CESAJ-CO-OR)
400 West Bay Street
P.O. Box 4970
Jacksonville, FL 32232-0019
   (904) 232-2907

Mobile District

Ron Krizman
U.S. Army Corps of Engineers
Mobile District (CESAM-OP-R)
P.O. Box 2288
Mobile, AL 36628-0001
   (205) 690-2658

Savannah District

Nick Ogden
U.S. Army Corps of Engineers
Savannah District (CESAS-OP-R)
P.O. Box 889
Savannah, GA 31402-0889
   (912) 652-5347

Wilmington District

G. Wayne Wright
U.S. Army Corps of Engineers
Wilmington District (CESAW-CO-R)
P.O. Box 1890
Wilmington, NC 28402-1890
   (910) 251-4630

South Pacific Division

Arizona, California, Colorado, Idaho, Nevada, New Mexico, Oregon, Utah, Wyoming

Theodore E. Durst
U.S. Army Corps of Engineers
South Pacific Division (CESPD-CO-O)
630 Sansome Street, Room 1216
San Francisco, CA 94111-2206
   (415) 705-1443

Los Angeles District

John Gill
U.S. Army Corps of Engineers
Los Angeles District (CESPL-CO-O)
P.O. Box 2711
Los Angeles, CA 90053-2325
   (213) 894-5606

Sacramento District

Art Champ
U.S. Army Corps of Engineers
Sacramento District (CESPK-CO-R)
1325 J Street
Sacramento, CA 95814-2922
   (916) 557-5250

San Francisco District

Calvin C. Fong
U.S. Army Corps of Engineers
San Francisco District (CESPN-CO-O)
211 Main Street
San Francisco, CA 94105-1905
   (415) 744-3036 ext. 233

Southwestern Division

Arkansas, Colorado, Kansas, Louisiana, Missouri, New Mexico, Oklahoma, Texas

Vicki Dixon
U.S. Army Corps of Engineers
Southwestern Division (CESWD-CO-R)
1114 Commerce Street
Dallas, TX 75242-0216
   (214) 767-2436

Albuquerque District

Andrew J. Rosenau
U.S. Army Corps of Engineers
Albuquerque District (CESWA-CO-R)
P.O. Box 1580
Albuquerque, NM 87103-1508
   (505) 766-2776

Fort Worth District

Wayne A. Lea
U.S. Army Corps of Engineers
Forth Worth District (CESWF-OD-M)
P.O. Box 17300
Fort Worth, TX 76102-0300
   (817) 334-2681

Galveston District

Marcos De La Rosa
U.S. Army Corps of Engineers
Galveston District (CESWG-CO-MO)
P.O. Box 1229
Galveston, TX 77553-1229
  (409) 766-3930

Little Rock District

Louie C. Cockmon, Jr.
U.S. Army Corps of Engineers
Little Rock District (CESWL-CO-L)
P.O. Box 867
Little Rock, AR 72203-0867
  (501) 324-5296

Tulsa District

Dave Manning
U.S. Army Corps of Engineers
Tulsa District (CESWT-OD-R)
P.O. Box 61
Tulsa, OK 74121-0061
  (918) 669-7400

WATERWAYS EXPERIMENT STATION

Russell F. Theriot, Manager
Wetlands Research Program
U.S. Army Corps of Engineers
Waterways Experiment Station
Environmental Laboratory (CEWES-EL-W)
3909 Halls Ferry Road
Vicksburg, MS 39180-6199
  (601) 634-2733
  (601) 634-3528 (FAX)

Appendix C

State Wetland Offices

STATE WETLAND AGENCIES AND OFFICES

Alabama

Dept. of Economic and Community Affairs
P.O. Box 2939
Montgomery, AL 36105
   (205) 284-8774

Field Operations Division
Alabama Department of Environmental Management
1751 Con. W.L. Dickinson Drive
Montgomery, AL 36130
   (205) 271-7700

Environmental Scientist
Alabama Dept. of Environmental Management
2204 Perimeter Road
Mobile, AL 36615
   (205) 479-2336

California

Federal Programs Manager
California Coastal Commission
45 Fremont St., Suite 2000
San Francisco, CA 94105
   (415) 904-5200

Wetlands Task Force
California Coastal Commission
640 Capitola Road
Santa Cruz, CA 95062
   (408) 479-3511

Connecticut

Division of Inland Water Resource Management
Department of Environmental Protection
Room 207, State Office Building
165 Capital Avenue
Hartford, CT 06106
   (203) 566-7280

Delaware

Dept. of Natural Resources and Envt'l Control
89 King's Highway
P.O. Box 1401
Dover, DE 19903
   (302) 739-4691

Florida

Division of Water Management
Department of Environmental Regulation
Twin Towers Office Building
2600 Blair Stone Road
Tallahassee, FL 32399-2400
   (904) 488-0130

Georgia

Marsh and Beach Section
Coastal Resources Division
Department of Natural Resources
One Conservation Way
Brunswick, GA 31523
(912) 264-7218

Hawaii

Office of State Planning
Office of the Governor
P.O. Box 2540
Honolulu, HI 96811
(808) 587-2833

Iowa

Wildlife Bureau
Iowa Department of Natural Resources
Wallace State Office Building
East 9th and Grand
Des Moines, Iowa 50319
(515) 281-6156

Governmental Liaison Bureau
Iowa Department of Natural Resources
Wallace State Office Building
East 9th and Grand
Des Moines, Iowa 50319
(515) 281-8973

Maine

Division of Natural Resources
Department of Environmental Protection
State House, Station 17
Augusta, ME 04333
   (207) 289-2111

State Planning Office
184 State Street
Augusta, ME 04330
   (207) 289-3261

Maryland

Nontidal Wetlands Division
Water Resources Administration
Department of Natural Resources
Tawes State Office Building, E-2
Annapolis, MD 21401
   (301) 974-3841

Tidal Wetlands Division
Department of Natural Resources
Tawes State Office Building, D-4
Annapolis, MD 21401
   (301) 974-3871

Chesapeake Bay Critical Area Commission
275 West Street, Suite 320
Annapolis, MD 21401
   (301) 974-2426

Massachusetts

Division of Wetland and Waterways Regulations
Department of Environmental Protection
1 Winter Street
Boston, MA 02108
   (617) 767-5518

Michigan

Land and Water Protection Section
Land and Water Management Division
Department of Natural Resources
P.O. Box 30028
Lansing, MI 48909
   (517) 335-2694

Great Lakes Shorelands Management Section
Land and Water Management Division
Department of Natural Resources
P.O. Box 20038
Lansing, MI 48909
   (517) 373-1950

Minnesota

Protected Waters and Wetlands Permit Program
Department of Natural Resources
500 Lafayette Road - Box 32
St. Paul, MN 55155-4032
   (612) 296-4800

Board of Water and Soil Resources
155 South Wabash St., Suite 104
St. Paul, MN 55107
   (612) 296-0879

Mississippi

Coastal Management Section
Bureau of Marine Resources
Dept. of Wildlife Fisheries & Parks
2620 Beach Boulevard
Biloxi, MS 39531

New Hampshire

N.H. Department of Environmental Services
Wetlands Bureau
P.O. Box 2008
Concord, NH 03301
   (603) 271-2147

New Jersey

Bureau of Freshwater Wetlands
Division of Coastal Resources
Department of Environmental Protection
CN-401
501 East State Street
Trenton, NJ 08625
   (609) 984-0853

New York

Freshwater Wetlands Program Manager
Division of Fish & Wildlife
Department of Environmental Conservation
50 Wolf Road
Albany, NY 12233
   (518) 457-9713

Bureau of Marine Habitat
Marine Regulatory Division
Department of Environmental Conservation
Building 40
SUNY at Stony Brook
Stony Brook, NY 11749
   (516) 751-7900

Coastal Erosion Section
Department of Environmental Conservation
50 Wolf Road
Albany, NY 12233
   (518) 457-3157

North Carolina

Division of Coastal Management
Dept. of Environment, Health, & Natural Resources
P.O. Box 27687
Raleigh, NC 27611
   (919) 733-2293

Oregon

Wetlands Program Manager
Division of State Lands
775 Summer Street, N.E.
Salem, OR 97310
　　(503) 378-3805

Pennsylvania

Division of Rivers and Wetlands Conservation
Department of Environmental Resources
Environmental Review Section
Technical Assistance and Education Section
P.O Box 8761
Harrisburg, PA 17105-8761
　　(717) 541-7803

Division of Waterway and Storm Waters Management
Bureau of Dams and Waterway Management
Department of Environmental Resources
One Ararat Boulevard, Room 149
Harrisburg, PA 17110
　　(717) 541-7904

Rhode Island

Division of Freshwater Wetlands
Department of Environmental Management
291 Promenade Street
Providence, RI 02908-6820
　　(410) 277-6820

South Carolina

Executive Director
South Carolina Coastal Council
AT&T Capital Center
1201 Main Street, Suite 1520
Columbia, SC 29201
   (803) 737-0881

Permit Administrator
South Carolina Coastal Council
4130 Faber Place
Charleston, SC 29405
   (803) 744-5838

Vermont

Wetlands Coordinator
Water Quality Division
Department of Environmental Conservation
10-North Building
103 South Main Street
Waterbury, VT 05676

Virginia

Habitat Management Division
Marine Resources Commission
P.O. Box 756
Newport News, VA 23607
   (804) 247-2200

Washington

Wetlands Management and Planning Section
Department of Ecology
State of Washington
P.O. Box 47600
Olympia, WA 98504-7600
 (206) 459-6790

Wisconsin

Water Regulation Section
Bureau of Water Regulation and Zoning
Department of Natural Resources
P.O. Box 7921
Madison, WI 53707
 (608) 266-7360

Appendix D

Clinton Administration's Wetlands Plan

*PROTECTING AMERICA'S WETLANDS:
A FAIR, FLEXIBLE,
AND EFFECTIVE APPROACH*

WHITE HOUSE OFFICE
ON ENVIRONMENTAL POLICY

August 24th, 1993

TABLE OF CONTENTS

I. Introduction

II. A Divisive Debate

III. The Interagency Working Group on Federal Wetlands Policy

IV. Five Principles for Federal Wetlands Policy

V. A Comprehensive Package of Reforms

    A. Addressing Landowner Concerns
    B. Advance Planning and Watershed Management
    C. Agriculture
    D. Categorization
    E. Geographic Jurisdiction
    F. Mitigation and Mitigation Banking
    G. Restoration
    H. Roles of Federal Agencies
    I. Roles of State, Tribal, and Local Government
    J. Scope of Regulated Activities
    K. State of Alaska
    L. Takings

VI. Conclusion

VII. Postscript: Lessons From the Flood

I. INTRODUCTION

The Clinton Administration is proposing a comprehensive package of improvements to the Federal wetlands program that reflects a new broad-based consensus among Federal agencies. For years, many have argued that the Federal government badly needed to improve its wetlands program to make it fairer and more effective. But for too long, contradictory policies from feuding Federal agencies have blocked progress, creating uncertainty and confusion. This wetlands package reflects a sharp break through the past gridlock caused by warring Federal agencies and contains a balanced, common sense, workable set of improvements that will make the program simpler, fairer, better coordinated with state and local efforts and more effective at protecting wetlands.

The Nation's wetlands perform many functions that are important to society, such as improving water quality, recharging groundwater, providing natural flood control, and supporting a wide variety of fish, wildlife and plants. The economic importance of wetlands to commercial fisheries and recreational uses is also enormous. The Nation has lost nearly half of the wetland acreage that existed in the lower 48 States prior to European settlement. The Nation's wetlands continue to be lost at a rate of hundreds of thousands of acres per year due to both human activity and natural processes. This continued loss occurs at great cost to society.

Notwithstanding the importance of wetland resources, efforts to protect wetlands have caused considerable controversy. It is estimated that 75 percent of the Nation's wetlands in the lower 48 States are located on private property. It is, therefore, imperative to recognize and consider fully the impacts of wetlands protection policies on individuals who own wetland property. Statutory, regulatory, and policy objectives should be accomplished in a manner that avoids unnecessary impacts upon such landowners.

Given the environmental and economic significance of wetlands, the alarming rate of wetlands loss, and concerns for private landowners, the Interagency Working Group on Federal Wetlands Policy began developing a comprehensive package of initiatives in June. The policy positions contained in this paper strongly support the effective protection and restoration of the Nation's wetlands, while advocating much-needed reforms to increase the fairness and flexibility of Federal regulatory programs.

II. A DIVISIVE DEBATE

Federal programs to protect the Nation's wetlands have been the focus of considerable controversy in recent years. Much of the attention focused upon the 1989 Interagency Wetlands Delineation Manual (1989 Manual). The 1989 Manual was prepared jointly by the U.S. Army Corps of Engineers (the Corps), the Environmental Protection Agency (EPA), the Fish and Wildlife Service (FWS) of the Department of the Interior, and the Department of Agriculture's Soil Conservation Service (SCS). It was developed in response to criticism that Federal agencies were not using a single set of common procedures to "delineate" -- or identify -- wetlands under the jurisdiction of programs administered by these agencies.

But rather than alleviating concerns about inconsistency, the 1989 Manual only further fueled the controversy. Critics claimed that the 1989 Manual represented a major expansion of regulatory jurisdiction without opportunity for public participation. In response, the Bush Administration embarked upon a closed-door effort to revise the 1989 Manual. This process resulted in the technically flawed 1991 Manual that would have dramatically and indefensibly reduced the amount of wetlands subject to protection. The proposed 1991 Manual generated even further controversy and resulted in even greater polarization of the debate on Federal wetlands policy.

In addition to assailing the 1989 Manual, critics of Federal wetlands regulatory programs effectively characterized those programs as unfair, inflexible, inconsistent, and confusing. Supporters of wetlands protection responded -- with equal effectiveness -- by emphasizing the environmental and economic benefits associated with protecting the Nation's wetlands.

As both sides voiced their strongly held opinions, the debate over Federal wetlands policy became increasingly divisive. The opposition that developed to both the 1989 and 1991 Manuals demonstrated the policy deadlock that had developed. Wetlands policy has become one of the most controversial environmental issues facing the Federal government, just as Congress embarks upon the reauthorization of the Clean Water Act.

III. THE INTERAGENCY WORKING GROUP ON FEDERAL WETLANDS POLICY

The Administration convened the Interagency Working Group on Federal Wetlands Policy in early June with the goal of developing a package of Clinton Administration initiatives to break the deadlock over Federal wetlands policy. The group has been chaired by the White House Office on Environmental Policy and has included the participation of the EPA, the Army (the Corps of Engineers), the Office of Management and Budget, and the Departments of Agriculture, Commerce, Energy, Interior, Justice, and Transportation.

The working group sought the views of a broad range of stakeholders representing all perspectives in the wetlands debate. For example, the working group has received presentations that have included: a bipartisan group of eight members of the U.S. Congress; representatives of State and local government; environmentalists; the development community; agricultural interests; scientists and others.

After listening to this broad range of interests, the working group began its policy deliberations by establishing the following five principles that serve as the framework for the Administration's comprehensive package of wetlands reform initiatives.

IV. FIVE PRINCIPLES FOR FEDERAL WETLANDS POLICY

1) The Clinton Administration supports the interim goal of no overall net loss of the Nation's remaining wetlands, and the long-term goal of increasing the quality and quantity of the Nation's wetlands resource base;

2) Regulatory programs must be efficient, fair, flexible, and predictable, and must be administered in a manner that avoids unnecessary impacts upon private property and the regulated public, and minimizes those effects that cannot be avoided, while providing effective protection for wetlands. Duplication among regulatory agencies must be avoided and the public must have a clear understanding of regulatory requirements and various agency roles;

3) Non-regulatory programs, such as advance planning; wetlands restoration, inventory, and research; and public/private cooperative efforts must be encouraged to reduce the Federal government's reliance upon regulatory programs as the primary means to protect wetlands resources and to accomplish long-term wetlands gains;

4) The Federal government should expand partnerships with State, Tribal, and local governments, the private sector and individual citizens and approach wetlands protection and restoration in an ecosystem/watershed context; and

5) Federal wetlands policy should be based upon the best scientific information available.

V. A COMPREHENSIVE PACKAGE OF REFORMS

Building upon these principles, the working group has developed a comprehensive package of initiatives that will significantly reform Federal wetlands policy, while maintaining protection of this vital natural resource. This package includes regulatory reforms and innovative, non-regulatory policy approaches; it includes administrative actions that will take effect immediately, and legislative recommendations for Congress to consider during the reauthorization of the Clean Water Act. The Clinton Administration looks forward to working closely with the Congress to implement this new approach to Federal wetlands policy. In addition, the Administration will establish an ongoing interagency working group, to be chaired by the Office on Environmental Policy, to monitor the implementation of the initiatives contained in the reform package.

The reform package includes the following initiatives:

- **To affirm its commitment to conserving wetlands resources, the Administration will issue an Executive Order embracing the interim goal of no overall net loss of the Nation's remaining wetlands resource base, and a long-term goal of increasing the quality and quantity of the Nation's wetlands;**

- To increase fairness in the wetlands permitting process, the Corps will establish an administrative appeals process so that landowners can seek recourse short of going to court;

- To increase fairness and efficiency in the wetlands permitting process, the Corps will establish deadlines for wetlands permitting decisions under the Clean Water Act;

- To reduce uncertainty for American farmers, yesterday the Corps and EPA issued a final regulation ensuring that approximately 53 million acres of prior converted cropland -- areas which no longer exhibit wetlands characteristics -- will not be subject to wetlands regulations;

- To reduce duplication and inconsistency for American farmers, the Soil Conservation Service will be the lead Federal agency responsible for identifying wetlands on agricultural lands under both the Clean Water Act and the Food Security Act;

- To close a loophole that has led to the degradation and destruction of wetlands, yesterday the Corps and EPA issued a final regulation to clarify the scope of activities regulated under the Clean Water Act;

- To emphasize that all wetlands are not of equal value, yesterday EPA and the Corps issued guidance to field staff highlighting the flexibility that exists to apply less vigorous permit review to small projects with minor environmental impacts;

- To ensure consistency and fairness, the Army Corps of Engineers, the Environmental Protection Agency, the Soil Conservation Service, and the Fish and Wildlife Service will all use the same procedures to identify wetland areas;

- To increase the predictability and environmental effectiveness of the Clean Water Act regulatory program and to help attain the no overall net loss goal, the Administration endorses the use of mitigation banks;

- To reduce the conflict that can result between wetlands protection and development when decisions are made on a permit-by-permit basis, the Administration strongly supports incentives for States and localities to engage in watershed planning;

- To provide effective incentives for farmers to restore wetlands on their property, the Administration will continue to support increased funding for the USDA's Wetland Reserve Program; and

• To attain the long-term goal of increasing the quantity and quality of the Nation's wetlands, the Administration will promote the restoration of damaged wetland areas through voluntary, non-regulatory programs.

The complete package of reform initiatives follows. (Some initiatives are listed under more than one heading for the sake of clarity.) By proposing an approach based upon effective protection and restoration of the Nation's wetlands, while adopting much-needed reforms to increase the fairness and flexibility of regulatory programs, the Administration's reform package offers a tremendous opportunity to move beyond the divisiveness that has characterized the wetlands policy debate in recent years.

A. ADDRESSING LANDOWNER CONCERNS

Issue Definition: The program that regulates wetlands under Section 404 of the Clean Water Act has been criticized as being slow, unpredictable and unfair. For example, it has been claimed that permits take too long to obtain; that wetlands delineations are sometimes slow, inaccurate, and inconsistent; and that it is unfair that the Corps does not provide a process by which landowners can appeal a jurisdictional determination or the denial of a wetlands permit short of suffering the expense of going to court.

Administration Position: The Clinton Administration believes that the Federal government has a responsibility to the public to conduct such regulatory programs in a manner that is efficient, responsive and fair. Therefore, the Administration supports the following reforms that will reduce the impact of regulation on the public, while meeting our objectives to protect wetlands:

•*Deadlines for Permit Action* Within one year the Corps will modify its regulations, through a public rulemaking process, to establish regulatory deadlines for reaching decisions regarding permit applications. The regulations will generally require the Corps to reach permit decisions within 90 days from the date of issuance of the public notice, unless precluded by other laws, such as the National Environmental Policy Act. The Administration will strongly support the additional personnel and funding necessary to meet these deadlines for permit action.

•*The Adoption of an Appeals Process* Within one year, the Corps will develop an administrative appeals process under the Section 404 regulatory program. The process, which will be implemented after a public rulemaking, will be designed to allow for administrative appeals of the Corps' determination that it has regulatory jurisdiction over a particular parcel of property, permit denials, and administrative penalties. The process will allow third parties to participate in applicant appeals of permit denials and will require that applicants exercise their right to appeal before initiating judicial action. The Administration will strongly support the additional personnel and funding necessary to implement successfully the appeals process.

The USDA already has an appeals process in place and landowners will be able to appeal SCS wetlands delineations through that administrative process.

- *Delineation Training and Certification* All employees of Federal agencies who conduct wetlands delineations will be required to complete the interagency wetlands delineation training program to improve accuracy and consistency in delineation in Federal wetlands programs or have comparable training and experience. As appropriate, State and Tribal agencies will also be encouraged to participate in the Federal training program. In addition, by the end of 1993, the Corps will propose regulations for implementing a certification program for private sector delineators.

By requiring training of Federal delineators, jurisdictional determinations can be done more accurately and consistently across the country. By encouraging the growth of a pool of certified private sector wetlands consultants, jurisdictional determinations can be performed far more quickly than if the job is solely the responsibility of Federal agency personnel. In addition, the Corps will streamline the process by which it considers and accepts delineations performed by certified wetlands consultants.

- *Promote Voluntary, Cooperative Programs.* With 75 percent of the Nation's remaining wetlands in the lower 48 States located on privately owned property, it is clear that cooperation with the private sector in implementation of wetlands protection and restoration activities is critical. Advance planning (see next issue) offers an excellent opportunity to involve the public in general, and property owners in particular, in developing and implementing wetlands protection and restoration plans. The Administration will support planning activities that include cooperative activities with property owners, and will increase support for programs that assist landowners in the implementation of such plans through restoration, technical assistance and information programs.

B. ADVANCE PLANNING AND WATERSHED MANAGEMENT

Issue Definition: Typically, decisions affecting wetlands are made on a project-by-project, permit-by-permit basis. This often precludes the effective consideration of the cumulative effects of piecemeal wetlands loss and degradation. It also hampers the ability of State, Tribal, regional, and local governments to integrate wetlands conservation objectives into the planning, management, and regulatory tools they use to make decisions regarding development and other natural resource issues. This can often result in inconsistent and inefficient efforts among agencies at all levels of government, and frustration and confusion among the public.

In contrast, advance planning, particularly comprehensive planning conducted on a watershed basis, offers the opportunity to have strong participation by State, Tribal, and local governments and private citizens in designing and implementing specific solutions to the most pressing environmental problems of that watershed. Advance planning generally involves at least the identification, mapping, and preliminary assessment of relative wetland functions within the planning area. More comprehensive advance planning may identify wetlands that merit a high level of protection and others that may be considered for development, and may also incorporate wetlands conservation into overall land use planning at the local level. Advance planning can provide greater predictability and certainty to property owners, developers, project planners, and local governments.

Administration Position: To encourage greater use of comprehensive advance planning, particularly with State, Tribal, regional, and local involvement, and to identify wetlands protection and restoration needs, opportunities, and concerns, the Administration supports the following actions:

● *Provide Incentives for States/Locals to Integrate Watershed and Wetlands Planning.* The Clean Water Act should authorize the development of State watershed protection programs, which should include local and regional involvement and Federal approval of the State programs. Wetlands should be incorporated into the overall watershed approach, with minimum standards for wetlands protection and restoration planning. Approved watershed plans would receive a high priority for technical and financial support for activities such as mitigation banking, advance identification, and watershed-based categorization under the Section 404 regulatory program. There would also be a high priority given to developing Programmatic General Permits that defer to local regulatory programs implementing approved watershed plans.

● *Endorse State/Tribal Wetlands Conservation Plans.* Congress should endorse the development of State/Tribal comprehensive wetland plans, with the goal of supporting State and Tribal efforts to protect and manage their wetlands resources. EPA is currently funding the development of 22 State Wetlands Conservation Plans; Congress should provide EPA the authority to use its Wetlands Grants program to fund both their development and implementation.

● *Provide for Greater Integration of Advance Planning Into the Section 404 Regulatory Program.* The Administration will support efforts to better integrate advance planning into the Section 404 regulatory program, including appropriate local or watershed-based categorization frameworks and regionalized improvements to implementation of the existing Nationwide Permit 26 in headwaters and isolated waters. Such opportunities are expected to grow as States, Tribes, and regional and local governments progress on watershed plans, State Wetlands Conservation Plans, and other wetlands-related planning processes. Where State, Tribal, regional, or local governments have approved watershed plans that address wetlands, EPA and the Corps will give high priority to assisting with the development of categorization of wetland resources for the purpose of Section 404. Categorization approaches should be local or regional in nature, and reflect the full range of impacts and functions that affect wetlands within the watershed or planning area.

- *Programmatic General Permits (PGPs) Under Section 404.* The Corps will issue guidance which specifies the circumstances under which State, Tribal, regional, and local governments with existing regulatory programs may assume a more active role in wetlands protection while reducing duplication with Federal programs. PGPs are extremely useful in reducing unnecessary duplication between Federal and non-Federal regulatory programs and in generally enhancing the role of State and local governments and of advance planning, in decisions regarding wetlands and other aquatic resources. The Administration recommends that Congress amend Section 404(e) of the Clean Water Act to provide explicitly for issuance of PGPs, with appropriate environmental safeguards, for approved State, Tribal, regional, and local regulatory programs.

- *Improve Nationwide Permit 26 Through Regionalization.* In order to improve the implementation of existing Nationwide Permit 26 (NWP 26) in isolated waters and in headwater areas, the Corps, in coordination with appropriate Federal, State, and Tribal agencies, and with the opportunity for public notice and comment, will undertake a field level review of NWP 26 to develop regional descriptions of the types of waters, and the nature of activities in those waters that will not be subject to authorization under NWP 26. Advance planning efforts that have assessed the functions and values of local isolated wetlands and headwaters, and have considered factors such as cumulative losses and scarcity of particular classes of waters, will be used to facilitate this effort.

- *Mitigation Banking.* Wetland mitigation banking refers to the restoration, creation, enhancement, and, in certain defined circumstances, preservation of wetlands expressly for the purpose of providing compensatory mitigation in advance of discharges into wetlands authorized under the Section 404 regulatory program. Advance planning can be used to identify appropriate locations for, and uses of, mitigation banks. EPA and the Corps have issued guidance to their field staff that clarifies the manner in which wetlands mitigation banking fits in the Section 404 regulatory program. Congress should endorse the appropriate use of banking, with environmental safeguards, as a compensatory mitigation option under the Section 404 regulatory program, and explicitly allow use of the State Revolving Fund to capitalize mitigation banks.

- *Promote Voluntary, Cooperative Programs.* With approximately 75 percent of the Nation's remaining wetlands in the lower 48 States located on privately owned property, it is clear that cooperation with the private sector in implementation of wetlands protection and restoration activities is critical. Advance planning offers an excellent opportunity to involve the public in general, and property owners in particular, in developing and implementing wetlands protection and restoration plans. The Administration will support planning activities that include cooperative activities with property owners, and will increase support for programs that assist landowners in the implementation of such plans through restoration, technical assistance, and education and information programs.

- *Revise the Executive Order on Wetlands.* The existing Executive Order on wetlands (E.O.11990) will be revised to direct the Federal agencies to take a watershed/ecosystem approach to wetlands protection and restoration. In addition, it will require Federal agencies that conduct or assist with multi-objective natural resource planning to incorporate wetlands protection into their programs to the extent practicable.

- *Provide Better and Coordinated Information and Technical Assistance on Wetland Issues.* The Federal agencies will coordinate efforts to provide States, Tribes, regional and local governments, and the public with timely, consistent information concerning wetlands programs. The agencies will develop a strategic plan for delivering information on regulatory programs, and encourage the development of innovative education and outreach materials and initiatives to assist the public in understanding wetlands issues.

The Administration will also direct the Wetlands Subcommittee of the Federal Geographic Data Committee to complete reconciliation and integration of all Federal agency wetland inventory activities. In addition, the Administration will coordinate wetlands restoration, research, inventory, monitoring, cooperative programs, and information and education activities.

C. AGRICULTURE

Issue Definition: Two Federal statutes regulate certain activities in wetlands on agricultural lands. The Food Security Act Wetlands Conservation provision, which is known as the Swampbuster program, is administered by the Soil Conservation Service (SCS) of the U.S. Department of Agriculture, in consultation with the Fish and Wildlife Service of the Department of the Interior. The Clean Water Act Section 404 program is administered jointly by the Department of the Army and the Environmental Protection Agency. American farmers have at times been subjected to needless duplication and frustrating inconsistency in the implementation of these two statutes.

<u>Administration Position:</u> The Administration recognizes the valuable contribution of agricultural producers to the Nation's economy and more generally to the American way of life. We also appreciate the challenges faced by farmers as they try to comply with wetlands regulations, as well as other environmental requirements affecting farm operations. As a result, the Administration is committed to ensuring that Federal wetlands programs do not place unnecessary restrictions or burdens on farmers and other landowners, while providing necessary environmental safeguards.

The Administration has identified a number of actions that can be taken to reduce the impact of these two wetlands protection programs on American agriculture. At the heart of this effort is a commitment on the part of all Federal agencies involved to work closely and cooperatively to coordinate their work under these two statutes so as to increase efficiency, minimize duplication, and reduce inconsistencies between the programs.

The following initiatives demonstrate our commitment to protect and restore the Nation's wetlands and eliminate unnecessary impacts on the farm community:

- *Prior Converted Cropland Rulemaking.* EPA and the Corps have just completed a rulemaking which assures American farmers that an estimated 53 million acres of prior converted cropland will not be subject to regulation under Section 404 of the Clean Water Act. These lands were converted from wetlands to croplands prior to the passage of the Food Security Act of 1985, which established the Swampbuster program, and no longer exhibit wetlands characteristics. The Administration is also recommending that Congress include in the Clean Water Act a definition of "waters of the United States" that explicitly excludes from Clean Water Act jurisdiction areas determined to be prior converted cropland.

- *A Package to Eliminate Duplication and Inconsistency*
The SCS, EPA, the Corps, and FWS signed an interagency agreement on August 23, 1993 that will reduce existing overlap and inconsistencies in the implementation of Federal wetlands programs affecting agricultural lands by undertaking, within 120 days, the following initiatives:

  · *Make the SCS the Lead Agency on Agricultural Lands.* The SCS, the Corps, EPA, and FWS will develop procedures to provide that SCS wetland delineations will represent the final government position on the extent of Swampbuster and Clean Water Act jurisdiction on agricultural lands. Interagency training programs will be developed to ensure that agency field staff are properly trained, that standard, agreed-upon methods are utilized in making delineation and mitigation determinations, and that EPA and the Corps, consistent with their statutory authorities, have the ability to monitor SCS determinations on a programmatic basis. SCS, EPA and the Corps will also coordinate enforcement responsibilities on agricultural lands to ensure that the Federal government's activities are equitable, and consistent.

  · *Guarantee Consistency in Delineations on Agricultural Lands.* In order to ensure consistency in identifying wetlands on agricultural lands, the Corps, EPA, SCS, and FWS will all use the same procedures to delineate wetlands. The agencies will develop field guidance for implementing the 1987 Wetlands Delineation Manual to establish procedures for identifying wetlands in areas managed for agriculture. The agencies will also expedite current efforts to revise the SCS Food Security Act Manual to eliminate inconsistencies between wetlands delineation procedures in the FSA Manual and the 1987 Manual.

  ·*Greatly Increase Farmers' Certainty in Agency Decisions.* The Corps, in coordination with EPA, SCS, and FWS, will propose a Nationwide General Permit for discharges associated with "minimal effects" and "frequently cropped with mitigation" conversions determined by SCS and FWS to qualify for exemption from Swampbuster provisions. This will provide greater certainty to the Nation's farmers that they can rely on SCS/FWS mitigation determinations. While the Nationwide permit will include appropriate conditions to protect valuable wetlands, an individual review by the Corps and EPA will generally not be required.

• *Clarify that Certain Man-Made Wetlands Are Not Jurisdictional.* The Corps and EPA will incorporate examples of certain man-made wetlands, such as non-tidal drainage and irrigation ditches excavated on upland, and irrigated lands that would revert to upland if irrigation ceased, into their regulations to clarify the types of waters that are generally not subject to Clean Water Act jurisdiction because they are created out of upland.

• *Wetlands Reserve Program.* The Wetlands Reserve Program (WRP) offers a significant opportunity to assist farmers who are interested in restoring wetlands on their property. Response by farmers to the nine State pilot program was overwhelming, with proposals for 250,000 acres of restoration by over 2300 farmers. The 1994 Appropriations conference report provides for 75,000 new acres to be enrolled in the WRP. When passed this will more than double -- to 20 -- the number of states where producers can participate in the program. The recent Midwest flood has created a particularly pressing need to assist farmers in the voluntary restoration of wetlands that have historically provided valuable flood protection. Congress should fully fund the Administration's budget requests for the WRP in 1995, and should expand the program in the 1995 Farm Bill.

D. CATEGORIZATION

Issue Definition: A persistent criticism of the Section 404 regulatory program is that the permit process is inflexible to the extent that "all wetlands are treated the same" from a regulatory perspective. Such criticisms have led to calls for a nationwide categorization system to rank wetlands based upon their relative function and importance to society.

One proposed approach would require that all of the Nation's wetlands be mapped and categorized "up front" as either "high-", "medium-", or "low-value." The ranking based upon this *a priori* categorization would, in turn, govern the regulatory response at the time of a specific permit application.

Administration Position: While conceptually *a priori* categorization and ranking may seem attractive, its technical, fiscal and environmental implications make it unworkable. For example, simply mapping the lower 48 States at a scale suitable for detailed regulatory use would involve a mammoth undertaking yielding nearly 14 million maps and costing in excess of $500 million. Assessing the functions of every wetland in the country would be a far larger and more complicated task and would require staffing and funding many times that necessary to complete mapping alone.

There is currently no scientific basis for a nationwide ranking of functionally distinct and diverse wetland types; any such scheme would be extremely difficult and require many years to develop. The suggestion contained in one legislative proposal that the Federal government buy all "high-value" wetlands would be infeasible from a budgetary standpoint. The Congressional Budget Office estimates the acquisition costs alone for the lower 48 States to range between $10 billion and $45 billion.

Finally, an *a priori* categorization and ranking approach would not provide for consideration of the individual impacts associated with specific projects. This makes little sense from the standpoint of either development or wetlands protection. For example, small projects with minor impacts would be arbitrarily prevented from proceeding in a "high-value" wetland area. At the same time, large and environmentally damaging projects would be automatically approved if they were located in "low-value" wetland areas. A nationwide *a priori* categorization scheme would further complicate the Section 404 program and would conflict with the Administration's goals of administering a scientifically sound regulatory program that is efficient, predictable and understandable.

In contrast to nationwide *a priori* categorization, opportunities exist to provide greater predictability and certainty in the regulatory process while increasing participation at the State and local levels. Local or regionally developed advance planning at the watershed level can provide a scientifically sound and workable framework for early consideration of variations in wetland functions within the Section 404 program. Appropriate functional assessment techniques can be applied to all wetlands within the boundaries of a particular watershed or planning area, and reasonably foreseeable development needs can be superimposed upon this inventory and assessment to identify appropriate regulatory responses in advance of specific permit applications. Highly functional and ecologically significant wetlands can be identified as deserving a very high standard of protection; conversely, wetlands with limited function and ecological significance, or activities that would cause minimal environmental harm, can be identified as appropriate for general permits or other regulatory streamlining methods.

In the context of individual permit reviews, the Section 404(b)(1) Guidelines currently provide the Corps and EPA with the flexibility to appropriately scale the regulatory response to reflect the relative function of the affected wetland, the character of the proposed discharge, and the probable environmental impact.

The Administration recognizes that "all wetlands are not the same" and that permit applicants deserve a timely and predictable regulatory response that is appropriate for the project being proposed. To this end, the Administration proposes the following actions:

- *Issue Section 404(b)(1) Guidelines Flexibility Guidance.* EPA and the Corps have issued guidance to their field staff to clarify and standardize implementation of the flexibility afforded by the 404(b)(1) Guidelines to make regulatory decisions regarding the analysis of project alternatives based on the relative severity of the environmental impact of proposed discharges. This guidance clarifies that small projects with minor impacts are subject to less rigorous permit review than larger projects with more substantial environmental impacts.

• ***Develop Improved Analytical Tools for Wetlands Functional Assessment.*** The agencies will expedite development of a new approach for wetland functional assessment known as the Hydrogeomorphic Classification System (HGM). The HGM methodology is being developed by the agencies and the academic community as an improved analytical tool to make timely and accurate assessments of wetland functions. This tool will assist the agencies in assessing the relative severity of environmental impact of proposed discharges to determine an appropriate regulatory response consistent with the 404(b)(1) Guidelines flexibility guidance referenced above.

• ***Encourage Advance Planning Efforts.*** The agencies will provide technical assistance for advance planning efforts addressing wetlands conservation, and will counsel planning participants on methods to link local or regional planning with Section 404 regulatory decision making. Wetland categorization will be supported within the context of an approved advance plan to provide landowners with early identification and characterization of wetlands on their property, streamlined permit review, and more flexible mitigation sequencing where appropriate.

• ***Regionalize General Permits for Activities in Defined Categories of Waters.*** The Section 404 program already embodies a form of wetlands categorization through use of Nationwide Permit 26 (NWP 26), a "category of waters" general permit that authorizes discharges into isolated waters and headwaters. The Corps will undertake, in close coordination with relevant State and Federal agencies, a field level review and evaluation of NWP 26 for the purpose of regionalizing and improving its use. Congress should amend Section 404(e) to recognize the concept of regionalized "category of waters" general permits.

E. GEOGRAPHIC JURISDICTION

The term "geographic jurisdiction" encompasses a set of wetlands issues that concern the determination of which waters fall within the jurisdiction of the Section 404 program of the Clean Water Act. These issues include the delineation manual that specifies the methodology by which wetlands are identified; the definitions of "wetlands" and "waters of the United States;" "artificial" wetlands; and isolated waters. (For "Delineation Training and Certification" see ADDRESSING LANDOWNER CONCERNS.)

Issue Definition: Delineation Manual
As previously indicated, there has been a great deal of controversy surrounding the manuals that Federal agencies use in the field to delineate wetlands. The 1989 Manual was strongly criticized by some who claimed that it was an attempt by the bureaucracy to greatly *expand* the geographic

jurisdiction of wetlands regulation without opportunity for public involvement. The proposed 1991 Manual that followed was roundly criticized by those who claimed that it would greatly *reduce* the scope of geographic jurisdiction applied to wetlands. In an attempt to resolve this controversy, in the fall of 1992 the Congress directed EPA to fund a National Academy of Science (NAS) study of wetlands delineation. That study is expected to be completed in the Fall of 1994. Since January 1993, both the Corps and EPA have adopted the 1987 Manual, which was in use in some parts of the country prior to the issuance of the 1989 Manual.

Administration Position: The Clinton Administration supports the use of the 1987 Wetlands Delineation Manual by the Corps, EPA, SCS, and FWS pending the evaluation of the NAS study. (See "Guarantee Consistency in Delineations on Agricultural Lands" under AGRICULTURE.) The use of the 1987 Manual by the Corps and EPA has increased confidence and consistency in identifying wetlands and has diminished the controversy associated with the 1989 and 1991 manuals. If the Federal agencies jointly conclude that the 1987 Manual should be revised to respond to recommendations of the NAS, any proposed changes will be the subject of a process that will provide full opportunity for public comment. In addition, any proposed changes will be field tested by the agencies prior to final adoption to determine their impact in the real world.

To increase public confidence in the Section 404 regulatory program, the Administration recommends that the Congress endorse the continued use of the 1987 Manual in the reauthorization of the Clean Water Act, pending recommendations that may result from the NAS study.

Issue Definition: Defining "Waters of the U.S." and "Wetlands"
The Clean Water Act regulates discharges to "navigable waters," which are defined in the statute as "waters of the United States." However, the Act does not contain a definition of "waters of the United States." Similarly, while the Act refers to "wetlands," the statute does not define the term. Explicit definitions of these terms in the statute, consistent with longstanding regulatory definitions, would clarify Congressional intent with regard to the scope of geographic jurisdiction under the Act.

Administration Position: The Administration recommends that Congress incorporate the definition of "waters of the United States" contained in existing EPA and Corps implementing regulations. To provide additional consistency among Clean Water Act and Food Security Act programs, Congress should also incorporate the definition of "wetlands" contained in the Clean Water Act regulatory definitions, which is essentially identical to the wetlands definition in the 1990 Farm Bill. (The Clean Water Act regulatory definition of wetlands is preferable because some States have used the definition in State wetlands statutes. To adopt a different definition at Federal and State levels of government would only create further confusion in the regulatory program.)

The EPA/Corps definition of "waters of the United States" explicitly includes recently promulgated language clarifying that "prior converted croplands" are not waters of the

United States for purposes of the Clean Water Act. Congress should include this clarifying language in statute as well.

The Administration also recommends that Congress add examples of "isolated waters" (e.g., prairie potholes, vernal pools, and playa lakes) to the statutory definition of wetlands. From a scientific standpoint, isolated wetlands perform many of the same vital functions performed by other aquatic areas widely accepted as wetlands, such as flood control and groundwater recharge, as well as providing critical habitat for migratory waterfowl and other wildlife, and contribute to achieving the objectives of the Clean Water Act both individually and as a class.

Issue Definition: "Artificial" Wetlands

Neither the Clean Water Act nor its implementing regulations distinguishes between natural and created wetlands. However, certain "artificial" wetlands do not normally exhibit the values and functions typically attributed to natural wetlands. These artificial wetlands are created inadvertently from upland by human activity and would revert to upland if such activity ceased. The fact that these areas are not specifically excluded from the jurisdiction of the Clean Water Act in either statute or regulation has caused confusion.

Administration Position: The EPA and the Corps will incorporate examples of artificial wetlands, such as non-tidal drainage and irrigation ditches excavated on upland, into their regulations to clarify the types of waters that are generally not subject to Clean Water Act jurisdiction because they are created out of upland.

F. MITIGATION AND MITIGATION BANKING

Issue Definition: Mitigating the harmful effects of necessary development actions on the Nation's waters is a central premise of Federal wetland regulatory programs. The Section 404 regulatory program relies upon a sequential approach to mitigating these harmful effects by first avoiding unnecessary impacts, then minimizing environmental harm, and, finally, compensating for remaining unavoidable damage to wetlands and other waters through, for example, the restoration or creation of wetlands.

Mitigation banking refers to a wetland restoration, creation, or enhancement effort undertaken expressly for the purpose of compensating for unavoidable wetland losses in advance of development actions, when compensatory mitigation is not appropriate, practicable, or as environmentally beneficial at the development site. Units of restored or created wetland are expressed as "credits", and accumulated credits are subsequently withdrawn to offset "debits" incurred at the development site.

Administration Position: The sequential approach to mitigation provides a logical, predictable, and reasonable framework for mitigating impacts associated with proposed development actions. The Administration supports the use of mitigation banking in appropriate circumstances as a means of compensating for authorized wetland impacts.

The Administration is proposing the following actions to ensure that mitigation of environmental impacts within the Section 404 program is effective, predictable, and consistent with a watershed management perspective:

- *Issue Mitigation Planning Guidance.* The Corps, in coordination with EPA, FWS, SCS, and the National Marine Fisheries Service (NMFS), will issue guidance to their field staff to clarify the requirements for developing compensatory mitigation conditions in Section 404 permits. This guidance is intended to increase the success of mitigation projects in offsetting impacts to wetlands and other waters resulting from permitted activities. This guidance will assist permit applicants by providing greater consistency and certainty with regard to how Section 404 mitigation requirements are applied.

- *Endorse the Use of Mitigation Banking Under the Section 404 Regulatory Program.* While a number of technical and procedural questions regarding the establishment and long term management of mitigation banks remain, conceptually mitigation banking, with appropriate environment safeguards, offers numerous advantages. Banking provides for greater certainty of successful compensatory mitigation in the permit process by requiring mitigation to be established before permits are issued. Banks are often ecologically advantageous because they consolidate fragmented wetland mitigation projects into one large contiguous parcel that can more effectively replace the lost wetland functions within the watershed. Mitigation banks also provide a framework for financial resources, planning and technical expertise to be brought together in a fashion often not possible with smaller mitigation projects.

Recognizing the advantages offered by mitigation banking to compensate for wetlands losses, Congress should endorse the appropriate use of banking as a compensatory mitigation option under the Section 404 regulatory program, within environmentally sound limits. Congress should also explicitly allow use of the State Revolving Fund by States to capitalize mitigation banks.

- *Issue Mitigation Banking Guidance.* EPA and the Corps, in coordination with FWS, NMFS, and SCS have issued guidance to their field staff to clarify the manner in which wetlands mitigation banking is appropriately used within the Section 404 regulatory program. This guidance provides interim direction pending the results of additional studies, but will encourage, within environmentally sound limits, the use of mitigation banks for compensatory mitigation under Section 404.

- *Develop Improved Analytical Tools.* The agencies will expedite current efforts being coordinated by the Corps Waterways Experiment Station to develop an improved wetland functional assessment tool, the Hydrogeomorphic Classification System, to assist in conducting impact analysis and determining appropriate and effective mitigation measures.

G. RESTORATION

Issue Definition: This Nation has lost nearly half of the wetland acreage that existed in the lower 48 States prior to European settlement. Much of this loss was due to Federal policies from an earlier era that encouraged the drainage of wetlands. The effect of this wetland loss is reflected in declining populations of fish, waterfowl, and other living things dependent upon the aquatic environment; in degraded water quality; and, most recently, in the extent of flooding in the Midwest.

The Section 404 regulatory program under the Clean Water Act and the Swampbuster provisions under the Food Security Act are attempts to stem this loss of wetlands. At best, the regulatory approach can ensure no further overall net loss. But to achieve a positive increase in the Nation's wetlands will require the restoration of some damaged wetlands.

Our ability to restore wetlands, particularly inland wetlands in agricultural areas, has been well-established over the last decade. A number of private and governmental entities have successfully restored degraded or lost wetlands to productive status. For example, the Fish and Wildlife Service, in cooperation with private landowners across the Nation, has implemented 9,500 restoration projects affecting 200,000 acres. Last year, a 50,000 acre pilot of the USDA Wetlands Reserve Program received proposals from 2,300 farmers to restore 500,000 acres.

Administration Position: Restoring some former wetlands that have been drained previously or otherwise destroyed to functioning wetlands is key to achieving the Administration's interim goal of no overall net loss of the Nation's remaining wetlands, and its long term goal to increase the quality and quantity of the Nation's wetlands base.

In support of a broad-based effort to restore a portion of the Nation's historic wetlands base that has been destroyed or degraded in the past, the Administration proposes to take the following actions:

● *Wetlands Reserve Program.* The fiscal year 1994 Agriculture Appropriations conference report provides for 75,000 new acres to be enrolled in the Wetlands Reserve Program. When passed this will also more than double – to 20 – the number of States eligible for participation in the program. The Administration will also use this program in the Midwest to restore wetlands in the course of providing financial assistance to farmers and improved flood protection for all those affected by the recent flooding. The Administration will also pursue full funding of the President's budget request for the Wetlands Reserve Program in FY 1995, and will seek to have this program expanded in the 1995 Farm Bill.

● *Promote Wetlands Restoration through Voluntary, Cooperative Programs and Outreach Activities.* Wetlands conservation efforts have historically focused largely on wetlands regulation and acquisition. These programs continue to be essential to a comprehensive strategy for achieving the Administration's wetlands goals. However, stemming the net loss of the Nation's wetlands base and achieving a long-term increase in wetlands acreage is dependent upon restoring wetlands that have been drained, diked, or otherwise destroyed in the past.

The universe of restorable former wetlands is predominantly on private lands, and the Administration presently has in place a number of Federal programs that focus on or incorporate voluntary, cooperative efforts to restore wetlands on private lands (e.g., FWS's Partners for Wildlife program, Bay and Estuary program, and North American Waterfowl Management Plan Joint Ventures; USDA's Wetlands Reserve, Water Bank, Water Quality Incentives, Forestry Incentives, and Stewardship Incentives programs.) The Administration will review existing Federal programs that seek to restore wetlands through cooperative, voluntary agreements and outreach efforts with private and other non-Federal landowners, and will examine opportunities to expand such programs, including education and outreach activities.

- *Revise the Executive Order on Wetlands.* The existing executive order on wetlands will be revised to incorporate the Administration's interim and long term wetland goals and to establish wetlands restoration as an essential vehicle for Federal and quasi-Federal agencies to achieve those goals through a voluntary approach.

H. ROLES OF FEDERAL AGENCIES

Issue Definition: Public support for Federal wetlands protection programs, such as the Clean Water Act Section 404 regulatory program and the Food Security Act Swampbuster program, has suffered during recent years from a perception that multiple agency roles in the Administration of these programs has contributed to confusion, delays, overlap, and a general sense that no single agency is "in charge".

Administration Position: The Administration is initiating steps to streamline the implementation of Federal wetlands protection programs by reducing duplication, overlap, and delay. For example, a memorandum of agreement has recently been signed to give the Soil Conservation Service, in consultation with the Fish and Wildlife Service, the lead agency for making wetlands delineations and mitigation decisions on agricultural land (see AGRICULTURE).

The Administration is committed to providing for effective and timely participation by the agencies with roles in Federal programs affecting wetlands while emphasizing the ultimate role of a single Federal agency decisionmaker. This increased coordination among the relevant agencies will be accomplished through the following mechanism:

- *Continue Implementation of the 1992 Interagency Section 404(q) MOAs.* EPA, the Corps, FWS, and NMFS have issued guidance to their field staff to improve interagency coordination procedures established in the 1992 Memoranda of Agreement under Section 404(q). These MOAs define a process for expedited review and resolution of agency concerns regarding individual permit decisions. The MOAs also establish procedures for resolving concerns involving the implementation of Section 404 program policy that can be accomplished without delaying individual permit decisions.

The agencies will continue to use the 1992 MOAs and, based on this experience, determine whether additional guidance or revisions to the MOAs are necessary. It is critical to the ultimate effectiveness of the Section 404 program to preserve the responsibilities of Federal resource agencies such as the EPA, FWS and NMFS to reflect their relative expertise and authorities while reducing duplication, overlap, and delay. It is equally critical to recognize and understand the Corps' leadership and final decision-making role as "project manager" for the evaluation of permit applications under the Section 404 regulatory program.

I. ROLE OF STATE, TRIBAL, AND LOCAL GOVERNMENT

Issue Definition: Decisions on where and how to protect or restore wetlands can be often most appropriately made at State, Tribal, or local levels. However, the current Section 404 regulatory program is run at the Federal level, except for certain waters in one State (Michigan). Many States, Tribes, and local governments have their own wetlands programs, which often overlap, are inconsistent with, or are simply distinct from Federal programs. This has resulted in inefficiency, frustration by the regulated public, and significant confusion.

Administration Position: The Administration is committed to increasing State, Tribal, and local government roles in Federal wetlands protection and restoration efforts. To increase consistency and clarity and reduce the confusion generated by the current relationship between the Federal government and State, Tribal, and local governments in wetlands protection and restoration, and to bring decision making to more appropriate levels, the Administration is taking the following actions:

• *Assist States, Tribes, and Local Governments in Taking a Stronger Role in Wetlands Protection.* The Administration will provide technical and financial assistance and guidance to States, Tribes, and local governments to assist them in taking more of a leadership role in wetlands protection, e.g., through State/Tribal assumption of Section 404, development of comprehensive State/Tribal Wetland Conservation Plans, application of State/Tribal Section 401 Certification authority to wetlands, development of Programmatic General Permits under Section 404, and better coordination between State, Tribal, and local permit programs and the Section 404 program.

• *Provide Incentives for States, Tribes, and Regional and Local Governments to Integrate Watershed and Wetlands Planning.* The Clean Water Act should authorize the development of State/Tribal watershed protection programs, requiring local and regional involvement and Federal approval of the State/Tribal programs. Wetlands should be incorporated into the overall watershed approach, with minimum requirements for wetlands protection and restoration planning. Approved watershed plans would receive a high priority for technical and financial support for activities such as mitigation banking, advance identification, and categorization under the Section 404 regulatory program. There would also be a high priority given to developing Programmatic General Permits that defer to local regulatory programs implementing approved watershed plans.

- *Increase Deference to State, Tribal, Regional, and Local Wetlands Decisionmaking.* The Corps will issue guidance which specifies the circumstances under which State, Tribal, regional, and local programs can effectively regulate Section 404 activities, through issuance of Programmatic General Permits (PGPs). The guidance will also clarify the safeguards required to ensure that these programs adequately protect wetlands and other waters.

The use of PGPs is designed to increase the roles of State, Tribal, regional, and local governments in wetlands protection, provide an incentive for watershed planning efforts, and reduce redundancy and overlap between these programs and the Federal Section 404 program. The Administration recommends that Congress amend Section 404(e) of the Clean Water Act to provide explicitly for issuance of PGPs with appropriate environmental safeguards for approved State, Tribal, regional, and local regulatory programs.

- *Endorse State/Tribal Wetlands Conservation Plans.* Congress should endorse the development of State/Tribal comprehensive wetland plans, with the goal of supporting State and Tribal efforts to protect and manage their wetlands resources. EPA is currently funding the development of 22 State Wetlands Conservation Plans; Congress should provide EPA the authority to use its Wetlands Grants program to fund both their development and implementation.

- *Encourage State/Tribal Assumption of Section 404.* Congress should provide EPA the authority to use its Wetlands Grants program to fund both development and implementation of State assumption of the Section 404 program. In addition, Congress should authorize partial assumption of the Section 404 program by States and Tribes as an interim step toward full assumption. By authorizing partial assumption of discrete areas within State or Tribal jurisdiction, the State/Tribe can get experience with the program as it develops full statutory equivalency, and the Federal government can defer to the State/Tribe as early as possible.

- *Provide States/Tribes with Access to Wetlands Delineation Training.* State and Tribal agencies will be encouraged to participate in the Federal interagency wetlands delineation training and certification programs to strengthen their abilities to conduct wetlands delineations, and to improve consistency in wetlands identification among State and Federal wetlands programs.

J. SCOPE OF REGULATED ACTIVITIES

Issue Definition: The Clean Water Act Section 404 program regulates "discharges" of dredged and fill material to wetlands and other waters of the United States. In the past, these terms have been interpreted in a way that created regulatory "loopholes" under which certain projects could be designed, using expensive and sophisticated methods, so that they did not require Section 404 authorization.

The environmental effects of these projects on wetlands are no different than less sophisticated projects involving discharges of dredged or fill material, which have been regulated under Section 404. Also, these loopholes have led to inconsistencies in how the Section 404 program has been implemented around the country.

    <u>Administration Position:</u> The Administration has issued a final regulation, and is asking Congress to take corresponding legislative action, to close these regulatory loopholes by clarifying the types of activities that involve discharges of dredged or fill material subject to Section 404 review.

    The following actions will result in better protection of wetlands, and improve the fairness, predictability, and consistency of the Section 404 program.

    ● *Clarify Definition of "Discharge of Dredged Material."* Under the final rule, this term is defined to ensure that discharges into wetlands and other waters of the United States will be consistently regulated when they are associated with excavation activities, such as ditching, channelization, or mechanized landclearing, that have environmental effects of concern. The rule explicitly excludes from Section 404 regulation discharges associated with activities that have only *de minimis*, or inconsequential, environmental effects. In an effort to reduce the impact of these changes on the regulation of minor activities with only minimal adverse environmental effects, the Corps will coordinate with EPA to develop additional general permits authorizing such minor activities. The revised definition does *not* affect the existing exemptions in Section 404(f) for ongoing farming, ranching, and silvicultural activities.

    ● *Clarify Definition of "Discharge of Fill Material."* The agencies also are clarifying the definition of "discharge of fill material" to ensure that activities in waters of the United States that involve the non-traditional use of pilings (e.g., shopping malls, parking garages) will require Clean Water Act authorization. In an effort to reduce the impact of these changes on the regulation of minor activities with only minimal adverse environmental effects, the Corps will coordinate with EPA to develop additional general permits that authorize such activities.

- *Legislative Clarification of Scope of Activities Regulated Under Section 404.* Congress should amend the Clean Water Act to make it consistent with the agencies' rulemaking.

K. STATE OF ALASKA

Issue Definition: The extent and nature of Alaska wetlands reflect, in part, climatological and physiographic conditions found in no other State. More than 99 percent of Alaska's wetlands remain, and much of the State's developable lands are wetlands. This abundance of wetlands in combination with Alaska's short building season, leads some to claim that the Section 404 program places a heavier burden on Alaskans than on the rest of the country.

The previous Administration attempted to address some of these concerns by proposing the "Alaska 1% rule" which would have exempted wetlands in Alaska from mitigation requirements until one percent of Alaska's wetland resources had been developed. The "Alaska 1% rule" was published for public comment in November 1992, and 83 percent of the over 6,500 comments received objected to the rule, raising concerns about its potential impact on the environment.

Objections to the proposed rule focused on several key considerations:

- An additional 1.5 million acres of Alaska's wetlands would be destroyed before the one percent threshold would be met, including potentially all of Alaska's 345,000 acres of extremely valuable coastal wetlands. Wetlands losses in Alaska have historically been greatest in coastal areas where the State's population is concentrated. For example, losses of high value coastal wetlands near the cities of Anchorage and Juneau are estimated to exceed 50 percent of their historic base.

- The proposed rule would hinder management efforts for several Federally listed or proposed threatened and endangered species that utilize Alaska's coastal wetlands, as well as hastening the listing of additional candidate species.

- Although full in-kind compensation is often not possible or practicable, opportunities do exist for restoration or rehabilitation of disturbed areas in proximity to a proposed development that have the potential to benefit affected fish and wildlife populations.

- There is enough flexibility in the existing Section 404 regulatory program to respond to Alaska's unique concerns administratively. During the last 20 years, of the approximately 4,000 permit applications received by the Corps' Alaska District, only 108 (2.7 percent) were denied; the remaining applications were either issued as individual or general permits, or withdrawn. Of the more than 3,000 individual permits issued, only 15 (0.5 percent) required compensatory mitigation.

Administration Position: Because of the significant adverse environmental consequences that it would allow, the "Alaska 1% rule" will be withdrawn. The best way to address Alaska-specific concerns regarding the Section 404 program is through targeting the specific areas where questions about program policies or implementation have been raised. Finalizing the proposed "Alaska 1% rule" would have far broader and avoidable adverse environmental consequences.

The EPA and the Corps will, within the next 90 days, initiate meetings with the Federal resource agencies, State and local government agencies, representatives of native villages, industry groups including oil and fishing interests, and environmental groups, to consider other environmentally appropriate means to assure regulatory flexibility and the feasibility of alternative permitting procedures in Alaska.

In addition, the Administration is proposing a number of actions to improve implementation of the Section 404 regulatory program nationwide (e.g., issuing guidance on flexibility in the Section 404(b)(1) Guidelines, mitigation banking, mitigation planning, advance planning, programmatic general permits; establishing an administrative appeals process; providing for more explicit consideration of wetland functions; and regionalizing Nationwide Permit number 26. See earlier discussion for details). These actions, in combination with any Alaska-specific proposals developed as a result of the process outlined above, should contribute significantly to addressing Alaska's concerns with implementation of the Section 404 regulatory program.

L. TAKINGS

Issue Definition: Some critics of the Section 404 regulatory program have asserted that Federal efforts to protect wetlands constitute a "taking" of private property and require compensation under the Fifth Amendment of the Constitution. Critics of the program have proposed legislation that would characterize permit denial decisions, and other Section 404 regulatory actions, as "takings" requiring compensation.

Administration Position: The Administration strongly supports private property rights. The equitable administration of any Federal regulatory program involves more than strict technical considerations and must include sensitivity to the rights and expectations of citizens. Implementation of the Section 404 program often requires a balancing of environmental protection, public interests, and individual interests.

Many activities undertaken on wetlands either are not regulated at all, are explicitly exempted from regulation, or are authorized by general permits. In situations where individual permits are required, the Federal agencies can work with permit applicants to design projects that meet the requirements of the law and protect the environment and public safety, while protecting the property rights of the applicant.
However, in rare instances the public interest in conserving wetlands may substantially interfere with the rights of landowners. In such instances, Federal action will be based

on the proposition that restrictions on the actions of the property owners in question are called for in order to protect the property rights, safety, environmental or economic interests of other individuals or the community at large.

In those situations where the necessary restrictions on use amount to a taking of the property, the owner will, of course, be entitled to compensation. Moreover, where a property owner believes that government action amounts to a taking, the courts are available to review such claims and to determine whether compensation is due. Due to the unique nature of each situation, these issues must be considered on a case-by-case basis. Therefore, the Administration does not support a legislative approach to this issue.

The Administration is strongly committed to reducing the impact of the 404 program on landowners. Many of the Administration positions that have been described in this paper are designed to make the program as efficient, predictable, consistent, and equitable as possible (see ADDRESSING LANDOWNER CONCERNS, AGRICULTURE and CATEGORIZATION).

VI. CONCLUSION

This comprehensive reform package represents a tremendous opportunity to move beyond the unnecessary polarization that has characterized the wetlands policy debate in recent years. While divisive, that debate has not been without value.

The critics of the wetlands regulatory program have performed a service to the country by highlighting the need for meaningful reform in the administration of wetland regulatory programs. Many of the much-needed reforms contained in this package — such as permit deadlines, an appeals process, the use of mitigation banks, and increasing the role of State and local government in wetlands regulation — have been proposed by critics of the current regulatory program.

The supporters of wetlands protection have also performed a service by helping to inform the Nation of the environmental and economic importance of wetlands, a vital natural resource that was once routinely destroyed. Their strong commitment to protecting and restoring this vital resource is also reflected in this package.

There will, no doubt, be individuals on each side of this divisive debate who will not be entirely pleased with every element of this reform package. But our approach provides effective protection of an important natural resource in a manner that is both fair and flexible, thus recognizing both the value of wetland resources and the need to minimize regulatory burdens.

VII. POSTSCRIPT: LESSONS FROM THE FLOOD

The entire Nation shares the pain of those Americans experiencing the physical destruction and economic loss caused by the disastrous floods that have devastated the Nation's heartland. Many lives have been lost, and billions of dollars in damage have been caused to property and crops. In the short term, we must use the tools available to us to assist those struggling to deal with severe economic hardship due to the floods. We must concentrate our attention on helping people rebuild their lives by protecting our riverfront communities and providing assistance to businesses and the agricultural community adversely affected by the floods.

We must also look to the future, and learn from these floods how to more effectively protect human health and safety, property, and the environment. Many scientists have concluded that past manipulation of the rivers in the Midwest has contributed to the current level of devastation by separating the river channels from their natural floodplains, eliminating millions of acres of additional flood storage capacity. Wetlands within the floodplain and higher in the watershed reduce floods by absorbing rain, snow melt, and floodwaters and releasing it slowly, thereby reducing the severity of downstream flooding.

We must be cautious not to repeat policies and practices which may have added to the destruction caused by these floods. One way to assist landowners while alleviating some flood risks is through funding wetlands restoration and acquisition programs targeted to help those in flood-ravaged areas. Programs such as the USDA Wetlands Reserve Program provide farmers with much needed support and increase the quantity of flood-absorbing wetlands in this region.

Of course, we recognize that wetlands and river system restoration and protection alone will not suffice. It will be critically important that we quickly rebuild many of the flood control structures. However, we have learned the importance of also looking at alternative non-structural measures that may provide as much or better flood damage reduction at the same or lower cost. Such measures would include using more natural river corridor systems and wetlands. In the longer term, it is important that *all* potential flood control measures, both structural and non-structural, be considered and evaluated from a pragmatic and cost-benefit standpoint.

It is not a question of whether to protect cities and farms; it is a question of how best to protect them. In the case of riverfront communities, protective levees may be the only reasonable answer, but in other circumstances, non-structural measures may make more sense. We can identify ways to protect and restore our river and wetlands systems so that they work *for* us, integrated with structural flood control measures. Of course, wetlands that provide flood control generally will also provide other important functions, such as fish and wildlife habitat, water quality improvement, and recreational opportunities. In our response to this flood-borne tragedy, the Administration will pursue measures that are the most effective means to prevent this catastrophe from happening again. Doubtless this will involve a combination of repair and construction of flood control structures together with restoration of natural flood attenuating river and wetlands systems.

Appendix E

Funding and Technical Assistance for Wetland Acquisition and Restoration

Many federal, state, and local programs, as well as private and nonprofit organizations offer cost-sharing, technical, and often direct payment assistance to private landowners to protect, restore, and create wetlands. Much of the information and funding involves agricultural-related activities in wetlands; however, ample resources also exist for landowners who engage in other activities. Options for private landowners include land banks, transferrable development rights, deed restrictions, easements to conservation organizations—all of which can provide tax breaks—and leases of rights to hunt, fish, harvest timber, and trap fur-bearing animals on the property.

The EPA Wetlands Information Hotline provides additional information about the agencies and program requirements discussed in this Appendix, as well as publications and regional contacts. Also, local Natural Resource Conservation Service offices (formerly the Soil Conservation Service) or county extension agent may know of other state and local programs.

GOVERNMENT AGENCIES

Natural Resource Conservation Service *(formerly known as the Soil Conservation Service)*

The Natural Resource Conservation Service (NRCS) is the technical arm of the USDA. NRCS administers programs such as the Wetlands

Reserve Program (WRP), the Water Bank Program, and the Forestry Incentives Program (FIP). Technical assistance is provided to landowners which they can request through local soil and water conservation districts. Landowners who sign agreements with local soil and water conservation districts can receive services for managing, using, enhancing, creating, and restoring wetlands. They must comply with the conservation provisions of the Food Security Act (see Chapter 3).

Forestry Incentives Program (FIP). The Forestry Incentives Program (FIP) is the major USDA forest tree planting program and can be used to help restored wooded wetlands. FIP provides technical and cost-sharing assistance to landowners participating in any one of four eligible national forestry practices. The overall goal of FIP is to increase the nation's supply of timber products from private non-industrial forest lands and preserve and improve the environment. FIP is jointly administered by the Farm Service Agency and the Forest Service.

Landowners apply for participation in the program at the county Farm Service Agency office. Upon request from the Farm Service Agency, the state forestry agency examines the property, develops the Forest Management Plan, and certifies the need for the practice. Forest management plans should specify the need for wetlands and riparian area protection measures. During the planning process, wetlands conservation and restoration opportunities, if any, should be discussed with the landowner and agreed-to measures incorporated into the final plan. The state forestry agency will also provide technical advice and help locate approved vendors for getting work accomplished.

Eligible forestry practices are divided into four forestry practice areas: tree planting (FP1); improving a stand of forest trees (FP2); site preparation for natural regeneration of trees (FP3); and special forestry practices (FP4). All FIP practices require a minimum 10-year maintenance agreement from the landowner.

The state forestry office must certify that the work has been completed in accordance with the approved plan before payment is made to the landowner by the county Farm Service Agency office. Cost-share assistance cannot exceed 65 percent of the actual, average, or estimated cost of performing the practice. The maximum cost-share that a participant can earn annually for forestry practices under FIP is $10,000. In some states, assistance is available under long-term agreements of three to ten years.

FIP is limited to landowners of 10 to 1,000 acres. Exceptions to the acreage limitation may be obtained for up to 5,000 acres. FIP is only offered in designated counties where a suitable number of ownerships exist which are each capable of producing at least 50 cubic feet of timber per year. Ornamental, Christmas tree production, and orchard tree plantings are not eligible for FIP funding.

Wetlands Reserve Program (WRP). The Wetlands Reserve Program (WRP) was authorized by the Food, Agriculture, Conservation, and Trade Act of 1990 (the 1990 Farm Bill). WRP is a voluntary program offering landowners a chance to receive payments for restoring and protecting wetlands on their property. Under WRP, landowners are provided cost-share funds to restore wetlands. They are paid up to the full market value of the land for granting the government a permanent easement and agreeing to maintain the wetland values in perpetuity. It is expected that by the year 2000, the WRP will have restored and protected nearly one million wetland acres nationwide.

Owners of eligible lands apply for enrollment at their local NRCS office by declaring their intent to participate during the specified enrollment periods. Following the declared intentions, the NRCS and the FWS will determine the eligibility of the acres offered, using national priority ranking factors, such as habitat for migratory birds and other wildlife, wetland functions, location significance, wetland management requirements, and physical conditions of the site. States may develop additional ranking factors.

The State Conservationist will then select the high priority intentions on which to extend offers. A Wetland Reserve Plan of Operations (WRPO) will be developed for each of the high priority areas. The NCRS, with the assistance of FWS, will help landowners develop the plans. Each plan will describe intentions and objectives as to restoration practices needed to accomplish the restoration, landowner requirements for maintaining the restored wetland values, and other details. The acceptable uses of the land after the easement is filed will also be spelled out in detail in the WRPO. They may include hunting, fishing, timber harvest, haying or grazing, and other uses depending on the situation. Duration and timing of these activities must be agreed upon and approved prior to completion of the WRPO. No activities may degrade or diminish the wetland functions and values of the land under easement.

After completion and approval of the plan by the agencies (including the conservation district) and the landowner, the landowner may accept the amount offered by NRCS for the easement. The government's offer will be based on the appraised agricultural value of the land. Up to 100 percent cost-share may be paid for restoring the wetlands and adjacent lands. State agencies and private conservation organizations may provide additional assistance and even incentives for enrollment. All legal costs associated with recording the easement will also be paid by the government. After the easement is filed and the restoration completed, a lump sum payment will be paid to the landowner.

The landowners will maintain full control over public access and use of the WRP easement lands. The WRP easement does not open the areas to public hunting, fishing, or other forms of recreation unless the landowner desires to do so. The landowner will be responsible for the minimal maintenance the area may require and for state and local taxes. However, taxes will likely be minimal as the land can no longer be used for crop production or developed. When lands are sold, the easement will follow the sale and the new owner assumes the easement obligations.

Eligibility for inclusion in the WRP are wetlands farmed under natural conditions, farmed wetlands, and wetlands converted to cropland prior to December 23, 1985. Adjacent land deemed necessary to protect the restored wetlands will also be included. Each WRP easement must be at least two acres in size and have been planted or considered planted to an agricultural commodity in at least one of the 1986-1990 crop years.

Riparian areas link wetlands protected by easement or similar device are also eligible for WRP irrespective of their land use. The protected areas being linked can be protected by a WRP easement entered in a previous sign-up or that is being offered at the same time, or it may be a wetland area owned and protected by a government agency or a private organization. Because of the multiplicity of these values provided by connecting riparian strips, riparian offers are generally given a top priority for acceptance.

Contact: USDA
NRCS
National Wetlands Team
P.O. Box 2890
Washington, DC 20013

Consolidated Farm Service Agency (CFSA). The Consolidated Farm Service Agent (CFSA) combines the functions of the Agricultural Stabilization and Conservation Service (ASCS), the Federal Crop Insurance Corporation (FCIC), and the farm-lending activities of the Farmers Home Administration (FmHA). The CFSA oversees such programs as the Agricultural Conservation Program (ACP) and the Conservation Reserve Program (CRP).

Agricultural Conservation Program (ACP). The Agricultural Conservation Program (ACP) encourages voluntary compliance with federal and state requirements for solving point and nonpoint source pollution on farms and ranches. ACP provides 50 percent to 75 percent cost-share funds for approved practices providing long-term and community-wide conservation benefits.

ACP agreements can be for one year or more. When entering into an agreement, the farmer pays the total cost of establishing the approved conservation practices and is then reimbursed for the government's share of the cost, which may range up to 75 percent of total costs for annual agreements. The maximum cost-share limitation for annual conservation management plans is $3,500 per year.

Long-term agreements require the development of a conservation plan by the Natural Resources Conservation Service and approval of the plan by the local soil and water conservation district and the county Farm Service Agency office. Lump sum payments in excess of $3,500 may be authorized for a long-term agreement under certain conditions. Farmers and ranchers may enter into pooling agreements to jointly solve mutual conservation problems. Pooling agreements could be used to restore a wetland area covering portions of several properties. The applicant must own between 10 and 1,000 acres to be eligible. Contact the nearest county Farm Service Agency office for details on a particular program.

Conservation Easement Debt Cancellation Program. Persons with Farm Service Agency (FSA) loans secured by real estate may qualify for cancellation of a portion of their indebtedness in exchange for a conservation easement. Easements may be established on wetlands, marginal cropland, and other environmentally sensitive lands for conservation, recreation, and wildlife purposes.

Borrowers who are up-to-date on their loan payments as well as those who are experiencing difficulty in keeping their loans current are eligible to participate. A conservation easement may be considered alone or in conjunction with FSA's Primary Loan Servicing Programs or new loans which are secured by real estate. By participating in the Conservation Easement Debt Cancellation Program, borrowers reduce their FSA debt, thereby improving their overall financial stability. In addition, borrowers can conserve wildlife habitat and improve the environmental and scenic value of their farms.

The process of easement establishment begins at the FSA County Office level when a borrower requests to be considered for a conservation easement. The County Supervisor determines if the borrower is eligible and contacts members of an easement review team. This team, consisting of representatives of the FSA, the NRCS, the U.S. Fish and Wildlife Service (FWS), and interested state and local conservation agencies, works with the borrower to conduct a field evaluation of the farm. Within 30 days of the site review, the team provides a report to the County Supervisor indicating the following:

- Which lands are eligible and potential easement boundaries.
- A finding of whether the land is suitable for conservation, recreation, and/or wildlife purposes.
- The name of the agency or entity that is willing to accept easement enforcement responsibility from the FSA.
- The recommended terms and conditions of the easement.
- A proposed management plan which is consistent with the easement purposes.

The County Supervisor evaluates the easement review team's report to determine if a conservation easement can be established on the farm in exchange for debt reduction.

In general, the amount of the borrower's FSA loan debt secured by real property that can be canceled is proportional to the amount of the farm that will be covered by the easement. However, for borrowers who are up-to-date on their loan payments or receiving a new loan secured by real estate, no more than 33 percent of the loan principal can be canceled in exchange for an easement. For delinquent borrowers, the amount of debt canceled may surpass this amount, provided it does not exceed the value of the land on which the easement is placed. The FSA County Supervisor can provide more detailed information on how much debt may be canceled.

The FSA will cover the cost of all surveys, appraisals, and recording fees associated with the conservation easement. However, the borrower must obtain written consent to the terms of the conservation easement from all prior and/or junior lien holders, if any exist.

In most cases, especially where wetlands and important wildlife habitat are involved, a permanent easement will be established. Under no circumstances will the terms and conditions apply for less than 50 years. In general, activities that are contrary to restoration and protection of the natural ecology of the area are prohibited by the easement.

The borrower retains the right to control public access to the easement area, and where compatible with the easement purpose, may use the area for hunting and fishing and other innocuous activities. The easement enforcement authority, in conjunction with the FSA, monitors the terms and conditions of the conservation easement.

The easement enforcement authority may designate a manager of the easement to conduct habitat management activities and to monitor the easement area. This may be a federal, state, or local government agency, a private conservation group, or an individual capable of carrying out the activities outlined in the easement management plan. The landowner may be eligible to serve as easement manager.

In most instances, the FWS provides technical and financial assistance to restore wetlands and other important habitats valuable to migratory birds and other wildlife on the easement area. Once these habitats are restored, the easement manager bears responsibility for maintenance.

Once a conservation easement is established, the property is subject to the easement for its duration, regardless of who owns the land. New owners of the property will be subject to the same restrictions and retain the same rights as the borrower who was originally granted the easement in exchange for the debt reduction.

Conservation Reserve Program (CRP). The Conservation Reserve Program (CRP) was introduced in the Food Security Act of 1985 and amended by the Food, Agriculture, Conservation, and Trade Act of 1990 to encourage farmers to enroll highly erodible cropland, and/or land contributing to a serious water quality problem, into the reserve for 10-15 years. In return, farmers receive annual rental payments for the land, cost-sharing, and technical assistance to plant vegetation for conservation. The major goals of CRP include reducing soil erosion and sedimentation, improving water quality, maintaining fish and wildlife habitat, and providing support income to farmers. The program is administered by the Consolidated Farm Service Agency in cooperation with the NCRS, Cooperative Extension Service, state forestry agencies, and local soil and water conservation districts.

Nationwide, farmers have entered over 36 million acres of mainly highly erodible cropland into the CRP and have established permanent vegetation on those lands. The enrollment of additional acreage into this program is not expected since it is likely that future funding will not be made available.

Lands in this program cannot be tilled or grazed until the end of the 10-year contract (only lands planted with trees may have a longer contract). Although most CRP lands are classified as "highly erodible," fields often include areas of former wetlands that could be restored. A small acreage of cropland fields containing mainly farmed wetlands or former wetlands was entered into the program in 1988 and 1989. Although landowners may return these lands to crop production at the end of the contract period, much of it is not economical to farm under the requirements for cropping of highly erodible lands.

Very few of these fields had their full wetlands values restored. Although CRP funds are no longer available to help restore wetlands on these lands, the landowner may do so at any time. Non-USDA funds can be used to assist in the restoration, provided that the plans for the restoration are included in the landowner's Conservation Plan maintained by the NRCS.

Contact: USDA
CFSA
Conservation and Environmental Protection Division
P.O. Box 2415
Washington, DC 20013

U.S. Forest Service (USFS). The U.S. Forest Service (USFS) administers the Forest Stewardship Program (FSP), the Stewardship Incentive Program (SIP), and the Forest Legacy Program.

Forest Stewardship Program (FSP). The Forest Stewardship Program (FSP) and the Stewardship Incentive Program (SIP) were established through the Food, Agriculture, Conservation, and Trade Act of 1990 (FACTA) to help landowners protect or enhance their forest lands and associated wetlands. FSP provides technical assistance to help landowners enhance and protect timber, fish and wildlife habitat, water quality, wetlands, and recreational and aesthetic values of their property. SIP provides cost-share assistance to private landowners for implementing the management plans developed under the FSP.

The guidelines for SIP define eight major categories for funding:

1. Management Plan Development.
2. Reforestation and Afforestation.
3. Forest and Agroforest Improvement.
4. Windbreak and Hedgerow Establishment.
5. Riparian and Wetlands Protection and Improvement.
6. Fisheries Habitat Enhancement.
7. Wildlife Enhancement.
8. Forest Recreation Enhancement.

SIP 6, Riparian and Wetlands Protection and Improvement, is the cost-share practice for restoring and protecting wetlands and riparian areas. Cost-share is authorized for purchase, installation, and establishment of plant materials, stream bank stabilization, fencing, and the restoration of natural hydrology.

FSP and SIP are administered by the State Forester for each state in cooperation with the Forest Service. The Consolidated Farm Service

Agency provides administrative assistance. Technical responsibilities for SIP practices may be assigned to various other agencies and resource professionals.

State forestry agency staff work with private landowners to develop a multi-use Forest Stewardship Resource Conservation Plan specifically for their forested properties. These plans outline a course of action that will enhance forest products, wildlife, soil and water quality, recreation, aesthetics, and environmental quality. Existing management plans can usually be modified to meet FSP guidelines. Once a forest management plan has been developed and approved, up to 65 percent cost-share is provided through SIP to fund the plan's projects. Payments to the landowner may not exceed $10,000 per landowner per fiscal year. Significant accomplishments are recognized by designating the landowner "Forest Steward" which gives public recognition to the landowner.

Eligible landowners must have an approved Forest Stewardship Plan and own 1,000 acres or less of qualifying land. Authorizations may be obtained for exceptions of up to 5,000 acres. Landowners must maintain and protect SIP-funded practices for a minimum of 10 years.

Contact: USDA
USFS
Cooperative Forestry Staff
Auditor's Building
201 14th Street, S.W.
Washington, DC 20250

U.S. Department of the Interior (USDOI). The USDOI helps private landowners through the U.S. Fish and Wildlife Service (FWS) with such programs as Partners for Wildlife and the North American Waterfowl Management Plan (NAWMP).

Partners for Wildlife

The Partners for Wildlife program offers technical and financial assistance to landowners who wish to restore degraded or converted wetlands, riparian, stream, and other critical habitats. The program focuses on reestablishment of original natural communities. Special consideration is given to projects that: (1) contribute to the survival of endangered, threatened, or candidate species, or migratory birds of management concern; (2) contribute to the objectives of the National Wildlife Refuge System or the North American Waterfowl Management Plan; (3) are located very close to existing habitats so that fragmentation of habitats would be reduced and recolonization by a full component of native plants and animals could easily occur; (4) contribute to the restoration of globally or nationally imperiled natural communities; or (5) will result in a self-sustaining system that is not dependent on artificial structures.

The assistance that the U.S. Fish and Wildlife Service (FWS) offers to landowners may take the form of informal advice on the design and location of potential restoration projects, or it may consist of designing and funding restoration projects under a formal cooperative agreement with the landowner. Restoration efforts may include, but are not limited to, plugging drainage ditches, installation of water control structures, dike construction, planting trees in formerly forested wetlands, restoring natural stream channel characteristics, fencing streams and rivers, and re-establishing natural riparian or prairie grassland vegetation.

If other considerations are roughly equal, cooperative agreements that are 25 years or longer in duration are preferable to those of shorter duration. In no case, however, may cooperative agreements be less than 10 years in duration. Cost-sharing may improve chances that the project will be funded, but it is not required. A restoration project that involves more than $10,000 of FWS funding for the initial restoration work must be justified in terms of biological significance of the work and (1) non-federal cost-sharing of at least 50 percent or (2) a very large acreage is proposed for restoration. Nationally, an average of 40 percent non-FWS cost-sharing is a program objective.

Subject to priority and preference factors stated above, any degraded or converted wetland or degraded riparian or stream corridor is eligible for restoration with technical and financial assistance by the FWS. Upland habitats are eligible for financial assistance only if their restoration will contribute to certain program goals.

North American Wetlands Conservation Act. The North American Wetlands Conservation Act (NAWCA), established in 1989, encourages partnerships among public agencies and other interests to: (1) protect, enhance, restore, and manage wetland ecosystems and other habitats for migratory birds, fish, and wildlife in North American; (2) maintain current or improved distribution of migratory bird populations; and (3) sustain an abundance of waterfowl and other migratory birds consistent with the goals of the North American Waterfowl Management Plan and international treaty obligations.

The NAWCA provides funding for wetlands conservation projects involving acquisition, restoration, and/or enhancement. Funding is approved by the Migratory Bird Conservation Commission (MBCC) based on recommendations from the North American Wetlands Conservation Council. The FWS coordinates with the Council and the NAWCA and can provide assistance to landowners to develop proposals for submission to the Council and the MBCC.

Proposals may be submitted by any group or individual by the second Tuesday in April and August for funding available October 1. A proposal must describe how the proposed work fits into a larger project (if applicable); the need for the proposal; where the work is to be done; the effect of the proposal on animals, plants, and wetland functions; how much the proposal will cost; and partner commitments and responsibilities. A grant application instruction booklet outlining the above information in more detail is available through FWS Regional Offices or the North American Wetlands Conservation Council.

NAWCA grants require a minimum one-to-one grant match from any non-federal source, such as a state, non-profit group, or the landowner. Annual payments for leases or easements require a minimum 10-year agreement.

Projects involving acquisition, restoration, enhancement, creation, management, and other activities that conserve wetland ecosystems and the fish and wildlife that depend on such habitats are eligible for funding.

North American Waterfowl Management Plan (NAWMP) is an agreement signed in 1986 between the United States and Canada to protect, restore, and enhance wetlands important to waterfowl and other wetland-dependent species. The NAWMP sets out objectives for returning waterfowl populations to levels observed in the 1970s. The plan is implemented at the grassroots level by unique partnerships called joint ventures. Wetlands identified under the NAWMP as "areas of major concern" for waterfowl habitat benefit from these joint ventures.

The FWS coordinates joint ventures with federal, state, and private agencies, and private individuals that cooperate and pool resources together to achieve objectives of the plan. Private landowners of wetlands significant to waterfowl may receive technical and financial assistance through a variety of cooperative programs undertaken within their geographic area. The Plan also entails research on wetlands restoration and the effects of contaminants on wetlands, wetland status surveys, and wetlands inventories. Landowners interested in learning about the joint venture NAWMP projects in their area should contact the joint venture coordinator in their area.

Contact: USDOI
USFWS
North American Waterfowl and Wetlands Office
4401 North Fairfax Drive
Arlington, VA 22203

U.S. Environmental Protection Agency (USEPA)

The U.S. Environmental Protection Agency (USEPA) offers information on current EPA wetland conservation, acquisition, and restoration initiatives through the Wetlands Division of its Office of Wetlands, Oceans, and Watersheds (OWOW) and the contractor-operated Wetlands Information Hotline.

Contact: USEPA
OWOW
Wetlands Division (4502F)
401 M Street, S.W.
Washington, DC 20460

The Office of Wetlands, Oceans, and Watersheds also provides financial assistance under Section 319(h) of the Clean Water Act for a number of wetland restoration and protection activities.

Contact: USEPA
OWOW
Nonpoint Source Control Branch (4503F)
401 M Street, S.W.
Washington, DC 20460

PRIVATE/NONPROFIT CONSERVATION GROUPS

Ducks Unlimited

Ducks Unlimited administers the Matching Aid to Restore States Habitat (MARSH) Program. The MARSH Program was begun in 1985 to provide matching funds to public agencies and private conservation groups for projects significantly benefiting waterfowl. Private landowners can benefit from the funding provided through MARSH if waterfowl and habitat restoration projects on their property qualify for the funding and is applied for by the agency or group working with the landowner.

MARSH project proposals should be developed and submitted to the MARSH coordinator by the agency or conservation group developing a habitat project. These proposals should include all pertinent information regarding location, legal description, ownership, management objectives, description of work, projected costs, and any supplementary support information pertinent to the project. Once the MARSH coordinator receives all of the necessary information, he will visit those sites with the most potential and prepare project evaluations.

Projects that lead to the protection and/or restoration of North American Waterfowl Management Plan (NAWMP) sites, benefiting non-game, threatened, or endangered species; unique habitats or ecosystems; and/or having high public visibility or interpretative values; in addition to providing substantial waterfowl values; will receive priority MARSH funding. Maximum cost-share assistance under the MARSH program is 50 percent.

Ducks Unlimited will consider proposals from any public agency or private conservation group that is: (1) able to execute a long-term habitat agreement; (2) capable of delivering and managing the proposed project; and (3) willing to assume all liability associated with the project. MARSH projects must be on lands under management control or oversight of a public agency or private cooperators.

Contact: Ducks Unlimited
MARSH Program Coordinator
1155 Connecticut Avenue, N.W., #800
Washington, DC 20036

The Nature Conservancy

The Nature Conservancy is an international, non-profit, science-based, membership organization whose mission is to preserve animals, plants, and natural communities by protecting the lands and waters they need to survive. The organization provides information to private landowners on methods of protecting natural areas, including acquisition, conservation easements, bargain sales, donations, and voluntary agreements. The Nature Conservancy also provides information of management practices and other scientific information.

Contact: The Nature Conservancy
2 Wisconsin Avenue
Chevy Chase, MD 20815

Trust for Public Land (TPL)

The Trust for Public Land (TPL) is a national nonprofit land conservation organization dedicated to conserving land for people to enjoy as parks, community gardens, and recreational and natural areas. The TPL is a problem-solving organization that helps communities, public agencies, and nonprofit groups acquire and protect open space for public use.

Contact: Trust for Public Land
312 Massachusetts Avenue, N.W.
Washington, DC 20002

American Farmland Trust (AFT)

The American Farmland Trust (AFT) is a nonprofit organization that works with farmers, business people, legislators, and conservationists to encourage sound farming practices and preserve America's most critical agricultural resources. AFT conducts on-farm research and demonstration projects with grassroots sustainable agriculture organizations and farmers to develop and encourage the use of sound environmental farming practices. AFT provides advice to private landowners on ways to include conservation strategies in land use and estate plans for farmers, and accepts donations of land and conservation easements for conservation purposes.

The Farm Legacy Program is a new AFT program that encourages individuals owning farms threatened by development to donate their lands to AFT. Farm Legacy is a very flexible program, allowing the prospective donor and AFT staff to structure gifts to meet the landowner's needs. Landowners donating their agricultural lands to AFT may retain lifetime use of the property. Donors may also receive significant income and estate-tax deductions. Upon receiving the donated property, AFT will sell the farm with conservation easements to guarantee the preservation of the property. Proceeds from the sale will then be used to protect other threatened farms.

The Farm Legacy Program, which will help to preserve wetlands located on agricultural lands that might otherwise be sold for development purposes, can potentially be coupled with other programs, such as the Conservation Reserve Program.

Contact: American Farmland Trust
1920 N Street, N.W.
Washington, DC 20036

Appendix F

EPA/Army Corps Memorandum of Agreement Concerning the Determination of Mitigation under the Clean Water Act Section 404(b)(1) Guidelines

**MEMORANDUM OF AGREEMENT
BETWEEN THE ENVIRONMENTAL PROTECTION AGENCY
AND THE DEPARTMENT OF THE ARMY CONCERNING
THE DETERMINATION OF MITIGATION UNDER THE
CLEAN WATER ACT SECTION 404(b)(1) GUIDELINES**

I. Purpose

The United States Environmental Protection Agency (EPA) and the United States Department of the Army (Army) hereby articulate the policy and procedures to be used in the determination of the type and level of mitigation necessary to demonstrate compliance with the Clean Water Act (CWA) Section 404(b)(1) Guidelines ("Guidelines"). This Memorandum of Agreement (MOA) expresses the explicit intent of the Army and EPA to implement the objective of the CWA to restore and maintain the chemical, physical, and biological integrity of the Nation's waters, including wetlands. This MOA is specifically limited to the Section 404 Regulatory Program and is written to provide guidance for agency field personnel on the type and level of mitigation which demonstrates compliance with requirements in the Guidelines. The policies and procedures discussed herein are consistent with current Section 404 regulatory practices and are provided in response to questions that have been raised about how the Guidelines are implemented. The MOA does not change the substantive requirements of the Guidelines. It is intended to provide guidance regarding the exercise of discretion under the Guidelines.

Although the Guidelines are clearly applicable to all discharges of dredged or fill material, including general permits and Corps of Engineers (Corps) civil works projects, this MOA focuses on standard permits (33 CFR 325.5(b)(1))[1]. This focus is intended solely to reflect the unique procedural aspects associated with the review of standard permits, and does not obviate the need for other regulated activities to comply fully with the Guidelines. EPA and Army will seek to develop supplemental guidance for other regulated activities consistent with the policies and principles established in this document.

This MOA provides guidance to Corps and EPA personnel for implementing the Guidelines and must be adhered to when considering mitigation requirements for standard permit applications. The Corps will use this MOA when making its determination of compliance with the Guidelines with respect to mitigation for standard permit applications. EPA will use this MOA in developing its positions on compliance with the Guidelines for

---

[1] Standard permits are those individual permits which have been processed through application of the Corps public interest review procedures (33 CFR 325) and EPA's Section 404(b)(1) Guidelines, including public notice and receipt of comments. Standard permits do not include letters of permission, regional permits, nationwide permits, or programmatic permits.

proposed discharges and will reflect this MOA when commenting on standard permit applications.

II. Policy

A. The Council on Environmental Quality (CEQ) has defined mitigation in its regulations at 40 CFR 1508.20 to include: avoiding impacts, minimizing impacts, rectifying impacts, reducing impacts over time, and compensating for impacts. The Guidelines establish environmental criteria which must be met for activities to be permitted under Section 404.[2] The types of mitigation enumerated by CEQ are compatible with the requirements of the Guidelines; however, as a practical matter, they can be combined to form three general types: avoidance, minimization and compensatory mitigation. The remainder of this MOA will speak in terms of these more general types of mitigation.

B. The Clean Water Act and the Guidelines set forth a goal of restoring and maintaining existing aquatic resources. The Corps will strive to avoid adverse impacts and offset unavoidable adverse impacts to existing aquatic resources, and for wetlands, will strive to achieve a goal of no overall net loss of values and functions. In focusing the goal of no overall net loss to wetlands only, EPA and Army have explicitly recognized the special significance of the nation's wetlands resources. This special recognition of wetlands resources does not in any manner diminish the value of other waters of the United States, which are often of high value. All waters of the United States, such as streams, rivers, lakes, etc., will be accorded the full measure of protection under the Guidelines, including the requirements for appropriate and practicable mitigation. The determination of what level of mitigation constitutes "appropriate" mitigation is based solely on the values and functions of the aquatic resource that will be impacted. "Practicable" is defined at Section 230.3(q) of the Guidelines.[3] However, the level of mitigation determined to be appropriate and practicable under Section 230.10(d) may lead to individual permit decisions which do not fully meet this goal because the mitigation measures necessary to meet this goal are not feasible, not practicable, or would accomplish only inconsequential reductions in impacts. Consequently, it is recognized that no net loss of wetlands functions and values may not be achieved in each and every permit action. However, it remains a goal of the Section 404 regulatory program to contribute to the national goal of no overall net loss of the nation's remaining wetlands base. EPA and Army are committed to working with others through the Administration's interagency task force and other avenues to help achieve this national goal.

---

[2](except where Section 404(b)(2) applies).

[3]Section 230.3(q) of the Guidelines reads as follows: "The term practicable means available and capable of being done after taking into consideration *cost, existing technology, and logistics in light of overall project purposes.*" (Emphasis supplied)

C. In evaluating standard Section 404 permit applications, as a practical matter, information on all facets of a project, including potential mitigation, is typically gathered and reviewed at the same time. The Corps, except as indicated below, first makes a determination that potential impacts have been avoided to the maximum extent practicable; remaining unavoidable impacts will then be mitigated to the extent appropriate and practicable by requiring steps to minimize impacts and, finally, compensate for aquatic resource values. This sequence is considered satisfied where the proposed mitigation is in accordance with specific provisions of a Corps and EPA approved comprehensive plan that ensures compliance with the compensation requirements of the Section 404(b)(1) Guidelines (examples of such comprehensive plans may include Special Area Management Plans, Advance Identification areas (Section 230.80), and State Coastal Zone Management Plans). It may be appropriate to deviate from the sequence when EPA and the Corps agree the proposed discharge is necessary to avoid environmental harm (e.g., to protect a natural aquatic community from saltwater intrusion, chemical contamination, or other deleterious physical or chemical impacts), or EPA and the Corps agree that the proposed discharge can reasonably be expected to result in environmental gain or insignificant environmental losses.

In determining "appropriate and practicable" measures to offset unavoidable impacts, such measures should be appropriate to the scope and degree of those impacts and practicable in terms of cost, existing technology, and logistics in light of overall project purposes. The Corps will give full consideration to the views of the resource agencies when making this determination.

1. **Avoidance.**[4] Section 230.10(a) allows permit issuance for only the least environmentally damaging practicable alternative.[5] The thrust of this section on alternatives is avoidance of impacts. Section 230.10(a) requires that no discharge shall be permitted if there is a practicable alternative to the proposed discharge which would have less adverse impact to the aquatic ecosystem, so long as the alternative does not have other significant adverse environmental consequences. In addition, Section 230.10(a)(3) sets forth rebuttable presumptions that 1) alternatives for non-water dependent activities that do not involve special aquatic sites[6] are available and 2) alternatives that do not involve special aquatic sites have less adverse impact on the aquatic environment.

---

[4]Avoidance as used in the Section 404(b)(1) Guidelines and this MOA does not include compensatory mitigation.

[5]It is important to recognize that there are circumstances where the impacts of the project are so significant that even if alternatives are not available, the discharge may not be permitted regardless of the compensatory mitigation proposed (40 CFR 230.10(c)).

[6]Special aquatic sites include sanctuaries and refuges, wetlands, mud flats, vegetated shallows, coral reefs and riffle pool complexes.

Compensatory mitigation may not be used as a method to reduce environmental impacts in the evaluation of the least environmentally damaging practicable alternatives for the purposes of requirements under Section 230.10(a).

2. **Minimization.** Section 230.10(d) states that appropriate and practicable steps to minimize the adverse impacts will be required through project modifications and permit conditions. Subpart H of the Guidelines describes several (but not all) means for minimizing impacts of an activity.

3. **Compensatory Mitigation.** Appropriate and practicable compensatory mitigation is required for unavoidable adverse impacts which remain after all appropriate and practicable minimization has been required. Compensatory actions (e.g., restoration of existing degraded wetlands or creation of man-made wetlands) should be undertaken, when practicable, in areas adjacent or contiguous to the discharge site (on-site compensatory mitigation). If on-site compensatory mitigation is not practicable, off-site compensatory mitigation should be undertaken in the same geographic area if practicable (i.e., in close physical proximity and, to the extent possible, the same watershed). In determining compensatory mitigation, the functional values lost by the resource to be impacted must be considered. Generally, in-kind compensatory mitigation is preferable to out-of-kind. There is continued uncertainty regarding the success of wetland creation or other habitat development. Therefore, in determining the nature and extent of habitat development of this type, careful consideration should be given to its likelihood of success. Because the likelihood of success is greater and the impacts to potentially valuable uplands are reduced, restoration should be the first option considered.

In the situation where the Corps is evaluating a project where a permit issued by another agency requires compensatory mitigation, the Corps may consider that mitigation as part of the overall application for purposes of public notice, but avoidance and minimization shall still be sought.

Mitigation banking may be an acceptable form of compensatory mitigation under specific criteria designed to ensure an environmentally successful bank. Where a mitigation bank has been approved by EPA and the Corps for purposes of providing compensatory mitigation for specific identified projects, use of that mitigation bank for those particular projects is considered as meeting the objectives of Section II.C.3 of this MOA, regardless of the practicability of other forms of compensatory mitigation. Additional guidance on mitigation banking will be provided. Simple purchase or "preservation" of existing wetlands resources may in only exceptional circumstances be accepted as compensatory mitigation. EPA and Army will develop specific guidance for preservation in the context of compensatory mitigation at a later date.

III. Other Procedures

A. Potential applicants for major projects should be encouraged to arrange preapplication meetings with the Corps and appropriate federal, state or Indian tribal, and local authorities to determine requirements and documentation required for proposed permit evaluations. As a result of such meetings, the applicant often revises a proposal to avoid or minimize adverse impacts after developing an understanding of the Guidelines requirements by which a future Section 404 permit decision will be made, in addition to gaining an understanding of other state or tribal, or local requirements. Compliance with other statutes, requirements and reviews, such as NEPA and the Corps public interest review, may not in and of themselves satisfy the requirements prescribed in the Guidelines.

B. In achieving the goals of the CWA, the Corps will strive to avoid adverse impacts and offset unavoidable adverse impacts to existing aquatic resources. Measures which can accomplish this can be identified only through resource assessments tailored to the site performed by qualified professionals because ecological characteristics of each aquatic site are unique. Functional values should be assessed by applying aquatic site assessment techniques generally recognized by experts in the field and/or the best professional judgment of federal and state agency representatives, provided such assessments fully consider ecological functions included in the Guidelines. The objective of mitigation for unavoidable impacts is to offset environmental losses. Additionally for wetlands, such mitigation should provide, at a minimum, one for one functional replacement (i.e., no net loss of values), with an adequate margin of safety to reflect the expected degree of success associated with the mitigation plan, recognizing that this minimum requirement may not be appropriate and practicable, and thus may not be relevant in all cases, as discussed in Section II.B of this MOA.[7] In the absence of more definitive information on the functions and values of specific wetlands sites, a minimum of 1 to 1 acreage replacement may be used as a reasonable surrogate for no net loss of functions and values. However, this ratio may be greater where the functional values of the area being impacted are demonstrably high and the replacement wetlands are of lower functional value or the likelihood of success of the mitigation project is low. Conversely, the ratio may be less than 1 to 1 for areas where the functional values associated with the

---

[7]For example, there are certain areas where, due to hydrological conditions, the technology for restoration or creation of wetlands may not be available at present, or may otherwise be impracticable. In addition, avoidance, minimization, and compensatory mitigation may not be practicable where there is a high proportion of land which is wetlands. EPA and Army, at present, are discussing with representatives of the oil industry, the potential for a program of accelerated rehabilitation of abandoned oil facilities on the North Slope to serve as a vehicle for satisfying necessary compensation requirements.

area being impacted are demonstrably low and the likelihood of success associated with the mitigation proposal is high.

C. The Guidelines are the environmental standard for Section 404 permit issuance under the CWA. Aspects of a proposed project may be affected through a determination of requirements needed to comply with the Guidelines to achieve these CWA environmental goals.

D. Monitoring is an important aspect of mitigation, especially in areas of scientific uncertainty. Monitoring should be directed toward determining whether permit conditions are complied with and whether the purpose intended to be served by the conditions actually achieved. Any time it is determined that a permittee is in non-compliance mitigation requirements of the permit, the Corps will take action in accordance with CFR Part 326. Monitoring should not be required for purposes other than these, although information for other uses may accrue from the monitoring requirements. For projects to be permitted involving mitigation with higher levels of scientific uncertainty, such as some forms of compensatory mitigation, long term monitoring, reporting and potential remedial action should be required. This can be required of the applicant through permit conditions.

E. Mitigation requirements shall be conditions of standard Section 404 permits. Army regulations authorize mitigation requirements to be added as special conditions to an Army permit to satisfy legal requirements (e.g., conditions necessary to satisfy the Guidelines) [33 CFR 325.4(a)]. This ensures legal enforceability of the mitigation conditions and enhances the level of compliance. If the mitigation plan necessary to ensure compliance with the Guidelines is not reasonably implementable or enforceable, the permit shall be denied.

F. Nothing in this document is intended to diminish, modify or otherwise affect the statutory or regulatory authorities of the agencies involved. Furthermore, formal policy guidance on or interpretation of this document shall be issued jointly.

G. This MOA shall take effect on February 7, 1990, and will apply to those completed standard permit applications which are received on or after that date. This MOA may be modified or revoked by agreement of both parties, or revoked by either party alone upon six (6) months written notice.

Robert W. Page (date) 2/6/90
Assistant Secretary of the Army
(Civil Works)

LaJuana S. Wilcher (date) 2/6/90
Assistant Administrator for Water
U.S. Environmental Protection Agency

Appendix G

Department of Agriculture, Environmental Protection Agency, Department of the Interior, and Department of the Army Memorandum of Agreement Concerning the Delineation of Wetlands for Purposes of Section 404 of the Clean Water Act and Subtitle B of the Food Security Act

MEMORANDUM OF AGREEMENT

AMONG THE DEPARTMENT OF AGRICULTURE, THE ENVIRONMENTAL PROTECTION AGENCY, THE DEPARTMENT OF THE INTERIOR, AND THE DEPARTMENT OF THE ARMY

CONCERNING THE DELINEATION OF WETLANDS FOR PURPOSES OF SECTION 404 OF THE CLEAN WATER ACT AND SUBTITLE B OF THE FOOD SECURITY ACT

I. BACKGROUND

The Departments of the Army, Agriculture, and the Interior, and the Environmental Protection Agency (EPA) recognize fully that the protection of the Nation's remaining wetlands is an important objective that will be supported through the implementation of the Wetland Conservation (Swampbuster) provision of the Food Security Act (FSA) and Section 404 of the Clean Water Act (CWA). The agencies further recognize and value the important contribution of agricultural producers to our society, our economy, and our environment. We are committed to ensuring that Federal wetlands programs are administered in a manner that minimizes the impacts on affected landowners to the fullest possible extent consistent with the important goal of protecting wetlands. We are also committed to minimizing duplication and inconsistencies between Swampbuster and the CWA Section 404 program. On August 24, 1993, the Administration announced a comprehensive package of reforms that will improve both the protection of wetlands and make wetlands programs more fair and flexible for landowners, including the Nation's agriculture producers. This Memorandum of Agreement (MOA) implements one of over 40 components of the Administration's Wetlands Plan.

II. PURPOSE AND APPLICABILITY

A. PURPOSE

The purpose of this MOA is to specify the manner in which wetland delineations and certain other determinations of waters of the United States made by the U.S. Department of Agriculture (USDA) under the FSA will be relied upon for purposes of CWA Section 404. While this MOA will promote consistency between CWA and FSA wetlands programs, it is not intended in any way to diminish the protection of these important aquatic resources. In this regard, all signatory agencies to this MOA will ensure that wetlands programs are administered in a manner consistent with the objectives and requirements of applicable laws, implementing regulations, and guidance.

B. APPLICABILITY

1. The Administrator of EPA has the ultimate authority to determine the geographic scope of waters of the United States subject to jurisdiction under the CWA, including the Section 404 regulatory program. Consistent with a current MOA between EPA and the Department of the Army, the Army Corps of Engineers (Corps) conducts jurisdictional delineations associated with the day-to-day administration of the Section 404 program.

2. The Secretary of the USDA, acting through the Chief of the Soil Conservation Service (SCS), has the ultimate authority to determine the geographic scope of wetlands for FSA purposes and to make delineations relative to the FSA, in consultation with the Department of the Interior, Fish and Wildlife Service (FWS).

III. DEFINITION OF AGRICULTURAL LANDS

For the purposes of this MOA, the term "agricultural lands" means those lands intensively used and managed for the production of food or fiber to the extent that the natural vegetation has been removed and cannot be used to determine whether the area meets applicable hydrophytic vegetation criteria in making a wetland delineation.

A. Areas that meet the above definition may include intensively used and managed cropland, hayland, pasture land, orchards, vineyards, and areas which support wetland crops (e.g., cranberries, taro, watercress, rice). For example, lands intensively used and managed for pasture or hayland where the natural vegetation has been removed and replaced with planted grasses or legumes such as ryegrass, bluegrass, or alfalfa, are considered agricultural lands for the purposes of this MOA.

B. "Agricultural lands" do not include range lands, forest lands, wood lots, or tree farms. Further, lands where the natural vegetation has not been removed, even though that vegetation may be regularly grazed or mowed and collected as forage or fodder (e.g., uncultivated meadows and prairies, salt hay), are not considered agricultural lands for the purposes of this MOA.

Other definitions for the purposes of this MOA are listed below in Section VI.

IV. ALLOCATION OF RESPONSIBILITY

A. In accordance with the terms and procedures of this MOA, wetland delineations made by SCS on agricultural lands, in consultation with FWS, will be accepted by EPA and the Corps for the purposes of determining Section 404 wetland jurisdiction. In addition, EPA and the Corps will accept SCS wetland delineations on non-agricultural lands that are either narrow bands immediately adjacent to, or small pockets interspersed among, agricultural lands. SCS is responsible for making wetland delineations for agricultural lands whether or not the person who owns, manages, or operates the land is a participant in USDA programs.

B. Lands owned or operated by a USDA program participant that are not agricultural lands and for which a USDA program participant requests a wetland delineation, will be delineated by SCS in coordination with the Corps, or EPA as appropriate, and in consultation with FWS. Final wetland delineations conducted by SCS pursuant to the requirements of this paragraph shall not be revised by SCS except where an opportunity for coordination and consultation is provided to the other signatory agencies.

C. SCS may conduct delineations of other waters for the purposes of Section 404 of the CWA, such as lakes, ponds, and streams, in coordination with the Corps, or EPA as appropriate, on lands on which SCS is otherwise engaged in wetland delineations pursuant to paragraphs IV.A or IV.B of this MOA. Delineations of "other waters" will not be made until the interagency oversight team convened pursuant to Section V.B.2 has agreed on appropriate local procedures and guidance for making such delineations.

D. For agricultural lands, the signatory agencies will use the procedures for delineating wetlands as described in the National Food Security Act Manual, Third Edition (NFSAM). For areas that are not agricultural lands, SCS will use the 1987 Corps Wetland Delineation Manual, with current national Corps guidance, to make wetland delineations applicable to Section 404.

E. Delineations on "agricultural lands" must be performed by personnel who are trained in the use of the NFSAM. Delineations on other lands and waters must be performed by personnel who are trained in the use of the 1987 Corps Wetland Delineation Manual. This MOA includes provisions for the appropriate interagency delineation training below in Section V.E.

F. In the spirit of the agencies' commitment to develop agreed upon methods for use in making wetland delineations, subsequent revisions or amendments to the Corps 1987 manual or portions of the NFSAM affecting the wetland delineation procedures upon which this agreement is based will require the concurrence of the four signatory agencies.

G. A final written wetland delineation made by SCS pursuant to the terms of this MOA will be adhered to by all the signatory agencies and will be effective for a period of five years from the date the delineation is made final, unless new information warrants revision of the delineation before the expiration date. Such new information may include, for example, data on landscape changes caused by a major flood, or a landowner's notification of intent to abandon agricultural use and the return of wetland conditions on a prior converted cropland. In accordance with Section 1222 of the FSA, SCS will update wetland delineations on this five-year cycle. Circumstances under which SCS wetland delineations made prior to the effective date of this agreement will be considered as final for Section 404 purposes are addressed in Paragraph V.C.

H. Within the course of administering their Swampbuster responsibilities, SCS and FWS will provide landowners/operators general written information (i.e., EPA/Corps fact sheets) regarding the CWA Section 404 program permit requirements, general permits, and exemptions. The SCS and FWS will not, however, provide opinions regarding the applicability of CWA Section 404 permit requirements or exemptions.

I. USDA will maintain documentation of all final written SCS wetland delineations and record the appropriate label and boundary information on an official wetland delineation map. USDA will make this information available to the signatory agencies upon request.

J. In pursuing enforcement activities, the signatory agencies will rely upon delineations made by the lead agency, as clarified below, providing a single Federal delineation for potential violations of Section 404 or Swampbuster. Nothing in this MOA will diminish, modify, or otherwise affect existing EPA and Corps enforcement authorities under the CWA and clarified in the 1989 "EPA/Army MOA Concerning Federal Enforcement for the Section 404 Program of the Clean Water Act." EPA, the Corps, and SCS may gather information based on site visits or other means to provide additional evidentiary support for a wetland delineation which is the subject of a potential or ongoing CWA Section 404 or Swampbuster enforcement action.

K. For those lands where SCS has not made a final written wetland delineation, and where the Corps or EPA is pursuing a potential CWA violation, the lead agency for the CWA enforcement action will conduct a jurisdictional delineation for the purposes of Section 404 and such delineations will be used by SCS for determining Swampbuster jurisdiction and potential Swampbuster violations. For those lands where the Corps has not made a final written wetland delineation, and where SCS is pursuing a potential Swampbuster violation, SCS will make a final written wetland delineation consistent with Sections IV.A, IV.B, and IV.C of this MOA and provide copies to the Corps and EPA. Such delineations will be used by the Corps and EPA for the purpose of determining potential violations of the CWA. In circumstances in which either the Corps or EPA is pursuing a potential CWA violation on land that is subject to an ongoing SCS appeal, a wetland delineation will be conducted by the Corps or EPA in consultation with SCS and FWS.

L. In making wetland delineations, the agencies recognize that discharges of dredged or fill material that are not authorized under Section 404 cannot eliminate Section 404 jurisdiction, and that wetlands that were converted as a result of unauthorized discharges remain subject to Section 404 regulation.

V. PROCEDURES

Accurate and consistent wetland delineations are critical to the success of this MOA. For this reason, the signatory agencies will work cooperatively at the field level to: 1) achieve interagency concurrence on mapping conventions used by SCS for wetland delineations on agricultural lands, 2) provide EPA and Corps programmatic review of SCS delineations, and 3) certify wetland delineations in accordance with Section 1222(a)(2) of the FSA, as amended. The following sections describe the procedures that will be followed to accomplish these objectives.

A. MAPPING CONVENTIONS

1. Each SCS State Conservationist will take the lead in convening representatives of the Corps, EPA, FWS, and SCS to obtain the written concurrence of each of the signatory agencies, within 120 calendar days of the effective date of this MOA, on a set of mapping conventions for use in making wetland delineations. Only mapping conventions concurred upon by all signatory agencies will be used by SCS for wetland delineations.

2. If interagency consensus on mapping conventions is not reached within 120 days of the date of this MOA, the State Conservationist will refer documentation of the unresolved issues to the Chief of SCS. The Chief of SCS will immediately forward copies of the State Conservationist's documentation of unresolved issues to the Corps Director of Civil Works; the EPA Director of the Office of Wetlands, Oceans, and Watersheds; and the FWS Director. Immediately thereafter, the Chief of SCS or an appropriate designee will lead necessary discussions to achieve interagency concurrence on resolution of outstanding issues, and will forward documentation of the resolution to the State Conservationist and the appropriate Headquarters offices of the signatory agencies.

3. Once interagency concurrence on mapping conventions is obtained, such mapping conventions will be used immediately in place of the earlier mapping conventions.

4. Agreed-upon mapping conventions developed at the state level will be documented and submitted, for each state, through the Chief of SCS to the Headquarters of each of the signatory agencies. State-level agreements will be reviewed by the Headquarters of the signatory agencies for the purpose of ensuring national consistency.

B. DELINEATION PROCESS REVIEW AND OVERSIGHT

1. This MOA emphasizes the need to ensure consistency in the manner in which wetlands are identified for CWA and FSA purposes, and provides a number of mechanisms to increase meaningful interagency coordination and consultation in order for the agencies to work toward meeting this goal. In this regard, the agencies believe it is critical that efforts for achieving consistency be carefully monitored and evaluated. Consequently, this MOA establishes a monitoring and review process that will be used to provide for continuous improvement in the wetland delineation process specified in this MOA.

2. EPA will lead the signatory agencies in establishing interagency oversight teams at the state level to conduct periodic review of wetland delineations conducted under the provisions of this MOA. These reviews will include delineations done by SCS pursuant to Sections IV.A, IV.B, and IV.C of this MOA and delineations done by EPA or the Corps pursuant to Section IV.K. of this MOA. These reviews also will include changes to wetland delineations resulting from the SCS appeals process, as well as disagreements regarding allocation of responsibility. These reviews will occur, at a minimum, on a quarterly basis for the first year, on a semi-annual basis for the second year, and annually thereafter. In addition, a review will be initiated whenever one or more of the signatory agencies believes a significant issue needs to be addressed. The purpose of each review will be to evaluate the accuracy of an appropriate sample of wetland delineations. When feasible, this will include actual field verifications of wetland delineations. Should the interagency oversight team identify issues regarding implementation of this MOA or wetland delineations conducted under the provisions of this MOA, the team will work to resolve those issues and reach agreement on any necessary corrective actions. Each review, and any necessary corrective action, will be documented in a report to be distributed to the signatory agencies' appropriate field and Headquarters offices.

3. In situations in which the interagency oversight team identifies and reports unresolved issues concerning wetland delineations conducted under the provisions of this MOA, including changes to wetland delineations resulting from the SCS appeals process, the Headquarters offices of the signatory agencies will informally review the issue and work to reach agreement on any necessary corrective actions. This informal process notwithstanding, the EPA Regional Administrator or the Corps District Engineer may, at any time, propose to designate a geographic area as a "special case".

4. Similar to the terms of the current Memorandum of Agreement between the Department of the Army and the EPA Concerning the Determination of the Geographic Jurisdiction of the Section 404 Program and the Application of the Exemptions under Section 404(f) of the CWA, the EPA Regional Administrator or the Corps District Engineer may propose to designate a geographic area, or a particular wetland type within a designated geographic area, as a special case. A special case may be designated only after the interagency oversight team (EPA, Corps, SCS, and FWS) has reviewed the relevant issues and been unable to reach a consensus on an appropriate resolution. Special cases will be designated by an easily identifiable political or geographic subdivision, such as a township, county, parish, state, EPA Region, or Corps division or district, and will be marked on maps or using some other clear format and provided to the appropriate EPA, Corps, FWS, and SCS field offices. Proposed designations of special cases will not be effective until approved by EPA or Corps Headquarters, as appropriate.

5. Upon proposing a special case, the EPA Regional Administrator or Corps District Engineer, as appropriate, will notify the appropriate SCS State Conservationist in writing. Following notification of the proposed designation, SCS will not make wetland delineations for the purposes of CWA jurisdiction within the proposed special case for a period of 20 working days from the date of the notification. SCS may proceed to make wetland delineations for CWA purposes in the proposed special case after the 20-day period if the SCS State Conservationist has not been notified by the EPA Regional Administrator or Corps District Engineer of approval of the proposed special case designation by EPA Headquarters or the Corps Director of Civil Works, as appropriate.

6. Following approval of the proposed special case, the Corps, or EPA as appropriate, will make final CWA wetland delineations in the special case area, rather than SCS. In addition, the referring field office (i.e., either the EPA Regional Administrator or Corps District Engineer) will develop draft guidance relevant to the specific issues raised by the special case and forward the draft guidance to its Headquarters office. The Headquarters office of the agency which designated the special case will develop final guidance after consulting with the signatory agencies' Headquarters offices. EPA concurrence will be required for final guidance for any special case designated by the Corps. Special cases remain in effect until final guidance is issued by the Headquarters office of the agency which designated the special case or the designation is withdrawn by the EPA Regional Administrator or Corps District Engineer, as appropriate.

C. RELIANCE ON PREVIOUS SCS WETLAND DELINEATIONS FOR CWA PURPOSES

1. Section 1222 of the FSA, as amended by the Food Agriculture Conservation and Trade Act, provides that SCS will certify SCS wetland delineations made prior to November 28, 1990. The intent of this process is to ensure the accuracy of wetland delineations conducted prior to November 28, 1990, for the purposes of the FSA. This certification process also will provide a useful basis for establishing reliance on wetland delineations for CWA purposes. All certifications done after the effective date of this MOA that are done using mapping conventions will use the agreed-upon mapping conventions pursuant to Section V.A of this MOA.

2. Written SCS wetland delineations for lands identified in Section IV.A of this MOA conducted prior to the effective date of this MOA will be used for purposes of establishing CWA jurisdiction, subject to the provisions of Section V.C.3 below. If such SCS wetland delineations are subsequently modified or revised through updated certification, these modifications or revisions will supersede the previous delineations for purposes of establishing CWA jurisdiction. Written SCS wetland delineations for lands identified in Sections IV.B and IV.C of this MOA conducted prior to the effective date of this MOA will require coordination with the Corps, or EPA as appropriate, before being used for purposes of determining CWA jurisdiction.

3. As part of the certification effort, SCS will establish priorities to certify SCS wetland delineations. In addition to responding to requests from individual landowners who feel their original wetland determinations were made in error, SCS will give priority to certifying those wetland delineations where at least two of the four signatory agencies represented on the interagency oversight team convened pursuant to Section V.B.2 of this MOA agree that SCS wetland delineations in a particular area, or a generic class of SCS wetland delineations in a particular area, raise issues regarding their accuracy based on current guidance. These priority areas will be identified only after mapping conventions are agreed upon pursuant to Section V.A of this MOA. Identification of these high priority certification needs shall be made at the level of the SCS State Conservationist, FWS Regional Director, EPA Regional Administrator, and the Corps District Engineer. Following identification of these high priority certification needs, the SCS State Conservationist will immediately notify the affected landowner(s), by letter, that the relevant SCS wetland delineations have been identified as a high priority for being certified under Section 1222 of the FSA. In addition, the notification will inform the landowner that while previous wetland delineations remain valid for

purposes of the FSA until certification or certification update is completed, the landowner will need to contact the Corps before proceeding with discharges of dredged or fill material. This communication by the landowner will enable the Corps to review the wetland delineation to establish whether it can be used for purposes of CWA jurisdiction. The SCS State Conservationist will initiate, within 30 calendar days of landowner notification, corrective measures to resolve the wetland delineation accuracy problem.

D. APPEALS

Landowners for whom SCS makes wetland delineations for either Swampbuster or Section 404 will be afforded the opportunity to appeal such wetland delineations through the SCS appeals process. In circumstances where an appeal is made and the State Conservationist is considering a change in the original delineation, the State Conservationist will notify the Corps District Engineer and the EPA Regional Administrator to provide the opportunity for their participation and input on the appeal. FWS also will be consulted consistent with the requirements of current regulations. The Corps and EPA reserve the right, on a case-by-case basis, to determine that a revised delineation resulting from an appeal is not valid for purposes of Section 404 jurisdiction.

E. TRAINING

1. SCS, in addition to FWS and EPA, will continue to participate in the interagency wetland delineation training sponsored by the Corps, which is based on the most current manual used to delineate wetlands for purposes of Section 404. Completion of this training will be a prerequisite for field staff of all signatory agencies who delineate wetlands on non-agricultural lands using the 1987 Corps Wetland Delineation Manual.

2. The interagency wetland delineation training will address agency wetland delineation responsibilities as defined by this MOA, including SCS NFSAM wetland delineation procedures.

3. Field offices of the signatory agencies are encouraged to provide supplemental interagency wetland delineation training (i.e., in addition to that required in paragraph IV.E), as necessary, to prepare SCS field staff for making Section 404 wetland delineations. For training on the use of the 1987 Corps Wetland Delineation Manual, such supplemental training will rely on the training materials used for the Corps delineation training program and will provide an equivalent level of instruction.

VI. DEFINITIONS

A. "Coordination" means that SCS will contact the Corps, or EPA as appropriate, and provide an opportunity for review, comment, and approval of the findings of SCS prior to making a final delineation. The Corps, or EPA as appropriate, will review the proposed delineation and respond to SCS regarding its acceptability for CWA Section 404 purposes within 45 days of receipt of all necessary information. SCS will not issue a final delineation until agreement is reached between SCS and the Corps or EPA, as appropriate.

B. "Consultation" means that SCS, consistent with current provisions of the FSA, will provide FWS opportunity for full participation in the action being taken and for timely review and comment on the findings of SCS prior to a final wetland delineation pursuant to the requirements of the FSA.

C. A "wetland delineation" is any determination of the presence of wetlands and their boundaries.

D. A "special case" for the purposes of this MOA refers to those geographic areas or wetland types where the Corps or EPA will make final CWA wetland delineations.

E. "Signatory agencies" means the EPA and the Departments of Army (acting through the Corps), Agriculture (acting through SCS), and Interior (acting through FWS).

F. "USDA program participant" means individual landowners/operators eligible to receive USDA program benefits covered under Title XII of the Food Security Act of 1985, as amended by the Food, Agriculture, Conservation and Trade Act of 1990.

VII. GENERAL

A. The policy and procedures contained within this MOA do not create any rights, either substantive or procedural, enforceable by any party regarding an enforcement action brought by the United States. Deviation or variance from the administrative procedures included in this MOA will not constitute a defense for violators or others concerned with any Section 404 enforcement action.

B. Nothing in this MOA is intended to diminish, modify, or otherwise affect statutory or regulatory authorities of any of the signatory agencies. All formal guidance interpreting this MOA and background materials upon which this MOA is based will be issued jointly by the agencies.

C. Nothing in this MOA will be construed as indicating a financial commitment by SCS, the Corps, EPA, or FWS for the expenditure of funds except as authorized in specific appropriations.

D. This MOA will take effect on the date of the last signature below and will continue in effect until modified or revoked by agreement of all signatory agencies, or revoked by any of the signatory agencies alone upon 90 days written notice. Modifications to this MOA may be made by mutual agreement and Headquarters level approval by all the signatory agencies. Such modifications will take effect upon signature of the modified document by all the signatory agencies.

E. The signatory agencies will refer delineation requests to the appropriate agency pursuant to this MOA.

_____ 1/6/94
James R. Lyons
Assistant Secretary for Natural
Resources and Environment
U.S. Department of Agriculture

_____ 1/5/94
George T. Frampton, Jr.
Assistant Secretary for Fish and
Wildlife and Parks
U.S. Department of the Interior

_____ 1-4-94
Robert Perciasepe
Assistant Administrator for Water
U.S. Environmental Protection Agency

_____ 1/6/94
G. Edward Dickey
Acting Assistant Secretary of the
Army for Civil Works
U.S. Department of the Army

Appendix H

EPA/Army Corps Memorandum to the Field: Appropriate Level of Analysis Required for Evaluating Compliance with the Section 404(b)(1) Guidelines Alternatives Requirements

United States Environmental Protection Agency
Office of Wetlands, Oceans and Watersheds
Washington, D.C. 20460

United States Department of the Army
U.S. Army Corps of Engineers
Washington, D.C. 20314

AUG 23 1993

MEMORANDUM TO THE FIELD

SUBJECT: APPROPRIATE LEVEL OF ANALYSIS REQUIRED FOR EVALUATING COMPLIANCE WITH THE SECTION 404(b)(1) GUIDELINES ALTERNATIVES REQUIREMENTS

1. **PURPOSE:** The purpose of this memorandum is to clarify the appropriate level of analysis required for evaluating compliance with the Clean Water Act Section 404(b)(1) Guidelines' (Guidelines) requirements for consideration of alternatives. 40 CFR 230.10(a). Specifically, this memorandum describes the flexibility afforded by the Guidelines to make regulatory decisions based on the relative severity of the environmental impact of proposed discharges of dredged or fill material into waters of the United States.

2. **BACKGROUND:** The Guidelines are the substantive environmental standards by which all Section 404 permit applications are evaluated. The Guidelines, which are binding regulations, were published by the Environmental Protection Agency at 40 CFR Part 230 on December 24, 1980. The fundamental precept of the Guidelines is that discharges of dredged or fill material into waters of the United States, including wetlands, should not occur unless it can be demonstrated that such discharges, either individually or cumulatively, will not result in unacceptable adverse effects on the aquatic ecosystem. The Guidelines specifically require that "no discharge of dredged or fill material shall be permitted if there is a practicable alternative to the proposed discharge which would have less adverse impact on the aquatic ecosystem, so long as the alternative does not have other significant adverse environmental consequences." 40 CFR 230.10(a). Based on this provision, the applicant is required in every case (irrespective of whether the discharge site is a special aquatic site or whether the activity associated with the discharge is water dependent) to evaluate opportunities for use of non-aquatic areas and other aquatic sites that would result in less adverse impact on the aquatic ecosystem. A permit cannot be issued, therefore, in circumstances where a less environmentally damaging practicable alternative for the proposed discharge exists (except as provided for under Section 404(b)(2)).

3. **DISCUSSION:** The Guidelines are, as noted above, binding regulations. It is important to recognize, however, that this regulatory status does not limit the inherent flexibility provided in the Guidelines for implementing these provisions. The preamble to the Guidelines is very clear in this regard:

> *Of course, as the regulation itself makes clear, a certain amount of flexibility is still intended. For example, while the ultimate conditions of compliance are "regulatory", the Guidelines allow some room for judgment in determining what must be done to arrive at a conclusion that those conditions have or have not been met.*

Guidelines Preamble, "Regulation versus Guidelines", 45 <u>Federal Register</u> 85336 (December 24, 1980).

Notwithstanding this flexibility, the record must contain sufficient information to demonstrate that the proposed discharge complies with the requirements of Section 230.10(a) of the Guidelines. The amount of information needed to make such a determination and the level of scrutiny required by the Guidelines is commensurate with the severity of the environmental impact (as determined by the functions of the aquatic resource and the nature of the proposed activity) and the scope/cost of the project.

a. Analysis Associated with Minor Impacts:

The Guidelines do not contemplate that the same intensity of analysis will be required for all types of projects but instead envision a correlation between the scope of the evaluation and the potential extent of adverse impacts on the aquatic environment. The introduction to Section 230.10(a) recognizes that the level of analysis required may vary with the nature and complexity of each individual case:

> *Although all requirements in § 230.10 must be met, the compliance evaluation procedures will vary to reflect the seriousness of the potential for adverse impacts on the aquatic ecosystems posed by specific dredged or fill material discharge activities.*

40 CFR 230.10

Similarly, Section 230.6 ("Adaptability") makes clear that the Guidelines:

> *allow evaluation and documentation for a variety of activities, ranging from those with large, complex impacts on the aquatic environment to those for which the impact is likely to be innocuous. It is unlikely that the Guidelines will apply in their entirety to any one activity, no matter how complex. It is anticipated that substantial numbers of permit applications will be for minor, routine activities that have little, if any, potential for significant degradation of the aquatic environment. <u>It generally is not intended or expected that extensive testing, evaluation or analysis will be needed to make findings of compliance in such routine cases.</u>*

40 CFR 230.6(9) (emphasis added)

Section 230.6 also emphasizes that when making determinations of compliance with the Guidelines, users:

must recognize the different levels of effort that should be associated with varying degrees of impact and require or prepare commensurate documentation. The level of documentation should reflect the significance and complexity of the discharge activity.

40 CFR 230.6(b) (emphasis added)

Consequently, the Guidelines clearly afford flexibility to adjust the stringency of the alternatives review for projects that would have only minor impacts. Minor impacts are associated with activities that generally would have little potential to degrade the aquatic environment and include one, and frequently more, of the following characteristics: are located in aquatic resources of limited natural function; are small in size and cause little direct impact; have little potential for secondary or cumulative impacts; or cause only temporary impacts. It is important to recognize, however, that in some circumstances even small or temporary fills result in substantial impacts, and that in such cases a more detailed evaluation is necessary. The Corps Districts and EPA Regions will, through the standard permit evaluation process, coordinate with the U.S. Fish and Wildlife Service, National Marine Fisheries Service and other appropriate state and Federal agencies in evaluating the likelihood that adverse impacts would result from a particular proposal. It is not appropriate to consider compensatory mitigation in determining whether a proposed discharge will cause only minor impacts for purposes of the alternatives analysis required by Section 230.10(a).

In reviewing projects that have the potential for only minor impacts on the aquatic environment, Corps and EPA field offices are directed to consider, in coordination with state and Federal resource agencies, the following factors:

i) Such projects by their nature should not cause or contribute to significant degradation individually or cumulatively. Therefore, it generally should not be necessary to conduct or require detailed analyses to determine compliance with Section 230.10(c).

ii) Although sufficient information must be developed to determine whether the proposed activity is in fact the least damaging practicable alternative, the Guidelines do not require an elaborate search for practicable alternatives if it is reasonably anticipated that there are only minor differences between the environmental impacts of the proposed activity and potentially practicable alternatives. This decision will be made after consideration of resource agency comments on the proposed project. It often makes sense to examine first whether potential alternatives would result in no identifiable or discernible difference in impact on the aquatic ecosystem. Those alternatives that do not may be eliminated from the analysis since Section 230.10(a) of the Guidelines only prohibits discharges when a practicable alternative exists which would have less adverse impact on the aquatic ecosystem. Because evaluating practicability is generally the more difficult aspect of the alternatives analysis, this approach should save time and effort for both the applicant and the regulatory agencies.[1] By initially focusing the alternatives analysis on the question of impacts on the aquatic ecosystem, it may be possible to limit (or in some instances eliminate altogether) the number of alternatives that have to be evaluated for practicability.

iii) When it is determined that there is no identifiable or discernible difference in adverse impact on the environment between the applicant's proposed alternative and all other practicable alternatives, then the applicant's alternative is considered as satisfying the requirements of Section 230.10(a).

iv) Even where a practicable alternative exists that would have less adverse impact on the aquatic ecosystem, the Guidelines allow it to be rejected if it would have "other significant adverse environmental consequences." 40 CFR 230.10(a). As explained in the preamble, this allows for consideration of "evidence of damages to other ecosystems in deciding whether there is a 'better' alternative." Hence, in applying the alternatives analysis required by the Guidelines, it is not appropriate to select an alternative where minor impacts on the aquatic environment are avoided at the cost of substantial impacts to other natural environmental values.

v) In cases of negligible or trivial impacts (e.g., small discharges to construct individual driveways), it may be possible to conclude that no alternative location could result in less adverse impact on the aquatic environment within the meaning of the Guidelines. In such cases, it may not be necessary to conduct an offsite alternatives analysis but instead require only any practicable onsite minimization.

This guidance concerns application of the Section 404(b)(1) Guidelines to projects with minor impacts. Projects which may cause more than minor impacts on the aquatic environment, either individually or cumulatively, should be subjected to a proportionately more detailed level of analysis to determine compliance or noncompliance with the Guidelines. Projects which cause substantial impacts, in particular, must be thoroughly evaluated through the standard permit evaluation process to determine compliance with all provisions of the Guidelines.

---

[1] In certain instances, however, it may be easier to examine practicability first. Some projects may be so site-specific (e.g., erosion control, bridge replacement) that no offsite alternative could be practicable. In such cases the alternatives analysis may appropriately be limited to onsite options only.

b. **Relationship between the Scope of Analysis and the Scope/Cost of the Proposed Project:**

The Guidelines provide the Corps and EPA with discretion for determining the necessary level of analysis to support a conclusion as to whether or not an alternative is practicable. Practicable alternatives are those alternatives that are "available and capable of being done after taking into consideration cost, existing technology, and logistics in light of overall project purposes." 40 CFR 230.10(a)(2). The preamble to the Guidelines provides clarification on how cost is to be considered in the determination of practicability:

> *Our intent is to consider those alternatives which are <u>reasonable in terms of the overall scope/cost of the proposed project</u>. The term economic [for which the term "cost" was substituted in the final rule] might be construed to include consideration of the applicant's financial standing, or investment, or market share, a cumbersome inquiry which is not necessarily material to the objectives of the Guidelines.*

Guidelines Preamble, "Alternatives", 45 <u>Federal Register</u> 85339 (December 24, 1980) (emphasis added).

Therefore, the level of analysis required for determining which alternatives are practicable will vary depending on the type of project proposed. The determination of what constitutes an unreasonable expense should generally consider whether the projected cost is substantially greater than the costs normally associated with the particular type of project. Generally, as the scope/cost of the project increases, the level of analysis should also increase. To the extent the Corps obtains information on the costs associated with the project, such information may be considered when making a determination of what constitutes an unreasonable expense.

The preamble to the Guidelines also states that "[i]f an alleged alternative is unreasonably expensive to the applicant, the alternative is not 'practicable.'" Guidelines Preamble, "Economic Factors", 45 <u>Federal Register</u> 85343 (December 24, 1980). Therefore, to the extent that individual homeowners and small businesses may typically be associated with small projects with minor impacts, the nature of the applicant may also be a relevant consideration in determining what constitutes a practicable alternative. It is important to emphasize, however, that it is not a particular applicant's financial standing that is the primary consideration for determining practicability, but rather characteristics of the project and what constitutes a reasonable expense for these projects that are most relevant to practicability determinations.

4. The burden of proof to demonstrate compliance with the Guidelines rests with the applicant; where insufficient information is provided to determine compliance, the Guidelines require that no permit be issued. 40 CFR 230.12(a)(3)(iv).

5. A reasonable, common sense approach in applying the requirements of the Guidelines' alternatives analysis is fully consistent with sound environmental protection. The Guidelines

clearly contemplate that reasonable discretion should be applied based on the nature of the aquatic resource and potential impacts of a proposed activity in determining compliance with the alternatives test. Such an approach encourages effective decisionmaking and fosters a better understanding and enhanced confidence in the Section 404 program.

6. This guidance is consistent with the February 6, 1990 "Memorandum of Agreement Between the Environmental Protection Agency and the Department of the Army Concerning the Determination of Mitigation under the Clean Water Act Section 404(b)(1) Guidelines."

ROBERT H. WAYLAND, III (date) 8/23/93
Director,
Office of Wetlands, Oceans,
  and Watersheds
U.S. Environmental Protection Agency

MICHAEL L. DAVIS (date) 8/23/93
Office of the Assistant Secretary
  of the Army (Civil Works)
Department of the Army

Appendix I

EPA/Army Corps Memorandum to the Field: Establishment and Use of Wetland Mitigation Banks in the Clean Water Act Section 404 Regulatory Program

 United States Environmental Protection Agency
Office of Wetlands, Oceans and Watersheds
Washington, D.C. 20460

United States Department of the Army
U.S. Army Corps of Engineers
Washington, D.C. 20314

AUG 23 1993

MEMORANDUM TO THE FIELD

SUBJECT: ESTABLISHMENT AND USE OF WETLAND MITIGATION BANKS IN THE CLEAN WATER ACT SECTION 404 REGULATORY PROGRAM

1. This memorandum provides general guidelines for the establishment and use of wetland mitigation banks in the Clean Water Act Section 404 regulatory program. This memorandum serves as interim guidance pending completion of Phase I of by the Corps of Engineers' Institute for Water Resources study on wetland mitigation banking[1], at which time this guidance will be reviewed and any appropriate revisions will be incorporated into final guidelines.

2. For purposes of this guidance, wetland mitigation banking refers to the restoration, creation, enhancement, and, in exceptional circumstances, preservation of wetlands or other aquatic habitats expressly for the purpose of providing compensatory mitigation in advance of discharges into wetlands permitted under the Section 404 regulatory program. Wetland mitigation banks can have several advantages over individual mitigation projects, some of which are listed below:

   a) Compensatory mitigation can be implemented and functioning in advance of project impacts, thereby reducing temporal losses of wetland functions and uncertainty over whether the mitigation will be successful in offsetting wetland losses.

   b) It may be more ecologically advantageous for maintaining the integrity of the aquatic ecosystem to consolidate compensatory mitigation for impacts to many smaller, isolated or fragmented habitats into a single large parcel or contiguous parcels.

---

[1] The Corps of Engineers Institute for Water Resources, under the authority of Section 307(d) of the Water Resources Development Act of 1990, is undertaking a comprehensive two-year review and evaluation of wetland mitigation banking to assist in the development of a national policy on this issue. The interim summary report documenting the results of the first phase of the study is scheduled for completion in the fall of 1993.

c) Development of a wetland mitigation bank can bring together financial resources and planning and scientific expertise not practicable to many individual mitigation proposals. This consolidation of resources can increase the potential for the establishment and long-term management of successful mitigation.

d) Wetland mitigation banking proposals may reduce regulatory uncertainty and provide more cost-effective compensatory mitigation opportunities.

3. The Section 404(b)(1) Guidelines (Guidelines), as clarified by the "Memorandum of Agreement Concerning the Determination of Mitigation under the Section 404(b)(1) Guidelines" (Mitigation MOA) signed February 6, 1990, by the Environmental Protection Agency and the Department of the Army, establish a mitigation sequence that is used in the evaluation of individual permit applications. Under this sequence, all appropriate and practicable steps must be undertaken by the applicant to first avoid and then minimize adverse impacts to the aquatic ecosystem. Remaining unavoidable impacts must then be offset through compensatory mitigation to the extent appropriate and practicable. Requirements for compensatory mitigation may be satisfied through the use of wetland mitigation banks, so long as their use is consistent with standard practices for evaluating compensatory mitigation proposals outlined in the Mitigation MOA. It is important to emphasize that, given the mitigation sequence requirements described above, permit applicants should not anticipate that the establishment of, or participation in, a wetland mitigation bank will ultimately lead to a determination of compliance with the Section 404(b)(1) Guidelines without adequate demonstration that impacts associated with the proposed discharge have been avoided and minimized to the extent practicable.

4. The agencies' preference for on-site, in-kind compensatory mitigation does not preclude the use of wetland mitigation banks where it has been determined by the Corps, or other appropriate permitting agency, in coordination with the Federal resource agencies through the standard permit evaluation process, that the use of a particular mitigation bank as compensation for proposed wetland impacts would be appropriate for offsetting impacts to the aquatic ecosystem. In making such a determination, careful consideration must be given to wetland functions, landscape position, and affected species populations at both the impact and mitigation bank sites. In addition, compensation for wetland impacts should occur, where appropriate and practicable, within the same watershed as the impact site. Where a mitigation bank is being developed in conjunction with a wetland resource planning initiative (e.g., Special Area Management Plan, State Wetland Conservation Plan) to satisfy particular wetland restoration objectives, the permitting agency will determine, in coordination with the Federal resource agencies, whether use of the bank should be considered an appropriate form of compensatory mitigation for impacts occurring within the same watershed.

5. Wetland mitigation banks should generally be in place and functional before credits may be used to offset permitted wetland losses. However, it may be appropriate to allow incremental distribution of credits corresponding to the appropriate stage of successful establishment of wetland functions. Moreover, variable mitigation ratios (credit acreage to

impacted wetland acreage) may be used in such circumstances to reflect the wetland functions attained at a bank site at a particular point in time. For example, higher ratios would be required when a bank is not yet fully functional at the time credits are to be withdrawn.

6. Establishment of each mitigation bank should be accompanied by the development of a formal written agreement (e.g., memorandum of agreement) among the Corps, EPA, other relevant resource agencies, and those parties who will own, develop, operate or otherwise participate in the bank. The purpose of the agreement is to establish clear guidelines for establishment and use of the mitigation bank. A wetlands mitigation bank may also be established through issuance of a Section 404 permit where establishing the proposed bank involves a discharge of dredged or fill material into waters of the United States. The banking agreement or, where applicable, special conditions of the permit establishing the bank should address the following considerations, where appropriate:

a) location of the mitigation bank
b) goals and objectives for the mitigation bank project;
c) identification of bank sponsors and participants;
d) development and maintenance plan;
e) evaluation methodology acceptable to all signatories to establish bank credits and assess bank success in meeting the project goals and objectives;
f) specific accounting procedures for tracking crediting and debiting;
g) geographic area of applicability;
h) monitoring requirements and responsibilities;
i) remedial action responsibilities including funding; and
j) provisions for protecting the mitigation bank in perpetuity.

Agency participation in a wetlands mitigation banking agreement may not, in any way, restrict or limit the authorities and responsibilities of the agencies.

7. An appropriate methodology, acceptable to all signatories, should be identified and used to evaluate the success of wetland restoration and creation efforts within the mitigation bank and to identify the appropriate stage of development for issuing mitigation credits. A full range of wetland functions should be assessed. Functional evaluations of the mitigation bank should generally be conducted by a multi-disciplinary team representing involved resource and regulatory agencies and other appropriate parties. The same methodology should be used to determine the functions and values of both credits and debits. As an alternative, credits and debits can be based on acres of various types of wetlands (e.g., National Wetland Inventory classes). Final determinations regarding debits and credits will be made by the Corps, or other appropriate permitting agency, in consultation with Federal resource agencies.

8. Permit applicants may draw upon the available credits of a third party mitigation bank (i.e., a bank developed and operated by an entity other than the permit applicant). The

Section 404 permit, however, must state explicitly that the permittee remains responsible for ensuring that the mitigation requirements are satisfied.

9. To ensure legal enforceability of the mitigation conditions, use of mitigation bank credits must be conditioned in the Section 404 permit by referencing the banking agreement or Section 404 permit establishing the bank; however, such a provision should not limit the responsibility of the Section 404 permittee for satisfying all legal requirements of the permit.

ROBERT H. WAYLAND, III   (date)
Director
Office of Wetlands, Oceans,
  and Watersheds
U.S. Environmental Protection Agency

MICHAEL L. DAVIS   (date)
Office of the Assistant Secretary
  of the Army (Civil Works)
Department of the Army

Appendix J

EPA/Army Corps Memorandum for the Field: Individual Permit Flexibility for Small Landowners

United States Environmental Protection Agency
Office of Water
Washington, D.C. 20460

United States Department of the Army
Office of the Assistant Secretary
Washington, D.C. 20310-0103

MAR 6 1995

MEMORANDUM FOR THE FIELD

SUBJECT: Individual Permit Flexibility for Small Landowners

In order to clearly affirm the flexibility afforded to small landowners under Section 404 of the Clean Water Act, this policy clarifies that for discharges of dredged or fill material affecting up to two acres of non-tidal wetlands for the construction or expansion of a home or farm building, or expansion of a small business, it is presumed that alternatives located on property not currently owned by the applicant are not practicable under the Section 404(b)(1) Guidelines.

Specifically, for those activities involving discharges of dredged or fill material affecting up to two acres into jurisdictional wetlands for:
1) the construction or expansion of a single family home and attendant features, such as a driveway, garage, storage shed, or septic field;
2) the construction or expansion of a barn or other farm building; or
3) the expansion of a small business facility;
which are not otherwise covered by a general permit, it is presumed that alternatives located on property not currently owned by the applicant are not practicable under the Section 404(b)(1) Guidelines. The Guidelines' requirements to appropriately and practicably minimize and compensate for any adverse environmental impacts of such activities remain.

Discussion

The Clean Water Act Section 404 regulatory program provides that the Army Corps of Engineers evaluate permit applications for the discharge of dredged or fill material into waters of the U.S., including wetlands, in accordance with regulatory requirements of the Section 404(b)(1) Guidelines (Guidelines). The Guidelines are the substantive environmental criteria used in evaluating discharges of dredged or fill material.

The Section 404(b)(1) Guidelines establish a mitigation sequence that provides a sound framework to ensure that the environmental impacts of permitted actions are acceptable. Under this framework, there is a three-step sequence for mitigating potential adverse impacts to the aquatic environment associated with a proposed discharge -- first avoidance, then minimization, and lastly compensation for unavoidable impacts to aquatic resources.

The Guidelines' mitigation sequence is designed to establish a consistent approach to be used in ensuring that all practicable measures have been taken to reduce potential adverse impacts associated with proposed projects in wetlands and other aquatic systems. The Guidelines define the term "practicable" as "available and capable of being done [by the applicant] after taking into consideration cost, existing technology, and logistics in light of overall project purposes." (40 CFR 230.3(q)). The first step in the sequence requires the evaluation of potential alternative sites under §230.10(a) of the Guidelines, to locate the proposed project so that aquatic impacts are avoided to the extent practicable.

This policy statement clarifies that, for the purposes of the alternatives analysis, it is presumed that practicable alternatives are limited to property owned by the permit applicant in circumstances involving certain small projects affecting less than two acres of non-tidal wetlands. This presumption is consistent with the practicability considerations required under the Guidelines and reflects the nature of the projects to which the presumption applies -- specifically, the construction or expansion of a single family home and attendant features, the construction or expansion of a barn or other farm building, or the expansion of a business. For such small projects that would solely expand an existing structure, the basic project purpose is so tied to the existing structures owned by the applicant, that it would be highly unusual that the project could be practicably located on other sites not owned by the applicant. In these cases, such as construction of driveways, garages, or storage sheds, or with home and barn additions, proximity to the existing structure is typically a fundamental aspect of the project purpose.

In the evaluation of potential practicable alternatives, the Guidelines do not exclude the consideration of sites that, while not currently owned by the permit applicant, could reasonably be obtained to satisfy the project purpose. However, it is the experience of the Army Corps of Engineers and EPA that areas not currently owned by the applicant have, in the great majority of circumstances, not been determined to be practicable alternatives in cases involving the small landowner activities described above. Cost, availability, and logistical and capability considerations inherent in the determination of practicability under the Guidelines have been the basis for this conclusion by the agencies.

The agencies recognize that the presumption characterized in this policy statement may be rebutted in certain circumstances. For example, a more thorough review of practicable alternatives would be warranted for individual sites comprising a subdivision of homes, if following issuance of this policy statement, a real estate developer subdivided a large, contiguous wetlands parcel into numerous parcels. In addition, the presumption is applicable to the expansion of existing small business facilities. Small businesses are typically confined to only one location and with economic and logistical limitations that generally preclude the availability of practicable alternative locations to meet their expansion needs. Conversely, larger businesses with multiple locations and greater resources are expected to consider opportunities to practicably avoid adverse aquatic impacts by evaluating off-site alternatives.

Finally, it is important to note that this presumption of practicable alternatives is intended to apply to the individual permit process. Alternatives are not evaluated for activities covered by general permits. Many activities related to the construction or expansion of a home, farm, or business, are already covered by a general permit. In addition, in conjunction with the issuance of this policy statement, a nationwide general permit authorizing discharges related to single family residential development is being proposed and will be available for public comment.

If you have any questions regarding this memorandum, please contact Gregory Peck of EPA's Wetlands Division at (202) 260-8794 or Michael Davis of the Corps of Engineer's Regulatory Branch at (202) 272-0199.

Robert Perciasepe
Assistant Administrator for Water
U.S. Environmental Protection Agency

John Zirschky
Acting Assistant Secretary
of the Army (Civil Works)

Index

A

Advance Identification of Wetlands, 56
Army Corps of Engineers Offices, 191

C

Case Studies, *See* Mitigation Case Studies
Clean Water Act Section 401 Certification, 63
Clean Water Act Section 404 Program, 33
Clinton Administration's Wetlands Plan, 9, 215
Coastal Zone Management Act, 46
Corps/EPA 404(b)(1) Mitigation Guidelines, 92-93, 261, 283

E

Endangered Species Act, 54
EPA Wetlands Offices, 187

F

Federal Agriculture Improvement and Reform Act of 1996, 42
Federal Manual for Delineating Wetlands, 16
Field Testing
    Hydric Soil Indicators, 24
    Hydrology Indicators, 22
    Wetland Vegetation Indicators, 25
Food Security Act, *See* Swampbuster Program
Functions and Values of Wetlands
    Functional Value Analysis, 114
    Lost and Degraded Wetlands, Consequence of, 8
    Wetland Functions, 2
    Wetland Values, 6
Funding and Technical Assistance, 243

G

General and Nationwide Permits, 82

H

Habitat Evaluation Procedure, 115

I

Identification of Wetlands
    Federal Manual for Delineating Wetlands, 16
    Field Testing and Data Collection, 22
    National Academy of Sciences Wetland Study, 18
    Wetland Characteristics, 19
    Wetland Mapping Criteria, 26
    Wetlands Defined, 13

M

Mitigation Banking
    Advantages of Mitigation Banking, 135
    Concept of Mitigation Banking, 129
    Disadvantages of Mitigation Banking, 139

302 / WETLAND MITIGATION

Mitigation Banking (*continued*)
  Functional Value Assessment, 132
  How Mitigation Banking Works, 131
  Tenneco-LaTerre Wetland Mitigation Bank, 138
  Timing of Bank Credit Withdrawals, 133
  Types of Mitigation Banks, 134
    Private Banks, 134
    Publicly Owned Banks, 135
    Single-User Banks, 134
Mitigation Banking Guidance
  Criteria for Use of a Mitigation Bank, 152
    Crediting/Debiting/Accounting Procedures, 155
    Geographic Limits of Applicability, 153
    In-Kind vs. Out-of-Kind Mitigation Determinations, 155
    Party Responsible for Bank Success, 157
    Project Applicability, 152
    Relationship to Mitigation Requirements, 153
    Timing of Credit Withdrawal, 156
    Use of a Mitigation Bank vs. On-Site Mitigation, 154
  Establishment of Mitigation Banks, 149
    Agency Roles and Coordination, 150
    Application of Banking Instrument, 152
    Development of Banking Instrument, 151
    Dispute Resolution Procedure, 151
    Mitigation Banking Instruments, 149
    Role of the Bank Sponsor, 151
  Long-Term Management, Monitoring and Remediation, 157
    Bank Operational Life, 157
    Financial Assurances, 159
    Long-Term Management and Protection, 158
    Monitoring Requirements, 158
    Remedial Action, 159
  Planning Considerations, 145
    Goal Setting, 145
    Inclusion of Upland Areas, 148
    Mitigation Banking and Watershed Planning, 148
    Prospectus, 145
    Role of Preservation, 147
    Site Selection, 146
    Technical Feasibility, 146
  Policy Considerations, 144
  Purpose and Scope of Guidance, 143
Mitigation Case Studies
  Achieving Successful Wetland Mitigation, 182
  Case Study 1: Creation of Freshwater Wetland, 162
    Functional Value of Impacted Wetland, 163
    Implementation of Mitigation Plan, 166
    Mitigation as Condition of Permit Approval, 164
    Mitigation Project Design, 165
    Post-Construction Monitoring, 168
    Project Site, 162
    Selection of Mitigation Site, 164
    Submission of Mitigation Plan, 165
    Success of the Mitigation Project, 169
  Case Study 2: Creation of Tidal Wetland, 170
    Background and Setting, 170
    Design/Implementation of Mitigation Plan, 171
    Human Disturbance of Mitigation Site, 172
  Case Study 3: Payment of Fee In-Lieu of Mitigation, 172

Mitigation Case Studies (*continued*)
    Calculation of Fee Payment, 174
    Cost Estimate #1, 174
    Cost Estimate #2, 176
    Cost Estimate #3, 177
    Case Study 4: Wetland Mitigation Bank, 178
    Background, 179
    Bank Establishment, 181
    Location and Description of Bank Site, 179
    Mitigation is Attainable, 186
    Past Efforts at Mitigation, 184
    Pennsylvania Mitigation Guidelines Concerning Cash Contributions, 177
Mitigation Categories, 113
Mitigation Compliance
    Achieving Mitigation Compliance, 107
    Corps/EPA 404(b)(1) Mitigation Guidelines, 92
    EPA/Corps 1993 Memorandum Regarding Minor Impacts, 98
    EPA/Corps 1995 Memorandum Regarding Small Landowners, 101, 297
    EPA/Corps Mitigation MOA, 93
    Illustrative Mitigation Cases, 102
    Practicable Alternatives Test, 97
    Sequencing Requirement, 94
        Avoidance, 94
        Compensatory Mitigation, 95
        Exceptions to the Sequencing Requirement, 97
        Minimization, 95
    State Law Mitigation Requirements, 91
    Wetland Mitigation Policy, 89
Mitigation Options
    Alternatives for Compensatory Mitigation, 118
    Ensuring Mitigation Project Success, 120
    Functional Value Analysis, 114
    Kinds of Wetlands Losses Requiring Mitigation, 114
    Mitigation Categories, 113
    Specific Types of Mitigation, 118
    Wetland Restoration and Creation Checklist, 121
Mitigation Sequencing
    Avoidance, 94
    Compensatory Mitigation, 95
    Exceptions to the Sequencing Requirement, 97
    Minimization, 95

N

National Academy of Sciences Wetland Study, 18
National Environmental Policy Act, 45
National Flood Insurance Program, 52
National Wetland Inventory, 26

P

Permitting, 73
    General and Nationwide Permits, 82
    Permit Application Process, 77
        Army Corps Action on Permit Applications, 78
        Permit Decision, 81
        Public Comment, 80
        Public Hearing, 81
        Public Notice, 78
    Remedies for Permit Denials, 84
    Section 404 Permit Applications, 73
        Application Form, 75
        Exemptions, 77
Practicable Alternatives Test, 97, 283

R

Regulation of Wetlands
    Clean Water Act Section 404 Program, 33

Regulation of Wetlands (*continued*)
   Related Federal Environmental Laws, 43
      Coastal Zone Management Act, 46
      Endangered Species Act, 54
      National Environmental Policy Act, 45
      National Flood Insurance Program, 52
      River and Harbors Act of 1899, 46
      Water Resources Development Act, 49
   Special Approaches to Wetlands Management, 56
      Advance Identification (ADID) of Wetlands, 56
      Special Area Management Plans, 57
      Wetlands and Watersheds, 58
   State Wetland Regulatory Programs, 59
      Clean Water Act Section 401 Certification, 63
      State Assumption of the Section 404 Program, 62
      State Water Quality Standards for Wetlands, 64
      State Wetland Conservation Plans, 61
      State Wetland Offices, App. C, 205
      State Wetland Protection Laws, 60
      State Wetlands Grant Program, 60
Wetlands Enforcement, 35
   Administrative Enforcement, 36
   Civil Enforcement, 37
   Criminal Enforcement, 38
Wetland Regulation under the Swampbuster Program, 39
   Commenced Conversion Exemption, 41
   Conversion of Wetlands, 40
   Federal Agriculture Improvement and Reform Act of 1996, 42
   Swampbuster Sanctions, 40
   USDA Regulations, 41
   Wetland Delineation, App. G, 269
River and Harbors Act of 1899, 46

S

Sequencing, *See* Mitigation Sequencing
Special Area Management Plans, 57
State Wetland Regulatory Programs
   Clean Water Act Section 401 Certification, 63
   State Assumption of the Section 404 Program, 62
   State Water Quality Standards for Wetlands, 64
   State Wetland Conservation Plans, 61
   State Wetland Offices, App. C, 205
   State Wetland Protection Laws, 60
   State Wetlands Grant Program, 60
Swampbuster Program
   Commenced Conversion Exemption, 41
   Effectiveness of Swampbuster Sanctions, 40
   Federal Agriculture Improvement and Reform Act of 1996, 42
   USDA's Swampbuster Regulations, 41
   Wetland Conversion under the Swampbuster Program, 40

W

Water Resources Development Act, 49
Wetland Characteristics, 19
   Hydric Soils, 20
   Hydrology, 19
   Wetland Vegetation, 21

Wetland Evaluation Technique, 115
Wetland Losses, 7
Wetland Mapping, 26
Wetland Restoration and Creation
       Checklist, 121
Wetland Values, 6
Wetlands Defined, 13
Wetlands Enforcement
   Administrative Enforcement, 36
   Civil Enforcement, 37
   Criminal Enforcement, 38

Government Institutes Mini-Catalog

PC #	ENVIRONMENTAL TITLES	Pub Date	Price
629	ABCs of Environmental Regulation: Understanding the Fed Regs	1998	$49
627	ABCs of Environmental Science	1998	$39
585	Book of Lists for Regulated Hazardous Substances, 8th Edition	1997	$79
579	Brownfields Redevelopment	1998	$79
4088	CFR Chemical Lists on CD ROM, 1997 Edition	1997	$125
4089	Chemical Data for Workplace Sampling & Analysis, Single User Disk	1997	$125
512	Clean Water Handbook, 2nd Edition	1996	$89
581	EH&S Auditing Made Easy	1997	$79
587	E H & S CFR Training Requirements, 3rd Edition	1997	$89
4082	EMMI-Envl Monitoring Methods Index for Windows-Network	1997	$537
4082	EMMI-Envl Monitoring Methods Index for Windows-Single User	1997	$179
525	Environmental Audits, 7th Edition	1996	$79
548	Environmental Engineering and Science: An Introduction	1997	$79
643	Environmental Guide to the Internet, 4rd Edition	1998	$59
560	Environmental Law Handbook, 14th Edition	1997	$79
353	Environmental Regulatory Glossary, 6th Edition	1993	$79
625	Environmental Statutes, 1998 Edition	1998	$69
4098	Environmental Statutes Book/CD-ROM, 1998 Edition	1997	$208
4994	Environmental Statutes on Disk for Windows-Network	1997	$405
4994	Environmental Statutes on Disk for Windows-Single User	1997	$139
570	Environmentalism at the Crossroads	1995	$39
536	ESAs Made Easy	1996	$59
515	Industrial Environmental Management: A Practical Approach	1996	$79
510	ISO 14000: Understanding Environmental Standards	1996	$69
551	ISO 14001: An Executive Repoert	1996	$55
588	International Environmental Auditing	1998	$149
518	Lead Regulation Handbook	1996	$79
478	Principles of EH&S Management	1995	$69
554	Property Rights: Understanding Government Takings	1997	$79
582	Recycling & Waste Mgmt Guide to the Internet	1997	$49
603	Superfund Manual, 6th Edition	1997	$115
566	TSCA Handbook, 3rd Edition	1997	$95
534	Wetland Mitigation: Mitigation Banking and Other Strategies	1997	$75

PC #	SAFETY and HEALTH TITLES	Pub Date	Price
547	Construction Safety Handbook	1996	$79
553	Cumulative Trauma Disorders	1997	$59
559	Forklift Safety	1997	$65
539	Fundamentals of Occupational Safety & Health	1996	$49
612	HAZWOPER Incident Command	1998	$59
535	Making Sense of OSHA Compliance	1997	$59
589	Managing Fatigue in Transportation, *ATA Conference*	1997	$75
558	PPE Made Easy	1998	$79
598	Project Mgmt for E H & S Professionals	1997	$59
552	Safety & Health in Agriculture, Forestry and Fisheries	1997	$125
613	Safety & Health on the Internet, 2nd Edition	1998	$49
597	Safety Is A People Business	1997	$49
463	Safety Made Easy	1995	$49
590	Your Company Safety and Health Manual	1997	$79

Government Institutes
4 Research Place, Suite 200 • Rockville, MD 20850-3226
Tel. (301) 921-2323 • FAX (301) 921-0264
Email: giinfo@govinst.com • Internet: http://www.govinst.com

Please call our customer service department at (301) 921-2323 for a free publications catalog.

CFRs now available online. Call (301) 921-2355 for info.

GOVERNMENT INSTITUTES ORDER FORM

4 Research Place, Suite 200 • Rockville, MD 20850-3226
Tel (301) 921-2323 • Fax (301) 921-0264
Internet: http://www.govinst.com • E-mail: giinfo@govinst.com

3 EASY WAYS TO ORDER

1. **Phone:** (301) 921-2323
   Have your credit card ready when you call.
2. **Fax:** (301) 921-0264
   Fax this completed order form with your company purchase order or credit card information.
3. **Mail:** Government Institutes
   4 Research Place, Suite 200
   Rockville, MD 20850-3226   USA
   Mail this completed order form with a check, company purchase order, or credit card information.

PAYMENT OPTIONS

❑ **Check** *(payable to Government Institutes in US dollars)*
❑ **Purchase Order** *(This order form must be attached to your company P.O. <u>Note</u>: All International orders must be prepaid.)*
❑ **Credit Card** ❑ VISA ❑ MC ❑ AMEX

Exp.___/___

Credit Card No. _____

Signature _____

(Government Institutes' Federal I.D.# is 13-2695912)

CUSTOMER INFORMATION

Ship To: (Please attach your purchase order)
Name: _____
GI Account # *(7 digits on mailing label):* _____
Company/Institution: _____
Address: _____
(Please supply street address for UPS shipping)

City: _____ State/Province: _____
Zip/Postal Code: _____ Country: _____
Tel: ( ) _____
Fax: ( ) _____
Email Address: _____

Bill To: (if different from ship-to address)
Name: _____
Title/Position: _____
Company/Institution: _____
Address: _____
(Please supply street address for UPS shipping)

City: _____ State/Province: _____
Zip/Postal Code: _____ Country: _____
Tel: ( ) _____
Fax: ( ) _____
Email Address: _____

Qty.	Product Code	Title	Price

❑ **New Edition No Obligation Standing Order Program**
Please enroll me in this program for the products I have ordered. Government Institutes will notify me of new editions by sending me an invoice. I understand that there is no obligation to purchase the product. This invoice is simply my reminder that a new edition has been released.

Subtotal _____
MD Residents add 5% Sales Tax _____
Shipping and Handling (see box below) _____
Total Payment Enclosed _____

15 DAY MONEY-BACK GUARANTEE
If you're not completely satisfied with any product, return it undamaged within 15 days for a full and immediate refund on the price of the product.

Within U.S:
1-4 products: $6/product
5 or more: $3/product

Outside U.S:
Add $15 for each item (Airmail)
Add $10 for each item (Surface)

Now Order Online: www.govinst.com   **SOURCE CODE: BP01**